Gặp gỡ China

Встреча с Китаем

Meet China

សួស្តី ប្រទេសចិន

Gặp Gỡ Trung Quốc

Ontmoet vir Sjina

ПРИВЕТ, КИТАЙ

چین سے ملنا

កូន ជួប ប្រទេសចិន

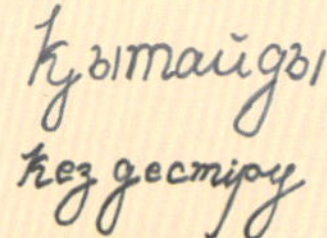

APA KHABAR CHINA

Қытай елімен танысу

SEVGILI ÇIN

ВСТРЕЧАЙ, КИТАЙ

遇見中國
중국과 만남

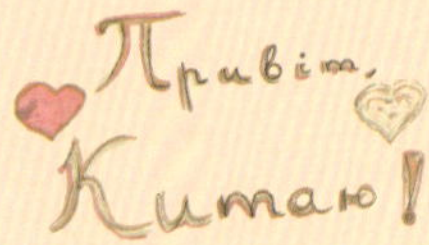

ជំនួបរវាង
ខ្ញុំ & ប្រទេសចិន

KAZIWAI CHINA

Selamat Temui China

សួស្តី ប្រទេសចិន

JUMPA CHINA

M'abehyia China!
M'abehunu China!
My encounters with China.

Kilalanin Ang Tsina

RENCONTRE AVEC LA CHINE

CONOCE A CHINA

မင်္ဂလာပါ တရုတ်နိုင်ငံ

HYTAY BILEN DUSUSYK

សួស្តី ប្រទេសចិន

Да срещнеш Китай

GẶP GỠ TRUNG QUỐC

我爱中国
I ♡ CN

Berjumpa Dengan China

Salutations, China!
Jiangsu Jiangxi Hubei Shandong Hainan Henan Fujian Yunnan Jilin Guizhou Shanxi Hebei Anhui Qinghai Gansu Guangdong Tibet Sichuan Hunan

中国に 巡り会う

တရုတ်ပြည်သူ့သမ္မတနိုင်ငံတော်နှင့် တွေ့ဆုံခြင်း

Gặp gỡ Trung Quốc

Gặp gỡ Trung Quốc

চীন পরিদর্শন

Gặp gỡ Trung Quốc

Знакомьтесь, Китай

중국을 만나다.

ค้นพบแดนมังกร

...พบกัน...
ประเทศจีน

Hytay bilen tanyşlyk

درود بر چین زیبا

Jumpa Tiongkok

چین سے ملیں

ちゅうごくに出会う
中国で出会う

سلام چین

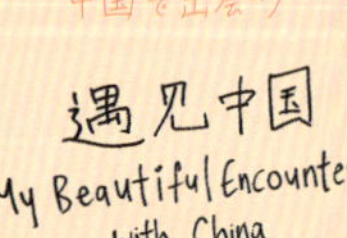

Conocer china!

我与中国的美丽邂逅

——我的2020

My Beautiful Encounter with China

— My 2020

教育部国际合作与交流司
教育部留学服务中心 编

Compiled by

Department of International Cooperation and Exchanges,
Ministry of Education of the People's Republic of China

Chinese Service Center for Scholarly Exchange,
Ministry of Education of the People's Republic of China

人民日报出版社
People's Daily Press

图书在版编目（CIP）数据

我与中国的美丽邂逅：我的 2020 / 教育部国际合作与交流司，教育部留学服务中心编 . — 北京：人民日报出版社，2020.11

ISBN 978-7-5115-6701-7

Ⅰ. ①我… Ⅱ. ①教… ②教… Ⅲ. ①留学生－学生生活－中国－文集－汉、英 Ⅳ. ① G648.9-53

中国版本图书馆 CIP 数据核字（2020）第 226088 号

书　　名：我与中国的美丽邂逅：我的 2020
WO YU ZHONGGUO DE MEILI XIEHOU: WO DE 2020
编　　者：教育部国际合作与交流司　教育部留学服务中心

出 版 人：刘华新
责任编辑：翟福军　梁雪云
版式设计：九章文化

出版发行：人民日报出版社
社　　址：北京金台西路 2 号
邮政编码：100733
发行热线：(010) 65369509　65369527　65369846　65369512
邮购热线：(010) 65369530　65363527
编辑热线：(010) 65369517　65369526
网　　址：www.peopledailypress.com
经　　销：新华书店
印　　刷：三河市华东印刷有限公司
法律顾问：北京科宇律师事务所　010-83622312

开　　本：710mm×1000mm　1/16
字　　数：380 千字
印　　张：26.5
版　　次：2020 年 11 月第 1 版　　2020 年 11 月第 1 次印刷

书　　号：ISBN 978-7-5115-6701-7
定　　价：99.00 元

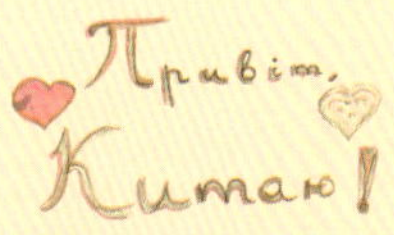

遇見中國
중국과 만남

ជំនួបរវាង
ខ្ញុំ & ប្រទេសចិន

KAZIWAI
CHINA

Selamat
Temui
China

RENCONTRE
AVEC LA
CHINE

မင်္ဂလာပါ
တရုတ်နိုင်ငံ

M'abehyia China!
M'abehunu China!
My encounters with China.

Kulalanin
ang Tsina

CONOCE A CHINA

序言
Preface

Without a doubt, the year 2020 is an unusual year. A sudden outbreak of novel corona-virus pneumonia has disrupted everyone's life and enabled all of us to see history in the making. As youngsters living in other countries, overseas students studying in China have suffered discomfort and anxiety, and gained strength and growth as well. In the past year, they have experienced home isolation, either long or short. Wearing masks, measuring temperature and showing "Health Code" have become their everyday "homework". Their exchange with teachers and classmates has also been moved onto the internet. All these unprecedented new lifestyles interweave with their daily study and life in China. Every international student has his own unique observation and understanding.

In order to record their special experiences and stories in 2020, promote the mutual understanding between Chinese people and foreign students, the Chinese Service Center for Scholarly Exchange, entrusted by the Ministry of Education, organized the 4th International Student Essay Contest. The contest has received warm response among Chinese universities, overseas students and graduates. A total of 1,100 essays have been received from more than 100 universities, Chinese embassies (consulates) in other countries, alumni organizations and individuals. Authors of these articles are from more than 100

2020年注定是不平凡的一年。一场突如其来的新冠肺炎疫情打乱了每个人的计划，也让所有人见证了历史。作为身在异乡的年轻人，来华留学生们经历了不安与焦虑，也收获了坚强与成长。一年中，来华留学生们在中国体验了或长或短的居家隔离，戴口罩、测体温、出示“健康码”成了每日必做的“功课”，与老师和同学的交流也搬到了网上。这些以前难以想象的新鲜生活方式与在华的学习生活交织在一起，让每一位来华留学生心中都有属于自己的独特体验与特殊感悟。

为了记录来华留学生2020年的这段特殊经历，增进来华留学生与中国人民的相互了解、讲述来华留学生所听、所看、所经历的中国故事，受教育部国际司委托，教育部留学服务中心组织举办了第四届“我与中国的美丽邂逅”来华留学生征文大赛，征文大赛得到了中国多所高校、广大来华留学生和留华毕业生的积极响应。据统计，征文期间共收到来自100余所高校、驻外使领馆教育处、留华校友组织以及个人投稿的1100余篇稿件，撰文的来华留学生遍及全球100多个国家。经过征文比赛组委会的评审，最终评出一等奖3篇、二等奖5篇、三等奖20篇、优秀奖32篇及特色奖若干篇。参赛作品均以中文写成，文笔流畅优美，内容丰富多彩，并作为《我与中国的美丽邂逅——来华留学生讲述中国

countries.

After the contest organizing committee's review, we have selected 3 essays as the first prize, 5 as the second prize, 20 as the third prize, 32 as outstanding award and certain featured award. All the winning works are written in fluent and vivid Chinese language. In the last three years, we have published three books titled *My Beautiful Encounter with China* with the subtitles of *The Chinese Stories Told by International Students*, *International Students' Stories on China's Reform and Opening-up* and *70 Years of Development in the Eyes of International Students*, respectively. This year's subtitle is My 2020.

In this book, students from different countries depict their unforgettable memories of 2020 and shared their study experiences and feelings in China.

Nusrat Qudrat, a student from Afghanistan whose Chinese name is Yang Kang, studies at the China University of Geosciences (Wuhan). Just before the lockdown of the capital of Hubei Province, he returned to Wuhan from Shanghai and joined the "Iron Man" volunteer team to provide services and assistance to 437 foreign students staying on the campus. "Although it may seem not to be a big deal to provide support and help them with their daily lives for international students, we have contributed all our courage and strength in this difficult time... Underneath the layers of stuffy protective clothing, in addition to the sweat in the harsh winter of Wuhan, there are traces of my hidden tear." he wrote, "What are these trifle things I did compared with those by the people around me? Heroic medics on the front lines built a healthy first-line with their bodies. The brave and fearless heroic people of Wuhan had allowed themselves to be 'trapped' in this heroic city. The heroic Chinese government and people, while fighting the epidemic themselves, also lend a helping hand to the world. My country has been given a large number of medical supplies from China..."

故事》《我与中国的美丽邂逅——来华留学生眼中的改革开放四十年》《我与中国的美丽邂逅——来华留学生见证壮丽 70 年》的姊妹篇，以《我与中国的美丽邂逅——我的 2020》为书名结集出版。

书中，来自不同国家的来华留学生以不同的视角记录 2020 年的难忘经历，分享自己来华留学的体验和感想。

就读于中国地质大学（武汉）的阿富汗留学生杨康同学在武汉封城前从上海赶回武汉，加入了学校留学生自发成立的志愿者组织——“钢铁侠”志愿服务队，为留校的 437 名留学生提供服务和帮助。他说：“虽然为留学生提供帮助、做好生活服务这些都是看起来微不足道的小事，但是在这个艰难时刻，我们用尽了全部的勇气和力气……层层防护服底下，除了记录在武汉严冬下闷出的汗水，还有我隐隐的泪水的痕迹……可比起周围的那些人，我做的这些小事又算得了什么呢？奋战在一线的英雄医护人员，用自己的身躯筑起健康的防线；勇敢无畏的英雄武汉人民，让自己‘困守’在

Đoàn Phuöng Hoa, a student from Vietnam who studies at the Guangxi Normal University, is a fervent lover of traditional Chinese poems and literature. Home quarantine during the epidemic gave her more time to learn Chinese poetry and appreciate the richness and beauty of Chinese culture. "In the first half of 2020, the COVID-19 epidemic trapped us at home for a long time. During the days of half isolation from the outside world, some people practiced hard at cooking, some did various exercises, some found ways to entertain themselves, while I happily immersed myself in the world of Tang Poetry. Several collections of Tang Poetry sit on my desk. Every time I read; I was reluctant to put it down. When I came across some wonderful lines, sometimes I cannot help clapping my hands for acclaim. Sometimes I signed sadly. Sometimes I held myself aloof from the world. Sometimes I shed my tears and sometimes I was impassioned," she wrote.

M Shujah Islam Sameem, a student from Pakistan, studies at the University of Science and Technology of China. After spending his 2020 Spring Festival in Malaysia, he met a dilemma, either return to his homeland Pakistan where no epidemic was reported, or return to China, which was then suffering from an outbreak. After one-night's struggling, he decided to follow his original plan and return to China. "During the period, I saw all functional departments of Chinese government were on duty every day; supermarkets were open as usual; community service staff set up virus-prevention stations to launch scientific virus prevention and control measures; even community guards were joining the fight and they helped measure temperatures for their community residents and register those going in and out of their communities; delivery people were delivering food supplies in a well-organized way door to door. The terror scenes in disaster movies did not occur at all and everyone was having their normal daily life. The sun still rises from the east and sets to the west every day,

这座英雄城市；英雄的中国政府和人民，在自己抗疫的同时还对世界伸出援手，我的祖国也获赠了大量来自中国的医疗用品……”来自越南的广西师范大学留学生段芳花是中国诗词文化爱好者，疫情期间的居家隔离，让她有了更多的时间学习中国的诗词，领略中华文化的博大精深。她在文中写道：“2020 年上半年，新冠肺炎疫情把我们困在了家中，在一个个与外界近乎隔绝的日子里，有的人苦练厨艺，有的人花式健身，有的人自娱自乐，而我则欣喜地把自己沉浸在了唐诗的世界里。几本唐诗的集子放在案头，每每让我手不释卷，读到精彩处，有时击节赞叹，有时扼腕叹息，有时神游物外，有时潸然泪下，有时慷慨激昂！”就读于中国科学技术大学的巴基斯坦留学生高兴同学的 2020 春节是在马来西亚度过的，2 月初春节假期结束时他面临两个选择，一个是回到还没有出现疫情的祖国巴基斯坦，另外一个是回到正处疫情的中国。经过了一夜的思想斗争，他还是按原计划返回了中国。他写道：“疫情期间我看到中国职能部门坚持每天在岗；

everyone was peaceful, without panic or crying and no one gave up." he wrote.

The COVID-19 epidemic broke out in winter vacation, when many foreign students have returned to their motherland. The repeated spread of the epidemic temporarily prevented them from returning to China. However, every student studying in China chose to fight against the epidemic in their own ways when facing the unprecedented human challenge. At the beginning of the outbreak, Bangladeshi student Mostak Ahmed actively collected surgical masks in the local market and nearby cities in his own country and managed to mail them to his Alma Mater – Beijing Institute of Technology. After the epidemic swept the whole world, he began to study the manufacture of mask machines. In order to help more people, he shot and uploaded the assembling of mask machines onto social media. "I realized that the little thinking and the few efforts I did were meaningful, not only to my country, but also to people in other countries. It is a great feeling to do something useful for human beings, and it is the true value of life," he said.

In May 2020, Chinese President Xi Jinping wrote a letter to Pakistani students studying at the University of Science and Technology Beijing. "I learned that many foreign students have expressed their support to the Chinese people in various ways during China's fight against COVID-19. A friend in need is a friend indeed. China will continue providing various help to all foreign students studying in the country." said Xi in the letter. "China welcomes excellent youth from other countries to study in the nation. They can learn more about the country, communicate more with their Chinese peers and tell the world more about the China they see." Xi wrote. Xi encouraged the students to communicate more with their Chinese peers and join hands with youth from all countries to contribute to promoting people-to-people connectivity and building a community with a shared future for humanity.

President Xi's letter is full of love and warmth, hoping after returning to

大型超市正常营业；社区街道工作人员在大街上成立大大小小的防疫站，向人们循环科普新型冠状病毒的防范措施；小区保安也加入抗疫的战斗中，每天坚持给小区居民测量体温并做好登记工作；外卖小哥更是有条不紊地给每个家庭送食物。而我以为的电影场景并没有发生，每个人都在正常生活不被打扰，太阳照常升起，夕阳照常西下，一切看上去都是那么平静，没有慌张、没有哭泣，更没有放弃。”

新冠肺炎疫情来袭于寒假，很多来华留学生回到了自己的祖国，疫情的反复蔓延暂时阻止了他们返回中国的脚步。但是，每一位来华留学生都以不同的方式抗击着疫情，共同面对这场百年未遇的人类挑战。疫情之初，北京理工大学的孟加拉国留学生心天积极在当地市场和邻近城市收集可用的医用外科口罩，克服重重困难寄送回母校；当世界都受到新冠肺炎疫情波及之时，他开始研究制造口罩机；为了帮助更多的人，他还拍摄了制作口罩机的分解视频上传到社交媒体。他说：“我意识到，我的一点思考和努力是有意义的，不仅对我的国家有意义，对其他国家的人也有意义。做一些对人类有用的事有一种很伟大的感觉，是生命真正的价值。”

2020 年 5 月，国家主席习近平在给北京科技大学全体巴基斯坦留学生的回信中写道：“我了解到，在抗击疫情期间，很多留学生通过各种方式为中国人民加油鼓劲。患难见真情。中国将继续为所有在华外国留学生提供各种帮助。中国欢迎各国优秀青年来华学习深造，也希望大家多了解中国、多向世界讲讲你们所看到的中国，多同中国青年交流，同世界各国青年一道，携手为促进民心相通、推动构建人类命运共同体贡献力量。”

习主席回信中的殷殷嘱托饱含深情，字字暖心，希望来华留学生朋友们在学成归国后，不仅能将在中国的所学、所得贡献到自己祖国的发

their motherland, international students can not only contribute what they have learned in China to the development and construction of their own country, but also keep eyes on China's development, actively introduce their views and understanding of China to their own people, so as to let the world know a more comprehensive and vivid China.

A bosom friend afar brings a distant land near. Dear friends of international students, no matter where you go in the future, the Chinese people will be your sincere friends. China's development will create a broader stage for you to display your talent.

Thanks to all the contestants who participated in the essay contest and short video competition to record the times and lives with their own pens and lenses. Thanks to the strong support of universities and education sections of embassies and consulates abroad; and to the hard work of teachers, experts and the judging panel. It is the efforts of each of us that made this event a success and encouraged us to move forward.

Time flies and 2020 is coming to an end. Different countries are striving to fight against the COVID-19 pandemic. Scientists are working round the clock to develop effective vaccines to tame the virus. Medical workers are still fighting in the frontline of anti-epidemic. Every ordinary person is still facing the extraordinary challenges of the human race. Let us conclude this preface with a sentence written by Tursynzhan Pariza from Kazakhstan. "The year 2020 is unprecedented for the mankind. We are all siblings of the Earth and heroes for each other. Let us pray for human kind's peace and unity. Wish you and I be brave and strong."

Editorial Committee

November 20, 2020

展建设中，也能继续关注中国的发展，积极向本国人民介绍自己在中国的所见、所感，让世界认识一个更加立体、更加鲜活的中国。

“海内存知己，天涯若比邻”。留学生朋友们，无论你们走到世界的任何一个地方，中国人民都是你们真诚的朋友，中国的发展将为你们提供展示才华的广阔舞台。

感谢所有参加本次征文比赛和短视频大赛的选手用自己的笔触和镜头记录时代，书写生活；感谢各高校、驻外使领馆教育处的大力支持；感谢各位老师、专家、评委的辛勤付出。正是我们每个人的努力，成就本次活动的成功举办，鼓励我们继续前行。

时间飞逝，2020 已近尾声。各国还在积极努力地与新冠肺炎疫情进行抗争，科学家们还在日以继夜地研制有效抑制病毒的疫苗，医护工作者依然奋战在战疫前线，每个平凡的普通人仍在应对着全人类不平凡的挑战。最后，让我们用征文中来自哈萨克斯坦的安迪同学的一段话作为结束语，“这是每个人独一无二的 2020，也是全人类共同的 2020，我们都是地球的孩子，也是彼此的英雄。愿人类平安、团结，愿你我勇敢、坚强！”

编委会

二〇二〇年十一月二十日

目录

CONTENTS

杨康

我的英雄梦

My Heroic Dream 002

白宇新

我把自己栽种在东方

I Planted Myself in the East 012

段芳花

离梦想更近

——我与唐诗的美丽邂逅

One Step Closer to My Dream 020

—A Beautiful Encounter with Tang Poetry

心天

阳光总在风雨后

——孟加拉国博士的抗疫进行曲

The Sun Always Shines After Storm 028

—The Anti-Epidemic Story of a Bangladeshi Ph.D. Candidate

阮红玲

武汉是我们青春的时光

Wuhan Defines My Youth 036

Contents

罗佩如
我和春天有个约会
I Have a Date with Spring 044

李江龙
我和中国
China and I 050

勒黑波妮
2020，我在中国
2020, I Am in China 058

王飒成
一封来自中国的邀约
An Invitation Letter from China 066

狄安娜
幸运的选择，美丽的邂逅
Lucky Choices, Beautiful Encounters 072

毕夏
生活，一键切换
One-Touch Life 078

陈嘉扬
印象华夏
My Impression of Huaxia 084

/ 目 录 /

黄美香
爱上一座城
The City I Fall in Love with 090

罗木
勇者无畏，行者无疆
The Brave Are Fearless and the Doers Are Boundless 096

阮庆玄
我的武汉故事
My Wuhan Story 102

陈文辉
方块字里读中国
Read China through Chinese Characters 110

高兴
重新出发看中国
Rediscover China 116

李米娜　方洁
从上网课到当主播，我们把中国歌声带给世界
——难忘的 2020 年故事
Singing Chinese Songs to the World 124

段兆嘉
我与北京
Beijing and I 130

Contents

苏逸
跟你谈场最“烧脑”的恋爱
A Brain-Burning Love with You 136

陈俐晴
少年游
Journey of a Youth 142

叶林特
破晓之春
——记 2020 年春校园生活
Dawn of Spring 148
—My Campus Life in the Spring of 2020

张小龙
我与中国的美丽邂逅
My Beautiful Encounter with China 154

李明涛
中国是我强大的后盾
A Strong China Stands Behind Me 160

申文燮
中国，我梦起航的地方
China, the Place Where My Dream Sets Sail 166

索克兰
我与中国人在特殊时期共同战疫
Fighting Pandemic Together with Chinese People 174

目 录

叶子琪

我用手机做公益

——留学生活中的特别收获

Charity with Mobile Phone 180

—A Special Gain of Studying in China

张博

我的中国梦

——我想成为“中国通”

My Chinese Dream 186

—To Become a Mr China

黄雯芳

中国，我把你藏在心里

China, I Cherish You in My Heart 192

李睿阳

给爸爸妈妈的一封信

A Letter to My Parents 198

安迪

我的 2020

My 2020 204

卡米拉

疫情与希望

Pandemic and Hope 210

阮春海

疫情无情人有情

Fighting Ruthless Pandemic with Love 216

Contents

崔志佑
生与死
Life and Death 222

塔蒂阿娜
我与中国美好的相遇
——千里之行，始于足下
My Beautiful Encounter with China 228
—The Journey of a Thousand Miles Begins with a Single Step

吕纯晶
唇齿留香，情暖心田
Delicious Food, Warm Love 236

伊森
透过疫情看中国
Witnessing China's Arduous Fight Against COVID-19 Pandemic 242

将森甫
邂逅中国，邂逅精彩
Encounter Splendid China 248

陈春
不同的家乡，同样的热爱
Different Hometown, Same Love 254

夏旋
停课不停学，隔离不隔爱
Suspend Schools but not Study, Isolate People but not Love 260

/ 目 录 /

阮氏秋恒
我的爱豆叫阿中
My Idol Is Called Brother Zhong 266

文武
2020，在抗疫中前行
2020 Records Progress and Victory in Battle Against Pandemic 274

黎氏浅
相思湖畔浅浅忆
Lakeside Memory 286

伊克巴尔
我的 2020
My 2020 292

夏小夕
“封闭”生活中的感动
Heart Touching Moments in Quarantine 298

岑冠浩
阿中的蒲公英
——给中国的一封信
Dandelion of Azhong 304
—A Letter to China

松叶佳子
我愿搭起中日桥梁
My Labor of Love: 310
Building Bridge between China and Japan

Contents

陈坤
中国！只想说爱你
China, I Just Want to Say I Love You! 316

陈诗吟
我看中国
China in My Eyes 322

马杜
我的中国情缘
My Attachment to China 328

艾金花
我的第二故乡
My Second Hometown 336

常德
魅力中国，我眼中最美的风景
Charming China, the most Beautiful Scenery in My Eyes 342

龚少杰
铁杆兄弟
Blood Brother 348

瑞吉娜
爱上温情的中国
Fall in Love with Tender China 354

阮氏庆璃
留学生活掠影
A Glimpse of My Study Life in China 362

/ 目 录 /

铃木雅子

邂逅中国，邂逅爱

Encounter China, Encounter Love 370

郑伊晴

我在中国的成长故事

Growing up in China 376

武扬

哦，我亲爱的中国

Oh, My Beloved China 382

张苏仪

我与中国的美丽邂逅

——志愿服务的变革力量

My Beautiful Encounter with China 388

—Change Power of Volunteering Services

阿福

美丽的邂逅

——我与中国的故事

A Beautiful Encounter 394

—My Story with China

我的英雄梦
My Heroic Dream

[阿富汗] 杨康 中国地质大学（武汉）
[Afghanistan] Nusrat Qudrat, China University of Geosciences (Wuhan)

Unlike most children in the world, I was born in a war-torn country. From childhood to adulthood, I have always had a dream – to see a peaceful, secure and developed Afghanistan. In the midst of the war, the seeds of studying abroad were secretly planted in my heart, I wanted to see the bigger world outside and feel the charm of the culture beyond the swords and spears. And I wanted to be a hero in the chaos, so that everything around me could be better.

In 2016, I was given the opportunity to make my dream come true in China. My first stop was the glamorous city of Shanghai! I fell even more madly in love with Chinese culture during my year of preparatory studies at Tongji University. At that time, language learning was intense and extracurricular life was filled with all kinds of Chinese novels. It was then that I became obsessed with Mr. Jin Yong's martial arts novels and the heroes of his novels. Yang Kang was one of the first fictional characters I came across, so I duly gave myself a Chinese name - Yang Kang. Later on, as my Chinese improved and my understanding of the novel grew, I loved the chivalrous Yang Guo even more than Yang Kang. But after all, people are used to call me Yang Kang, so I'll reluctantly continue to be

和世界上大多数的孩子不一样，我出生于一个战乱的国家，从小到大，我一直有一个梦想——看到一个和平、安全而发达的阿富汗。在战火硝烟中，我的心里悄悄埋下了出国留学的种子，我想去外面更大的世界看看，想感受一下刀枪剑戟之外的文化魅力，更想做一个乱世里的英雄，让我周围的一切能够好起来。

2016 年，我获得了来中国实现梦想的机会，第一站便去了魅力之都上海。在同济大学进行预科学习的那一年，我更加疯狂地爱上了中国文化。那时候语言学习紧张，课余生活被各种各样的中国小说填满。也就在那时候，我迷上了金庸先生的武侠小说和小说里的英雄人物。杨康，是我最早接触的小说人物之一，于是我也像模像样地给自己取了个中文名——杨康。后面随着我汉语水平的提高，对小说的理解也越来越深，比起杨康，我更爱侠肝义胆的杨过，不过毕竟这名字也叫得顺口了，那我就勉强还是继续做这个“英雄之父”吧。

2017 年 9 月，我进入中国地质大学（武汉）土木工程专业开始学习。

专业学习真是让我大开眼界。中国的工程技术老厉害了，特别是道路桥梁工程，那可是全世界第一！中国的科学技术已经达到世界领先水

the "father of heroes".

In September 2017, I entered China University of Geosciences (Wuhan) majoring in the civil engineering.

The study on my major really opens my eyes. Engineering technology of China is amazing. China is especially good at the road and bridge projects, which are the best in the world. The science and technology level of China is already at the top of the world. I am determined to study hard and bring advanced technology to my country so that more people can benefit from it. Although my undergraduate schedule is very full, I still make time to study Chinese on my own and get close to Chinese culture. I took a lot of traditional Chinese culture classes, Chinese calligraphy, Chinese painting, seal carving and more. I joined the school's dragon dance team and participated in a dragon dance competition of China. With the cooperation of the Chinese and foreign students, the feeling of the dragon soaring and jumping in our hands was so cool!

A beautiful encounter with Chinese culture excitated my love for China and its people. In the past four years, I have been taking the "fast and accurate" high-speed train, enjoying the beauty of China's rivers and mountains, getting to know many of Chinese buddies and gaining a deep respect for this civilization that has been passed down for 5,000 years.

The beginning of 2020 is also the start of my 24-year-old life. According to Chinese custom, this is my "year of fate". As soon as the winter holidays started, I set up a "travel plan of year of fate" for myself to learn more about the scenery, people and geography of China before I graduate.

On January 20, I began my trip to Shanghai with two other fellow

杨康在地大校碑前留影

平。我暗下决心好好儿学习，把先进的技术带到我的国家，让更多人受益。虽然本科生的课程安排得很满，但是我仍然会挤出时间来自学汉语，亲近中国文化。我选修了很多中国传统文化课程，中国书法、中国画、篆刻等，我还加入了学校的舞龙队，参加了中国的舞龙大赛。在中外同学们的合作下，巨龙在我们手中飞腾跳跃，那种感觉真是太酷了！

与中国文化的美丽邂逅，碰撞出了我对中国和中国人的热爱。这四年间，我坐着“快准稳”的高铁，饱览中国的秀美河山，结识了不少中国“老铁”，更让我对这传承五千年的文明有了深深的敬畏之情。

2020 年伊始，我的 24 岁也到来了。按照中国的习俗，今年可是我的“本命年”，寒假刚刚开始，我就给自己设定了一个“本命年旅行计划”，我想在毕业前更多地了解中国的风光景色、人文地理。

1 月 20 日，我和另外两位在武汉高校留学的同胞好友开始了上海之行。我们第一站去了母校同济大学，原本打算游完上海再去杭州、重庆，

countrymen who were also international students studying in colleges and universities of Wuhan. Our first stop was at my alma mater, Tongji University. We had planned to travel to Hangzhou and Chongqing after Shanghai to experience the excitement of Chinese New Year in depth, but a sudden epidemic disrupted all.

On January 22, my friends and I were getting ready to rest at 11:00 pm in our hotel when I suddenly noticed the news that Wuhan would be closed the next day. That's when I realized the seriousness of the " pneumonia of unknown cause" that had been on the news. We were outside of Wuhan and relatively safe, so my fellow compatriots and friends urged me to go straight home with them. But I made a decision that made them very surprised. I would go back to Wuhan!

I knew that this was a difficult and critical time for Wuhan. As one who grew up in a war-torn land, as one who did not fear death and vowed to be with my friends, how could I go alone when my teachers and classmates were suffering? No! I want to stay in Wuhan! Side by side with everyone! I want to do my part to help Wuhan fight the epidemic! After discussing with my two compatriots, they confirmed my idea and we immediately booked tickets for the next day's high speed train back to Wuhan.

Back at the school, the city, the school and the building were all closed. Strict measures followed step by step. Four hundred foreign students of the school were suddenly in a panic. Teachers of the school and colleges stood forward to divide the students into different groups for corresponding management at this critical moment, caring our lives and learning all the time. I couldn't stay idle either and tried to contact my fellow students and relevant

深度体验一下中国春节的热闹，没想到一场突如其来的疫情打乱了这一切。

1月22日晚上11点多，我和朋友在入住的酒店正准备休息，突然在手机上看到了武汉将于第二天封城的消息，这时我才意识到之前新闻里说的那个“不明原因肺炎”的严重性。当时我们身处武汉以外地区，相对安全，同行的同胞好友劝我一起直接回国。但是，当时我却做了一个让他们惊掉下巴的决定：回武汉！

我知道，现在是武汉的困难时期、关键时刻。作为一个在战乱之地长大的人，作为一个无惧死亡、誓与朋友共进退的人，我怎能在我的老师和同学们遭受苦难之时独自离去？不！我要留在武汉！与大家并肩作战！我要为武汉抗击疫情尽自己的一分力量！我和两位同胞商量后，他们也肯定了我的想法，我们当下就预订了隔天回武汉的高铁票。

回到学校，封城封校封楼，一步步严密措施接踵而来，学校400多

中国地质大学（武汉）/ 杨康提供

organizations that I could work together with to fight the epidemic.

On January 25, under the call of Da Ming, an international student from Benin, the international students in our school set up a volunteer service team known as "Iron Man". Under the guidance of the school authorities and teachers, it provided services and assistance to 437 international students who stayed on campus. When I learned this news, I was so excited that I immediately signed up to join the "Iron Man" volunteer team. At that time, I didn't know what I could do, but I knew I had to do something.

Day after day, we gradually found the direction and motivation. Although it may seem not to be a big deal to provide support and help them with their daily lives for international students, we have contributed all our courage and strength in this difficult time. Sometimes, when my voluntary service was not understood by everyone and there were some small conflicts, I also felt aggrieved and sad. Underneath the layers of stuffy protective clothing, in addition to the sweat in the harsh winter of Wuhan, there are traces of my hidden tears.

It is gratifying that, with the joint efforts of everyone, Wuhan is once again welcoming a warm spring. Our efforts have not been in vain. There hasn't been a single case of infection among international students throughout the school. Everyone was healthy and happy to see the Yellow Crane Tower light up again! As for me, at the moment I took off my protective suit and goggles, I felt the strength that courage and responsibility empowered me.

Later, reporters interviewed us and the students called us "heroes" when meeting us. What? Is this the "hero" I've been dreaming of? The role I had hoped to become so many times, the sentiment I had held on to for so long, have all

名留学生一下子慌了神。学校和学院的老师们挺身而出，在这个危急时刻将大家网格式划分，时时刻刻为大家的生活和学习服务。我也坐不住了，试着去联系同学，联系可以共同战疫的组织。

1 月 25 日，在我们学校贝宁籍留学生大明的号召下，学院的留学生们自发成立了一个志愿者组织——“钢铁侠”志愿服务队，在学校和老师们的指导下，为留校的 437 名留学生提供服务和帮助。看到这个消息，我激动不已，立马报名加入了“钢铁侠”志愿服务队。那时的我，还不知道自己能做些什么，但是我知道：我一定要做点儿什么。

日复一日的坚持，我们逐渐找到了行动的方向和动力。虽然为留学生提供帮助、做好生活服务这些都是看起来微不足道的小事，但是在这个艰难时刻，我们用尽了全部的勇气和力气。有时候，志愿服务碰上了小矛盾，甚至不被大家理解时，我也有委屈、有难过。层层防护服底下，

中国地质大学（武汉）/ 杨康提供

中国地质大学（武汉）/ 杨康提供

come true at this moment!

But what are these trifle things I did compared to the people around me? Heroic medics on the front lines built a healthy first-line with their bodies. The brave and fearless heroic people of Wuhan had allowed themselves to be "trapped" in this heroic city. The heroic Chinese government and people, while fighting the epidemic themselves, also lend a helping hand to the world. My country has been given a large number of medical supplies from China......

Never forget why you started, and your mission can be accomplished. I came here with a dream of being a hero, and will continue to fulfill my hero's dream along the "the Belt and Road".

除了记录在武汉严冬下闷出的汗水，还有我隐隐的泪水的痕迹。

让人欣慰的是，在所有人的共同努力下，武汉再次迎来了温暖的春天。我们的努力也没有白费，整个学校的留学生没有一例感染病例，大家都健健康康、快快乐乐地看到了黄鹤楼上再次亮起的明灯。而我，在脱下防护服、摘下护目镜的那一刻，感受到了勇气和担当赋予我的力量。

后来，有记者采访了我们，还有同学们在看到我们时，都直呼我们为“英雄”。什么？这就是我心心念念的“英雄梦”吗？我曾无数次盼望成为的那个角色，我内心执着已久的情怀，竟然都在那一刻变成了现实！

可比起周围的那些人，我做的这些小事又算得了什么呢？奋战在一线的英雄医护人员，用自己的身躯筑起健康的防线；勇敢无畏的英雄武汉人民，让自己“困守”在这座英雄城市；英雄的中国政府和人民，在自己抗疫的同时还对世界伸出援手，我的祖国也获赠了大量来自中国的医疗用品……

不忘初心，方得始终。我怀揣着一个英雄梦而来，也会沿着这“一带一路”，把我的英雄梦继续做完。

我把自己栽种在东方
I Planted Myself in the East

[土耳其] 白宇新 西安外国语大学
[Turkey] Kucukagtas Bayram, Xi'an International Studies University

Fourteen years have passed since I came to China from Turkey. During these years, I grew up to be a Turkish teacher from a young student. Recalling my life in China and my stories in Xi'an International Studies University, I have a lot to say. The longer I stay here, the deeper I love it. China has been my second hometown. I have heard such a saying: "The hometown cannot settle down your body and the other places cannot settle down your soul." To this, I cannot agree. China is foreign land for me, but it has well placed both my body and soul, making me feel at home. The plants and trees, the local customs and hospitable people are all the reasons why I am deeply rooted here. There are so many precious and indelible memories.

Having studied in the Xi'an International Studies University for six years, I became a teacher after graduating with a master degree. I had been called "Xiao Bai" (Little Bai) by my teachers and now I am Teacher Bai in the eyes of my students. Time flies. Eight years passed since I became a teacher. A Chinese saying goes, "It takes 10 years to grow a tree but 100 to cultivate a person." My little saplings (students) are now in full bloom, which is my proudest

我从土耳其来到中国已经快14年了。14年中，在古城西安，我从一名青涩的学生成长为一位土耳其语教师。关于我的中国生活，关于我的西外故事，我有说不完的话。日久情深，中国已经成了我的第二故乡。我听过这样一句话："故乡安置不了肉身，他乡安置不了灵魂。"我并不认同这个说法，因为中国虽然是我的异乡，但却很好地安置下了我的肉体与灵魂，真正让我有一种宾至如归的亲切感。这里的一草一木，这里的风土人情，都是我在此深深扎根的原因，这里有着许多抹不掉的珍贵回忆。

我在西外留学6年，硕士毕业留校任教至今，开始是老师们口中的"小白"，接下来成为学生们喜欢的白老师，掐指算来，也已经8年了。中国人常说"十年树木，百年树人"。我的小树苗们如今已枝繁叶茂，花开朵朵，这是我最骄傲、最有成就感的事。课堂上，我比较严厉，学生们都会对我产生敬畏之情，甚至有时候对我有些小害怕，但是他们清楚这是我在为他们负责；一到课下，那气氛就不一样了，我对学生尽量做到平等相待，尽量去提高他们的素养，培养他们的兴趣。我们会一起吃泡馍，期末去郊游野餐，我也会邀请学生来到家里做客，一起做中国

fulfillment. I am relatively strict in the classes. The students are in awe of me and sometimes even a little afraid of me. However, they are clear that I am responsible for them by being harsh. Outside classes, the atmosphere differs. I try my best to treat the students as equals, to tap their potential and cultivate their interests. We eat mutton soup with bread together and go on a picnic at the end of the term. I also invite students to my home, cooking Chinese food and Turkish dessert together, and exchanging opinions on Chinese and Turkish culture. The students of each session are more like my friends and family members. The earliest graduates have left school for four years, but I still keep contacts with them. I try to learn their latest work, who has found their love and who meet troubles and need help. They are just like my children and I still care about them even if they are independent in the society.

It is the people and the things that are truly rooted in my spiritual world, that have fused my blood and flesh into this land. Being a teacher is my first job in this new city and country. This job brings me warmth and motivates me to stay here for a long time. From the beginning when I was nervous in the class to now when I teach them with ease and proficiency; From the beginning when I tried to build trust with students with great care to now when I teach them with enthusiasm, I devote myself to teaching with sweat and tears. The rolling towers and familiar faces in this city seem to have been planted in my world and imprinted in my mind, which I am far more familiar with than my hometown. After getting married in 2013, I brought my wife, Bai Ruoxuan to China. In 2016 our son Xiao Xiao Bai (Junior Xiao Bai) was born here. Somehow, I will never separate with this country and this city. Here is my second country and second hometown. My whole youth, my family, my friends and everything

西安外国语大学 / 白宇新提供

饭和土耳其甜点，交流中土文化。每一届的学生与其说是我的学生，倒不如说更像是我的朋友、家人。最早的一届离校已经 4 年了，但是我仍与他们保持联系，关心他们的近况，哪个同学如今在岗位上做了什么贡献，哪个同学有了人生伴侣，哪个同学遇到了麻烦需要帮助，这些我都依然了解，就像自己的孩子步入了社会一样，想要时时刻刻关心他们。

真正根植在我精神世界里的，将我的血与肉融合进这片土地里的，就是这里的人和事。“老师”是我一开始来到这个陌生国家、陌生城市的第一份工作。是这份工作带给了我温暖，让我有了在这里长久留下的念头。从一开始在三尺讲台上授课时的青涩紧张到现在授课时的轻松熟练，从一开始小心翼翼和学生建立信任关系到现在可以用自己的热情和态度去培育他们，这一步步走来，都倾注了我的心血，洒下了我的汗水和泪水。这座城市里连绵起伏的大厦，一张张熟悉的面孔，仿佛本身就生长在我的世界里，烙印在我的脑海里，熟悉的程度甚至远超过我自己的家乡。2013 年结婚之后我把爱人白若萱接来中国，2016 年我们的儿

西安外国语大学 / 白宇新提供

of me are planted here. This land bestows me with the feeling of homeland which I am unwilling to leave. Such feeling has nothing to do with identity and national boundaries.

I have been living here for 14 years and will carry on teaching on the platform I love. The longer I stay, the deeper my root goes. I have been travelling to many places in China, big and small. Xi'an is the city where I have lived for more than 10 years. It seems that I have become a typical Xi'an person by absorbing the culture aura of the city. I know more or less about various scenic spots, food and snacks, as well as bus routes, dialects and customs in Xi 'an. This understanding helps me truly perceive the charm of local culture and would like to share with more people so that they can see and experience.

The outbreak of the COVID-19 pandemic has made me more aware of the power of China as a strong nation with deep love and responsibility for

西安外国语大学 / 白宇新提供

子小小白出生在这里。冥冥之中，我知道我与这个国家、这座城市永远也分不开了，这里就是我的第二个国家、第二个家乡。我的整个青春，我的亲人，我的朋友，我一切的一切都扎根在了这里，无关身份，无关国界，这是这片土地所赠予我的，一种故土难离的观念。

我在这里已经生活了近 14 年，我还会继续在热爱的讲台上耕耘。时间只会使我的根扎得更深，情怀变得更浓。这些年来我去过中国大大小小许多地方，见证了中国的发展和改变，十几年来我一直生活在西安这个城市，汲取这座城市的文化气息，仿佛变成了一个地道的西安人。大到西安的各类景点、风俗小吃，小到西安的公交线路、方言习俗，我多多少少都了解一些，而这种了解使我真正感受到了本土文化的魅力，同时也想将它发扬传播出去，让更多的人看见，体会到这里的风土人情。

这次新冠肺炎疫情，让我更加见识到中华民族、中国情的力量，也让我更加意识到我完全把自己当成了一个中国人，每天关注新闻，了解

its people. It has also made me realize that I regard myself as a Chinese, who tracks the news every day and understands what is happening. I laugh with the Chinese people, cry with them, worry with them and feel proud with them. I also received care of many friends and students with feeling of warmth. No matter what takes place in the future and no matter I leave or not, I appreciate all what I have here. All what I cherish will be in my bones and blood. China, that I deeply love and am willing to commend to the whole world, is my second hometown where I contribute myself. It is an obvious fact that I love this land from the heart and no proof is needed.

Planting myself in this land, I grow happily with bathing of affection.

发生的事情，和中国人民一起哭一起笑，一起担心一起自豪。我也体会到了身边许许多多朋友和学生的关心，这让我倍感温暖。不管今后如何，不管我是否离开，这里的所有就是我的所有，我珍重的一切都将融进我的骨子里，流淌在我的血液里。这个我深深热爱着的中国，我想向全世界去称赞的中国，我把一切都留在了这里的中国，就是我的第二个故乡，我深深地热爱着这片土地，真的无须证明。

我把自己栽种在这片土地上，沐浴着深情，幸福成长。

离梦想更近
——我与唐诗的美丽邂逅
One Step Closer to My Dream
—A Beautiful Encounter with Tang Poetry

［越南］ 段芳花 广西师范大学
[Vietnam] Đoàn Phuöng Hoa, Guangxi Normal University

Time is a one-way arrow. Once launched, it never turns back; Time is a handful of dust. Once let go, it goes with the wind; Time is a journey. Once set out, you have to move forward with courage. If we waste time, it will leave us with endless regrets; if we treat it well, it will give us the beauty of life. Dear friends, time is a treasure for all of us, what do you do with your time? I spent my time quietly in realizing my dream, that is, to master Chinese language and culture so as to be a Chinese language teacher in Vietnam.

As a child, I knew that China was an ancient civilization with a long history, and that the Chinese nation was glorious, who had created a splendid culture. In 2017, I was fortunate enough to come to China to study Chinese. The teacher taught us a Tang poem by Du Fu, "The Thatched Cottage is Broken by the Autumn Wind". She read slowly but engagingly, transporting me into the colorful world of ancient poetry and the brilliant and magical world of Tang poetry. Since then, I bound up with and foster a deep love with Tang Poetry. I

时间是一支箭，一旦发射就永不回头；时间是一把沙尘，一旦放手就随风而去；时间是一场旅行，一旦启程就只能勇往直前。若虚度光阴，它将留给我们无尽的懊悔；若善待光阴，它将馈赠我们生命的华美。亲爱的朋友们，时间是我们每个人的财富，你会用自己的时间去干什么呢？我用自己的时间悄悄实现自己的梦想，那就是，学好汉语和中国文化，将来回自己的祖国越南当一名汉语教师。

儿时的我就知道，中国是一个有着悠久历史的文明古国，中华民族是一个创造出灿烂文化的光辉民族。2017 年，我有幸来到了中国学习汉语。在一次汉语课上，老师为我们讲了一首唐诗，是杜甫的《茅屋为秋风所破歌》，她读得很慢却很动人，让我走进了色彩斑斓的古诗世界，也把我带进了瑰丽神奇的唐诗世界，从此，我与唐诗结下了美丽的缘分。我爱上了唐诗，爱上了书写着唐诗的泛黄的纸张，也爱上了品读那朗朗上口、让人欲罢不能的动人诗篇。唐诗之美，是促进我向汉语和中国文化深处探寻的源源动力。

段芳花在越南

also fell in love with the yellow paper, on which Tang poetry was written, and with reading the catchy and touching poems. The beauty of Tang poetry is the endless power to motivate me to explore Chinese language and Chinese culture.

The poetry of Tang Dynasty is a magnificent heritage of Chinese culture and a precious artistic treasure that China has brought to the world. There are so many popular lines in Tang poetry. In China, few people can't recite a few Tang poems. The poets put their personal sentiments and their devotion to country and family in their poems. The exquisite words and expressions have already enchanted me. The rich and profound emotions have deeply touched my sensitive heart. I love reading poems. But because of the heavy work load, I could hardly find spare times to be immersed in the world of Tang poems.

In the first half of 2020, the COVID-19 epidemic trapped us at home. During the days of half isolation from the outside world, some people practiced hard at cooking, some did various exercises, some found ways to entertain themselves, while I happily immersed myself in the world of Tang Poetry. Several collections of Tang poetry sit on my desk. Every time I read; I was reluctant to put it down. When I came across some wonderful lines, sometimes I cannot help clapping my hands for acclaim. Sometimes I signed sadly. Sometimes I held myself aloof from the world. Sometimes I shed my tears and

广西师范大学（清晨）/ 段芳花提供

唐诗，是中国文化的瑰丽遗产，是中国带给世界的宝贵艺术财富。唐诗中有那么多脍炙人口的句子，有哪个中国人不会背诵几句唐诗呢？诗人把个人情怀与家国情怀寄托在他们的诗句里，词语的精雕细琢早已让我陶醉，情感的深沉厚重更是深深打动了我敏感的心灵。我爱读诗，但课业繁重，没那么多时间流连在唐诗的世界里。

2020年上半年，新冠肺炎疫情把我们困在了家中，在一个个与外界近乎隔绝的日子里，有的人苦练厨艺，有的人花式健身，有的人自娱自乐，而我则欣喜地把自己沉浸在了唐诗的世界里。几本唐诗的集子放在案头，每每让我爱不释手，读到精彩处，有时击节赞叹，有时扼腕叹息，有时神游物外，有时潸然泪下，有时慷慨激昂！

每每读懂一首诗，我对汉语的敏感就会提升一些，想象力也会更丰富一些。杜甫诗中说“安得广厦千万间，大庇天下寒士俱欢颜”，在战

广西师范大学（春日）/ 段芳花提供

sometimes I was impassioned.

Every time I understand a poem, my sensitivity to the Chinese language builds up a little more and my imagination grows a little richer. In Du Fu's poem, he said, "Could I get mansions covering ten thousand miles, I'd house all poor scholars and make them beam with smiles." How touching it is that a weak scholar in a time of war should had such a strong humanist sentiment! Du Mu's poem, "The candle has a wick just as we have a heart; all night long it sheds tears for us before we part." makes me deeply appreciate that people paint the world with their own moods. Li Bai's poem, "Its torrent dashes down three thousand feet from high; as if the Milky Way fell from azure sky.", makes me realize that with the wings of imagination, our world can be larger, more beautiful and more magical. Li Shangyin's poem, "Till the end of life a silkworm keeps spinning silk; Till burning itself out a candle goes on lighting us" is so sad and romantic. Wang Han's poem, "Don't laugh if we lay drunken on the battle

登山俯瞰桂林城 / 段芳花摄

乱年代，一个文弱的书生竟然具有这么厚重的人文主义情怀，多么令人动容！杜牧的“蜡烛有心还惜别，替人垂泪到天明”让我深深体会到人是用自己的心境描绘这个世界的；李白的“飞流直下三千尺，疑是银河落九天”让我深知只要插上想象的翅膀，我们的世界可以更大、更美、更神奇！李商隐的“春蚕到死丝方尽，蜡炬成灰泪始干”多么缠绵悱恻，而王翰的“醉卧沙场君莫笑，古来征战几人回”又是多么慷慨豪迈！“举头望明月，低头思故乡”，李白用寥寥几笔就勾起了我们的思乡泪；“人闲桂花落，夜静春山空”，王维幽静的山居生活何尝不能让我们收起名利之心、生出归隐之念？

唐诗之美，说不尽，也道不完。唐诗，让我更了解古代中国人的雅致生活。过着“柴米油盐酱醋茶”的日常，心中也要有着“琴棋书画诗酒花”的远方。现代人生活节奏快，当我们觉察到生活的疲惫，不妨像古人一样，用雅趣来给生活增添乐趣和情怀，生活不只是苟且，唐诗让我们心中有远方。

ground; how many soldiers ever came back safe and sound" is very passionate and heroic. "Raising my head, I see the moon so bright; withdrawing my eyes, my nostalgia comes around." Li Bai evoked people's tears of homesickness with several lines. "Osmanthus falls by the side of the idle poet; the spring mountain is empty in the quiet night." Does Wang Wei's quiet life in the mountains make us shift out attention from wealth and fame and long for seclusion?

There is no end to talking about the beauty of Tang poetry. Tang poetry has given me a better understanding of the elegant life of ancient Chinese people. Apart from the daily life surrounded by daily necessities (fuel, rice, oil, salt, soy, vinegar and tea), we can also pursue spiritual things (music, chess, painting, poetry, wine and flowers). Modern life is fast paced. When we feel tired, we may learn from the ancients who knew how to enrich the life with elegance and fun. Life not only has a single look. Tang poetry takes us to any place as far as our heart can reach.

In 2020, I devoted myself to Tang poetry. It is a beautiful encounter and a baptism of my soul. It was my Chinese teacher who brought me into the pretty world of Tang poetry in the first place, helping me go closer to my dreams. I hope that like my teacher, I can make my students encounter and fall in love with the Tang poetry that I encountered and loved so much!

在桂林两江四湖公园小径徜徉 / 段芳花提供

2020 年，我把时间交给了唐诗，这是一场美丽的邂逅，这是一次心灵的洗礼。当初是我的汉语老师把我带进了唐诗的美丽世界，让我离自己的梦想近一点、更近一点，我希望自己能像老师一样，让自己的学生也邂逅我邂逅过的唐诗，爱上我深爱着的唐诗！

阳光总在风雨后

——孟加拉国博士的抗疫进行曲

The Sun Always Shines After Storm

—The Anti-Epidemic Story of a Bangladeshi Ph.D. Candidate

[孟加拉国] 心天 北京理工大学

[Bangladesh] Mostak Ahmed, Beijing Institute of Technology

"There is a dragon in the far East." With a curious yearning, I came to China in 2013. I graduated with a master's degree with a good command of Chinese, and am currently doing my doctorate at Beijing Institute of Technology. Over the past 40 years of reform and opening up, drastic changes have taken place in China. I have really felt the changes in the past few years when I studied in China. More importantly, I have understood the Chinese spirit, that is, "help each other."

The COVID-19 epidemic broke out around the world in 2020. While actively responding to the domestic epidemic, China offered a helping hand to other countries, including sending anti-epidemic medical experts to help Bangladesh carry out the prevention and control of the COVID-19 epidemic.

"The Chinese friends have helped us in the time of difficulty." This is the common voice of many countries.

I have to do something, too!

I returned early to Bangladesh in the winter vacation, when I hadn't heard

“遥远的东方有一条龙”，怀着对美好中国的向往，2013 年我来到了中国。我硕士毕了业、学会了汉语，目前在北京理工大学读博士。改革开放 40 多年来，中国发生了翻天覆地的变化，留学中国的这几年我真切感受到了中国的变化，更重要的是我了解了中国精神，那就是互帮互助。

2020 年全球暴发了新冠肺炎疫情，中国在积极应对国内疫情的同时，主动向其他各国伸出援助之手，包括派出抗疫医疗专家组帮助孟加拉国开展新冠肺炎疫情的防控。

“在困难的时候，中国朋友帮助了我们”，这是很多国家共同的心声。

我也要做点什么！

因为学校放寒假，我提早回到了孟加拉国，那时还没听说过新冠肺炎病毒。回到家后我通过新闻得知形势比较严峻，开始在网上搜索了解更多信息。

of the COVID-19 virus. When I got home, I learned of the gravity of the situation from the media and began to search the internet for more information.

Purchase of Masks

When the World Health Organization declared the COVID-19 epidemic an "international public health emergency", there was a temporary shortage of medical supplies in China, so I quickly collected available medical surgical masks from the local market and all neighboring cities in Bangladesh and sent them to China. Transportation from Bangladesh to China was not easy, and many flights and freight services had been delayed. So, we shipped the goods from Dhaka to Hong Kong and then to Chongqing. I provided more than 70, 000 masks for Chongqing and also sent some to Beijing Institute of Technology, my alma mater.

The first case in my country was confirmed on March 8, after which more people were confirmed within a month. There was already a shortage of protective equipment in Bangladesh. I then managed to buy masks, gloves and protective equipment from abroad and gave them to hospitals, prime minister's offices, local governments, banks, relatives and friends, and so on.

Try to Make Masks for the First Time

Gradually, the whole world was affected by the COVID-19 epidemic. I realized that in Bangladesh, a country with a large population, it would be very difficult to control the epidemic. I wanted to do something for my country and people. I was neither a mechanical engineer, nor had any experience in making machines. But I believed that "where there is a will, there is a way."

So, I began to try to make mask machines. I wanted to distribute the

紧急购买口罩

当世界卫生组织宣布新冠肺炎疫情为“国际公共卫生紧急事件”时，中国出现医疗物资供应暂时短缺的现象，于是我赶快在当地市场和所有邻近城市收集可用的医用外科口罩，一起寄往中国。从孟加拉国到中国的运输很不容易，许多航班和货运服务被推迟。所以，我们将货物从达卡运到香港，然后运到重庆。我向重庆市提供了 7 万多个口罩，也给母校——北京理工大学，寄送了一些。

我们国家的第一例确诊病例是在 2020 年 3 月 8 日。此后一个月内又有一些人确诊，当时在孟加拉国当地市场上也出现了防护用品短缺的情况。我又想办法从国外买了口罩、手套和防护用品，送给医院、总理府、地方政府、银行和亲朋好友等。

北京理工大学 / 心天摄

中国文化——京剧 / 心天摄

masks among people for free. It's not easy for me. First, I collected relevant research and design, and then I started purchasing and manufacturing all the parts. Thinking that maybe a lot of people around the world were struggling to make mask machines, I made another decomposition video and uploaded it onto the social media. More than 300 companies from more than 50 countries contacted me for advice and support. I not only helped them and shared my experience with them, but also provided some parts for many countries. I realized that the little thinking and the few efforts I did were meaningful, not only to my country, but also to people in other countries. It is a great feeling to do something useful for human beings, and it is the true value of life.

Teach People the Method

Due to the spread of the epidemic, many people lost their jobs and were unable to support their families, so I donated the living expenses I saved while studying to more than 100 families and told them, "If you are in trouble, please feel free to contact me." In my opinion, donation is only an expedient measure, not a permanent solution. Many energetic young people were out of work. I called them to my house and taught them how to do business quickly. Then

第一次尝试制作口罩

渐渐地，全世界都受到了新冠肺炎疫情的波及。我意识到，在孟加拉国这个人口众多的国家，要控制疫情非常困难。我想为我的祖国和人民做点什么。我既不是机械工程师，也没有任何制造机器的经验，但我相信“有志者事竟成”。

于是我开始尝试制造生产口罩的机器，我想把口罩免费分发给老百姓。这对我来说并不容易，首先我收集了相关研究和设计，然后开始采购和制造所有的零部件。想到可能全世界很多人都在为制造口罩机而奋斗，我又制作了一个分解视频，并上传到了社交媒体。来自 50 多个国家的 300 多家公司联系我，请我提供咨询和支持。我不仅帮助了他们，和他们分享经验，也向许多国家提供了一些零部件。我意识到，我的一点思考和努力是有意义的，不仅对我的国家有意义，对其他国家的人也有意义。做一些对人类有用的事有一种很伟大的感觉，是生命真正的价值。

授人以渔

由于疫情扩散，许多人失去了工作，不能养家糊口，于是我把自己读书期间省吃俭用攒下来的生活费捐给了 100 多个家庭，告诉他们：“如果有困难，请随时与我联系。”在我看来，捐赠只是权宜之计，并不是永久性的解决办法。许多精力充沛的年轻人失业，我把他们叫到我家来，教给他们快速经商的点子。然后我创建了一家公司，招募了 15 个人，他们因此可以养家糊口。我正尝试通过网络来扩展短期培训，以便在全国范围内创造更多的就业机会。

尽己所长

除了力所能及地帮助别人，我还根据计算机的专业特长做了一些有

I started a company and recruited 15 people so that they could support their families. I am trying to expand short-term training through the Internet in order to create more jobs across the country.

Take Advantage of My Expertise

In addition to helping others as much as I can, I have also made some useful attempts on the basis of my computer expertise, such as online education and making health videos. I have made a complete online learning platform (www.banglatraining.com), which includes video lessons, real-time chat, homework submission, quizzes, automatic assessment, accreditation and many other functions. Some courses have been released and more courses are on the way. I hope to help more students. I have made some videos to raise public awareness in an attempt to build a correct public understanding of the novel coronavirus on the Internet.

The epidemic has taught us more about the value of life and what is more important to us. China has helped many countries fight the epidemic together. As international students, we sincerely appreciate and admire the great efforts made by the Chinese government, and we are especially grateful to the Chinese government for its help to Bangladesh in difficult times. We will never forget these helps. I will always remember the "Chinese spirit" of helping each other. I will also rely on my professional knowledge to help more people. I hope that more people will contribute their love and strength to protect the beautiful earth together.

"The sun always shines after the storm, there is a clear sky above the dark clouds, cherish all that moves you, every hope lies in your hands ..."

Let's keep moving. Come on!

益的尝试，比如在线教育和制作健康视频。我做了一个完整的网上学习平台（www.banglatraining.com），其中包含视频课、实时聊天、作业提交、测验、自动评估、资格认证和诸多其他功能，目前一些课程已经发布，更多课程也即将推出，希望能帮到更多的学生。我制作了一些提高公众意识的视频，尝试在网上建立公众对新冠病毒的正确认识。

因为疫情，我们更了解了生命的价值，也渐渐明白了哪些事情是更重要的。中国帮助很多国家共同抗疫，作为留学生，我们由衷赞赏和钦佩中国政府在抗疫方面做出的巨大努力，特别感谢中国政府在艰难的时刻给予孟加拉国的帮助。这些帮助我们永远不会忘记，我将永远铭记互帮互助的"中国精神"，我也会凭借自己的专业知识帮助更多人，希望更多的人一起献出爱心和力量，共同守护美好地球。

"阳光总在风雨后，乌云上有晴空，珍惜所有的感动，每一份希望在你手中……"

让我们行动起来，加油！

故宫 / 心天摄

武汉是我们青春的时光
Wuhan Defines My Youth

［越南］ 阮红玲　华中师范大学
[Vietnam] Nguyễn Hồng Linh, Central China Normal University

I am a Vietnamese girl and I love Chinese culture, especially ancient Chinese literature. I have been in Wuhan, Hubei Province for almost three years. It may not be so long, but enough to light up my thirst and eager for knowledge and research.

When I just finished the above paragraph, I naturally recalled the first day I arrived in Wuhan. It was a fresh morning. As I opened the window, I saw the tree-covered campus and breathed in the refreshing cool air. It was my biggest dream as a student to come to China to study, especially at Central China Normal University. From the Chinese class at my senior middle school and ancient Chinese literature class at college in Vietnam, I had learned that Wuhan consisted of three towns, that is, Hankou, Wuchang and Hanyang. Located at the confluence of the Yangtze River and Hanjiang River, Wuhan is known as "Gateway to Nine Provinces," where the fabled story of Yu Boya and Zhong Ziqi took place. This is a blessed land with great attractions, such as the Heptachord Terrace (*Guqin Tai*) and Yellow Crane Tower. You see, I had learned of Wuhan before I actually arrived in the city. On the second night, I smiled at the moon

我是一位热爱中国文化，尤其是中国古代文学的越南姑娘，来武汉至今快三年了。虽然时间不是很长，但对我来说，这段时间足够点燃自己内心求知若渴的神圣火焰。

当我写下这段话的时候，我怀旧的心思也随之回到来武汉的第一天。我仍然记得第一个来到武汉的清晨，我打开窗户，外面是一片绿树成荫的校园，空气十分凉爽。有机会来到中国，尤其能到华中师范大学读书，是我学习生涯中最大的愿望。从高中的语文课和大学中国古代文学教材中，我早已对武汉有所了解。“武汉三镇”为汉口、武昌和汉阳的合称，是长江和汉水的交汇之处的城市，九省通衢，伯牙子期“知音”故事的发生地，古琴台和黄鹤楼的所在地，等等。因此我对武汉的有名景区也有一定了解。在武汉的第二天晚上，我望着窗外的月亮，那里也是黄鹤楼的方向，有众多杰出的作家，优秀的作品都在这里发芽与繁荣。我微笑着，我的来华留学梦想实现了。好神奇啊！

一年之中有春夏秋冬，四季交替。在武汉，我感受到了四季的魅力与特征。秋天到来，黄叶与红叶也跟着来了。“红叶似火，黄叶如金”是武汉赏秋的最佳美景。冬天来临，对于一个来自东南亚国家的姑娘来

shining in the direction of the Yellow Crane Tower. Throughout the history men of letters gathered there and composed great essays and poems. I smiled, for my dream of studying in China was fulfilled. How amazing!

Wuhan has four clearly distinctive seasons, In Wuhan I experienced the features of the four seasons and the charms of spring, summer, autumn and winter. In autumn, there are yellow and red leaves all around. The city is well known for its great autumn scenery featuring the "flame-like red leaves and yellow-gold leaves." For a girl form Southeast Asia, I had longed for big snow in winter. Wuhan did not fail me. I saw snow last winter. It was so beautiful. I rushed to the stadium in high spirit and I made a snowman and had a snowball fight. For each foreign student, it was unforgettable happy time. When spring arrives and the cherry blossoms bloom in full glory. Wuhan becomes an ethereal realm, a picturesque fairyland. Due to the pandemic, I was away from Wuhan, thus unable to appreciate the cherry blossoms this spring. So I was even more eager for next spring's beautiful cherry blossoms.

华中师范大学提供

说，非常期待能看到一场大雪。武汉没有辜负我的希望。我去年冬天终于看到下雪了，雪景十分美丽。我们高高兴兴地来到体育场里，堆雪人，打雪仗，这是令每个留学生难以忘怀的时光。尤其在春天，当樱花盛开的季节，武汉更加美成一幅画，令人心动。今年由于疫情，无法欣赏武汉艳丽的樱花，更让我期待明年春天的美丽樱花。

如果你曾去过武汉，我相信你会像我一样深爱武汉。武汉不仅是著名的风景名胜之城，这里的人们更美。老师们非常体贴、周到，我从未忘记当我学完汉语课的时候，与班主任老师拥抱的那一刻。那一刻我内心生出一种温暖的情感，就像亲情一样。华师文学院中国古代文学专业都是专业素养深厚的优秀教授，而我们的导师也是其中之一。他们的指导和关怀，给我留下深刻的印象。甚至学校食堂的叔叔和阿姨们也非常细心，热情好客。这些平凡的人也给我们带来温暖、亲密的感觉。

我还记得当武汉封城时，中国的网站上有一句话："我们隔离病毒，却不隔离爱。"当家家户户关注武汉疫情的信息时，我在默默翻看旧照片。这些照片，记录了我和老师、同学们在一起的美好时光。

If you have ever been to Wuhan, I believe you will fall in love with the city just like I did. Wuhan is not only a charming city with great attractions, but a city of amazing people. My teachers are so kind and considerate. I still remember the warmths of kinship grew in my hear while my professor hugged me when I completed my Chinese course. Faculty of the Department of Ancient Chinese Literature at the School of Chinese Language and Literature consisted of highly qualified and well-learnt professors just like my tutor. Their guidance and care had left me with deep impression. Even the sirs and madams at the campus canteens were so attentive and friendly. They made me feel so warm and close to each other.

I remember when Wuhan was locked down, I've read from the Chinese media "We isolate diseases, but not love." When the world had its eyes on Wuhan fighting against the Convid-19 as the epicenter of the pandemic, I checked the old photos in silence. These photos recorded my happy time with teachers and classmates.

This city has become part of my youth. To me, Wuhan is truly a heroic city, which has tenaciously put the coronavirus under control and finally surmounted it. When trouble occurs at one spot, help comes from all quarters. Mobilized in solidarity, Chinese people plunged themselves into the fight against the pandemic, while overseas Chinese all over the globe made their due contributions to their motherland. In Wuhan, everyone shouldered his or her share of responsibility. Everyone endured hardships and made silent efforts. Wuhan has long become my land of promise and pride.

Due to the pandemic, I cannot return to the campus in Wuhan for the time being. But I still enjoy looking at the moon. And quite often I will recite Li

这座城市已经成为我青春的一部分。对我而言，武汉确实是一座英雄的城市。这场新冠肺炎疫情，武汉市顽强地控制住了，并战胜了疫情。一方有难八方支援，团结一致的中国人战疫，各大洲华人华侨朋友们也积极帮助祖国。在武汉，每个人都清楚地了解自己的责任，全民在艰苦的日子里默默努力。武汉，早已成为令我骄傲的土地！

由于全球战疫的需要，现在我暂时还不能返校，但我仍然喜欢看着月亮，常常朗读李白的《黄鹤楼送孟浩然之广陵》。我对这首诗中的地名非常熟悉，因为武汉早已成为我的第二故乡：

故人西辞黄鹤楼，
烟花三月下扬州。
孤帆远影碧空尽，
唯见长江天际流。

阮红玲在武汉黄鹤楼

Bai's poem *Seeing Meng Haoran off at Yellow Crane Tower.* I am so familiar with the places mentioned in the poem, for Wuhan has long become my second hometown:

My friend has left the west where the Yellow Crane towers,

For River Town veiled in green willows and red flowers.

His lessening sail is lost in the boundless blue sky,

Where I see but the endless River rolling by.

The heroic city of Wuhan is the big family shared by all foreign students. I love Wuhan so much and I am looking forward to returning to the city!

Wuhan, wait me back!

阮红玲在华中师范大学图书馆

这座英雄之城武汉，是我们全体留学研究生共同的大家庭。我非常想念武汉，我渴望能早日回去！

武汉，等我回来吧！

我和春天有个约会

I Have a Date with Spring

[柬埔寨] 罗佩如 北京工业大学

[Cambodia] Ngoun Mariya, Beijing University of Technology

"When I was young, 2020 seemed so far way. While imagining the great infinite changes in the future, I wished time pass faster and faster, so that I could embrace the spring I had longed for." Now that 2020 arrived, it was a cold winter. The COVID-19 pandemic was spreading all across the country. People were scared, they took protective measures. They were cautious. And every single day, they closely watched the latest developments of the pandemic.

I always have affection for the city of Wuhan. And I worried about horrible pandemic that hit Wuhan so hard. When COVID-19 broke out, it was around the Spring Festival, the most important festival for the Chinese people. Due to the unexpected and unwelcome virus, the city came to a standstill and people were panicked. To curb and control the spread of the pandemic, the megacity of Wuhan was locked down. Wuhan is a city with more than 10 million people, a gateway to nine provinces. It was suddenly silenced. And the streets and alleys became silent and empty. They looked familiar yet. What a surreal feeling!

It was a cold winter of ice and snow. After an unusual Spring Festival, there was a shortage of medical supplies in Wuhan, a city under lockdown. However,

“小时候觉得2020好遥远，想象那无限的变迁，总是忍不住想要拨快时间，去拥抱盼了很久的春天。”如今终于到了2020年，可它却是一个寒冷的冬天。新冠肺炎疫情在全国蔓延，人们担忧着，提防着，小心翼翼着，每天刷屏关注着最新疫情动态。

我一直对武汉这座城市充满感情，武汉遭遇的严重疫情牵动着我的心。疫情袭来正好是春节，春节对中国人来说是一个最重要的节日，却因为一位不速之客，而变得冷清，让人恐慌！疫情当下，一座千万人口的城市，一个四通八达的城市立刻被管制，整座城市一下子静了下来，大街小巷变得熟悉而陌生，有一种物是人非的感觉。

冰封雪飘，一个不平常的春节过后，被封城的武汉面临医疗用品等物资缺乏情况，全国各地纷纷支援湖北省的画面令人感动。不速之客四处掠夺人们的健康和生命，出现了无数的白衣战士，他们拼尽全力在阻击疫情。钟南山爷爷和李兰娟奶奶一再叮嘱大家减少不必要外出，而他们却不顾高龄亲自带领团队冲到了一线。除此之外，还有无数的工人师傅，放弃休假来到危险的一线，仅用10天就建成了一座可容纳1000张床位的医院。“火雷速度”中饱含着上万名中国建筑工人的辛勤奋斗，

the whole country was mobilized to give support to Hubei Province as donations and supplies kept flooding in. To fight against the deadly virus, angels in white had emerged. They were truly heroes in harm's way. For many times, Sir Zhong Nanshan and Madam Li Lanjuan warned people that they should stay at home and avoid going out. However, they themselves led the teams and worked at the very forefront with the patients and doctors. Many workers worked day and night at the center of the deadly coronavirus outbreak. In 10 days, a 1,000-bed hospital was miraculously built. This fantastic speed would not have been made possible without the incredibly hard work of over 10,000 Chinese construction workers. They were competing with the pandemic, racing against the clock. The sooner the hospitals were built, the more lives it would save.

China suspended all means of transport in and out of Wuhan and lots of key virus-hit areas. People co-operated well with the government in implementing the strict measures to control the pandemic. Some Wuhanese had no abnormal symptoms for the time being, however they chose to stay at home in Wuhan in order not to pass the virus to others once they ventured out. There was a vigorous flame in their hearts. Adults quarantined for days shouted "Long Live the Motherland" all together from different rooms in one building, while children saluted to the TV screen when it broadcast the scene of the national flag being hoisted up. Wuhan is a heroic city. And China is a heroic country. Chinese people have always been protected well by the bravest of them. Time and time again I was touched by the Chinese spirit of solidarity and sacrifice.

Now that China has successfully controlled the pandemic, but the virus keeps spreading all over the world. I am heartened that China keeps sharing its experiences, expertise and donating supplies and equipment to countries around the world. My

他们与疫情赛跑，争分夺秒筑就了火神山医院和雷神山医院，让更多患者能及时地得到救治。

国家限制大量人员流动，有效抗击疫情也少不了广大人民的配合，有的武汉人暂时没有发现身体异常，也坚决地选择留在武汉，避免出去后感染到其他人。人们的内心始终有一团火，他们可以在封闭多天的大楼里一起高声喊“祖国万岁”，孩子们看到电视上国旗升起向国旗敬礼。武汉本来就是一座很英雄的城市。中国本来就是一个很英雄的国家。中国人，总是被他们之中最勇敢的人保护得很好。我不断地被这种精神感动着。

眼下中国疫情控制进入稳定期，病毒却在全球严重蔓延，中国毫不吝啬对世界的支持和帮助。我们学校给身在海外的外国留学生寄口罩，关心学生的健康，老师们不分昼夜地帮助学生解决各种问题，线上教学一天都没有拖延。作为留学生的我，感受到学院对外国留学生满满的关

北京工业大学 / 罗佩如提供

university mailed facial masks to foreign students stranded in their home countries to protect their health. Teachers worked day and night, teaching online courses and helping students with their questions, without a single day of delay. As a foreign student, I felt the abundant care and love my college had for foreign students. During the period I plunged myself into study with full enthusiasm. I worked very hard because I had vowed never to fail my teachers and my university.

When its neighboring countries were sick, China offered generous support to help them fight against the pandemic. This had demonstrated China's global leadership. China had donated facial masks, nucleic acid detection kits and many other medical supplies to the world's hard-hit countries, such as Iran, Pakistan, Republic of Korea and Japan, and had sent medical teams to many countries, including my country, Cambodia. China shared its anti-pandemic experience and expertise with my country. The medical experts team worked at the forefront at Cambodian hospitals, sharing their experiences with local doctors and medical staff, proactively guiding my country's fight against the pandemic. The Chinese medical team had brought with them in a chartered plane the much-needed medical supplies to Cambodia. Posted at cardboard boxes containing the medical supplies were national flags of China and Cambodia and the heart-touching words "Together stronger, we help each other. China and Cambodia, our hearts beat together" in Chinese and Cambodian. Sincere thanks to China for her help when we needed it most. We will always remember China's great kindness in our heart of hearts.

The subway will be crowded with passengers like before, life will come back to the streets. The pandemic had brought us a very cold and dark winter. But I think spring will surely and finally arrive!

罗佩如

爱。不发奋读书就对不起学院和老师，这段时间我以百倍的热情全身心投入学习，发誓绝不辜负老师和学校。

周围的国家生病了，中国没有袖手旁观，援助各国抗击疫情，体现出中国的大国精神。中国向疫情较严重的伊朗、巴基斯坦、韩国和日本等国捐赠了口罩、核酸检测试剂盒等医疗用品，并向多国派遣医疗专家组，其中也有我的国家——柬埔寨。中国将自己防疫抗疫的经验带给我国，医疗专家组深入医院，与医务工作者交流，积极指导帮助我国的战疫行动。随同包机一道抵达的还有柬埔寨急需的抗疫医疗物资，物资包装纸箱上印着中柬两国国旗，以及用中柬两国文字标明的“守望相助、中柬同心”。感谢中国在我们最需要的时候，伸出援手。这份恩情，我们永远铭记于心！

地铁会回归拥挤，街道会重返热闹。虽然疫情的到来带给了我们一个格外黑暗寒冷的冬天，但是我们坚信，春天一定会来！

我和中国

China and I

[美国] 李江龙 三峡大学

[The United States] Ramsey, Thomas Stephen, China Three Gorges University

One of my colleagues is a teacher from Computer College of Sanxia University. When I learned that he stayed in the US during COVID-19 pandemic, I asked him the local conditions there. He said, "Awfully terrible!" Their food, money and daily supplies were in shortage. One of my family members who lives in east coast of the US told me that the capital city of their state was like a ghost city, and shelves in stores were all empty. He believed that the US would also carry out lockdown measures.

When the COVID-19 pandemic broke out, some leaders in the US and other countries neglected it. They stayed indifferent to what happened in China or even criticized China for what they were endeavoring to fight against the pandemic, which led to the final breakout of the pandemic in the world. The pandemic was spread without any country borders and humankind was its victims. Under no circumstance and no period should the pandemic be called as Wuhan Virus or Chinese Virus. Though a little bit worried during the pandemic period, the university never made me panic with their quick response. Chinese government reacted with the quickest speed, therefore the pandemic got

我有一位同事是三峡大学计算机学院的老师，与他交谈时我得知疫情期间他身在美国，当我询问他当地情况时，他说："情况十分糟糕，特别可怕！"他们的食物、钱，还有各种物资都面临着短缺问题。我还有一位住在美国东海岸的家人告诉我，他们的州府，也就是他所在的城市现在就像一个鬼城一样，商店里的货品被一扫而空，他还认为美国同样也会采取隔离措施。

我的国家的一些领导人以及世界上其他国家不仅在疫情初期对病毒坐视不理，甚至还指手画脚地诘难中国，于是导致了今天全球范围的不幸局面。病毒是无国界的，人类是这场疫情的受害者，在任何时候、任何情况下，这个病毒都不该被称作武汉病毒、中国病毒。疫情期间虽然我不免有些担心，但是学校从未让我感到恐慌，中国政府的反应也很迅速。好在中国的疫情已逐渐好转，然而现在我开始担心在美国的家人朋友。

作为一个在宜昌生活、工作多年的美国人，我对于一些西方国家，尤其是美国那些所谓的"领导人"口中那些不专业、满是偏见、毫无根据的言论（至今仍）感到万分惊讶和不安。这些言论纯粹是为了混淆视听、掩盖他们没有及时为疫情做好准备的错误，这种将病毒的起因归结

under complete control soon. However, I began to worry about my family and friends in the US.

As an American who has been living and working in Yichang, Hubei Province for many years, I was (still) greatly astonished and annoyed by those unprofessional and biased speeches of some so-called "leaders" in some Western countries especially in the US. Those speeches were only disguises for their decision mistakes for not getting themselves ready to fight the pandemic and for misleading the public. Their opinions of attributing the pandemic to China had no grounds to stand on itself.

My family and friends all opposed to these opinions and we all respected China and the Chinese people. Here I would like to take this opportunity to express my sincere wishes and support to the Chinese people. In addition, I also wanted to voice some opinions, that is, many Americans had been respecting China all the time and they had never blamed China for this pandemic. They were still hoping that they could travel to China after the pandemic. Many Americas saw through the disguise and evil minds behind all those spreading of terrifying news. Don't let our joy be robbed by a small number of ignorant people in the world.

李江龙

After the breakout of the pandemic,

李江龙

于中国的说法是根本站不住脚的，也没有任何意义。

在这里我想说，我的家人和朋友和我一样反对这种言论，我们都非常尊重中国和中国人民，我也想借此机会，向全体中国人民表达我衷心的祝愿和支持。此外我还想传递一些美好的声音，很多美国人一直都很尊重中国，从来没有把疫情归咎于中国，他们仍然盼望在疫情结束后的某一天能来中国游玩！所以有很多人看穿了那些散播恐怖言论的人的恶意与伪装，请大家不要让世界上少数无知的人掠夺我们的快乐。

疫情袭来后，为减少病毒的传播，中国政府迅速采取措施封锁城市、隔离人员，而一些西方国家却错误地将这种行为看作是对人权的侵犯。如果西方国家有人（尤其是那些所谓的“领导人”）认为中国政府在春节这个对中国人而言最重要、最能带动经济效益的节日里采取封城举措是为了侵犯人权的话，那意味着他们根本就不懂得什么是真正的领导能力。掌握了可靠数据后，中国政府迅速采取行动，保护了数十万甚至数

to effectively stop the spread of the virus, the Chinese government quickly took measures to block cities and put in quarantine those infected and suspected to prevent the infection. However, some Western countries accused China of violating humanity for these actions. If some people, especially those so-called leaders in Western countries, thought that efforts taken by the Chinese government, in the most important Chinese festival that had the highest economic values, were to violate human rights, they did not know what true leadership was. Based on reliable data, the Chinese government immediately took measures to block related cities so that they successfully protected millions of people from being infected by the virus. This was not violating human rights; however, these efforts were full respect and protection of humanity and they displayed the great leadership of the Chinese government!

After the breakout of the pandemic, China shared related information with the World Health Organization and other countries. That means, other countries had almost two months in advance to prepare themselves for the prevention of the COVID-19. However, what made us upset and angry was that leaders in some countries completely neglected the virus and kept accusing China. I wanted to apologize to Chinese people on behalf of some blind Americas. Most of American people respected China and its great Chinese people. Some anti-Chinese thoughts of people in the US and other countries made me agitated and I was ashamed of those actions and words. I wish all people in the world not blinded by fear of the pandemic and actively join China in fighting against the virus.

During the pandemic period, the university gave me full respect and care. I was greatly touched by the active cooperation of the Chinese people with

百万人民免受感染，这非但不是侵犯人权，反而显示出了对人权的充分尊重与保护，显示了中国政府的领导力！

疫情袭来后，中国及时与世卫组织、西方国家分享信息，这意味着其他国家有近乎两个月的时间来为防范病毒做准备，然而令人感到不安和愤怒的是，这些国家的领导人还不以为然，继续指责中国。我想代表部分盲目的美国人向中国人民道歉，大部分美国人都是尊重伟大的中国和中国人民的。美国及其他国家的仇华言论让人感到非常不安，我也为美国有些人的言行感到很羞愧。希望各国人民不要被疫情的恐惧所蒙蔽，并且尽快与中国合作抗疫。

疫情期间，学校给予了我充分的尊重与关心。看到中国人民积极配合政府工作，各界尽职尽责阻止病毒的传播，医院不分国界、尽心尽力地照顾所有患者，我深受感动。我想说，能够在这一艰难时期坚守在宜昌和我的中国朋友们、同事们，以及留下来的留学生们一起携手面对这

三峡大学求索溪畔 / 李江龙提供

the government, the full efforts of all social circles in preventing the COVID-19 pandemic and the devotion of medical professionals in taking care of all patients regardless of their nationalities. I felt greatly honored by joining my Chinese friends, colleagues and foreign students who stayed in Yichang at its tough period to fight against the crisis. After the breakout of the pandemic, I was in the middle of the crisis. However, I had never felt fearful because every day we were well communicated with real-time information about the pandemic and were supplied with enough food, water and all necessities. The Chinese government was trying their utmost to make our life comfortable and stay safe both physically and psychologically. The government staff, medical professionals and police forces were all working day and night in the first forefront of fighting against the pandemic. They put our health and safety in the highest priority and my deep respect and gratitude to their devotions was beyond words.

No man is an island, entire of itself. Our destiny is closely linked. Therefore, let's join hands to fight against the pandemic and to comfort those fearful souls. Let's march towards victory for China and the whole world. All bygones will be bygones and God will bless us!

宜昌龙泉镇民俗文化展
/李江龙提供

次危机，我感到无比荣幸，这种团结也是我们共同努力的象征。疫情以来，我身处危机中心，但我从未感到害怕，因为地方领导每天都在与我们大家不断沟通，确保我们有充足的食物、水和各种所需物资，并且努力让我们过得舒适安心。领导者、医务人员和警察们始终奋战在抗疫前线，将我们的健康与安全放在首位，我对他们的尊重和感激难以言表！

朋友们，我们的命运息息相关，让我们携手抗疫，抚慰那些恐惧的心灵，为了中国，为了世界，向着胜利前进！一切终将过去，愿上帝保佑我们！

2020，我在中国
2020, I Am in China

[法国] 勒黑波妮 武汉大学
[France] Leret Bonnie, Wuhan University

"There is such a lot of world to see." It was quite unexpected that it was finally my turn to go to China to have a look. I came to China from the far-away France, and with this beautiful encounter, I started a fresh life. The new environment brought me a new way of life. From life and study to work and consumption, earth-shaking changes were brought over my original habits. Before I came to China, I told myself never to walk into any inexperienced life with a cold attitude, but to believe that life is worth living. Now it seems that the experiences and feelings in China have really integrated themselves into my heart and filled me with more fun and memories. In 2020, I am in China enjoying life.

In China, the science and technology in daily life has made me witness the prosperity and strength of a country. It was another Singles' Day, and I joined in the shopping spree again. I searched among the Taobao goods with great expectation. After I made the payment on phone, I would just wait for the express delivery to arrive. It was a matter of less than three to five days, even though it was across China. It was many a time that I felt bored at home and

“世界那么大，我想去看看”，没想到最后终于轮到我，到中国看看。我从遥远的法国来到中国，这场美丽的邂逅，展开了我全新的生活。新的环境给我带来了新的生活方式，从生活、学习再到工作、消费方式，给我原有的习惯带来了翻天覆地的变化。到达中国之前，我告诉自己，不要冷漠地走入任何未经检验的生活，要相信生活值得一过，现在看来，在中国的体验和感受真真切切地融入了我的心中，给我装下了更多的趣味与回忆。2020 年，我在中国；2020 年，我在享受生活。

在中国，日常生活中的科技带我见证了一个国家的繁荣富强。又到了双十一狂欢购物之际，我再次加入了剁手团，兴致勃勃地浏览着淘宝商品，手机支付完成后便坐等快递的到来，即使横跨中国，不到三五天也可拿到商品；不知几回，在家无聊想去旅游之时，拿出手机，携程在手，说走就走，拿着最优惠的价格坐上最快捷的高铁；到达目的地，不怕没司机，就怕没滴滴，不到几分钟，滴滴快车即可为我提供接送服务，带我去已在网上预订好的酒店里；即使到了酒店太累不想动，美团 App 成了我最佳的点单选择，不仅能在平台上找到很多餐厅商家，而且套餐有优惠，配送费也没有那么贵。科技改变生活，而我有幸能体验到这种

武汉大学秋季枫林 / 勒黑波妮提供

wanted to travel. I took out my cell phone, logged on Ctrip, and was ready to go. I would get on the fastest high-speed rail with the most favorable price. When I arrived at my destination, I wouldn't be afraid of there being no taxi around, but I would be really afraid that there was no Didi service there. In just a few minutes, Didi Express Taxi would pick me up and take me to the hotel I booked online. Even if I was too tired to move in the hotel, Meituan APP would be my best ordering choice. Not only would I be able to find many restaurants and businesses on the platform, but also enjoy package discounts, and cheap delivery fee. Technology has changed my life, and I am fortunate to be able to experience this different life, immerse into it, and enjoy it.

In China, the construction and development of new media provides me with more possibilities to communicate and witness. WeChat has become a tool for me to communicate with my family in France. WeChat moments constantly refresh the life stories of my Chinese friends and I; Weibo is a platform for me to learn dynamically about hot Chinese topics in my spare time. In Weibo, I can not only express my opinions, but also learn more about Chinese values and outlook on life. Meanwhile, I also feel

与众不同的生活，并融入其中，享受其中。

在中国，新媒体的建设与发展给我提供了更多交流与看见的可能。微信成了我与远在法国的家人交流的工具，微信朋友圈在不断刷新中呈现了我与中国朋友们的生活故事；微博是我闲暇之时通过动态去了解中国热点话题的平台，在微博中，我可以发表我的意见和看法，也可以去更多地了解中国人的价值观和人生观。与此同时，我也感受到了直播电商在这个特殊时期的发展。我们老师说，2020 年是直播电商元年，不得不承认，数字经济在疫情期间发挥了核心作用。封锁限制、社交疏远以及其他措施，这些外部环境的变化推动了消费者网上购物的频率增加，电子商务交易的营销方式一时变得愈加火热，而我本人也深深感受到了直播电商给我的消费生活带来的便利。除此之外，中国的短视频平台也给了我更多看见的力量。存在即是完美，看见即是体验，有时我会打开抖音、快手等短视频平台去欣赏中国人各式各样的生活，在这里，我看到了中国古老手艺如何惊艳时光，翩翩少年如何奋发图强，耄耋老人如何白头偕老，芸芸众生如何逆风飞翔。技术的进步给更多人提供了看见的可能，那些原来沉默的大多数就可以不沉默，那些原来普通的人就可以不普通，因为看见，让我觉得生活值得一过。

勒黑波妮在桂林攀岩

在中国，疫情改变了我的

the development of live streaming e-commerce in this special period. Our teacher said that 2020 was the first year of live streaming e-commerce. We have to admit that digital economy played a central role during the epidemic. Such changes in the external environment as lockdown, social distancing and other measures have promoted the increase in the frequency of consumers' online shopping, and the marketing method of e-commerce transaction has become more and more popular. And I have also deeply felt the convenience that live streaming e-commerce has brought to my consumption. In addition, China's short video platforms also give me more opportunities to watch. Existence is perfection, and seeing is experience. At times, I would open the short video platforms such as Tiktok and SnackVideo to enjoy the various lives of Chinese people, where I see how amazing is the ancient Chinese craftsmanship, how hard young people work, how elder people grow old together, and how ordinary people fly against the wind. The progress of technology has provided more people with the possibility to see, can help the silent majority break silence, and those who are originally ordinary be extraordinary. Seeing makes me feel life is worth living.

In China, the outbreak of the epidemic has not only changed my living habits, but also made me feel the unity and care of the Chinese people. I stayed in China during the COVID-19 epidemic. The spread of the virus was full of threats, but the unity of the Chinese people made me feel this strength of resistance. At the beginning of the epidemic, I happened to be in Guangxi province, where I have some family and friends. Because I studied in Wuhan, many people were concerned about me, not only my

生活习惯，也让我感受到了中国人的团结与关爱。新冠肺炎疫情期间，我留在了中国。病毒的肆虐充满着威胁，但中国人的团结让我感受到了这股反抗的力量。疫情之初，我刚好在中国的广西，这里有我的一些家人和朋友。因为我上学期间在武汉读书，因此很多人关心我，不仅是我的家人，还有我的老师、朋友、同学，甚至是牙医也送来了问候，这让我深深地感受到了来自中国人的关爱与呵护。除此之外，健康码的推出改变了我的一些生活习惯，省外出行、景区或超市的出入，只需出示健康码即可，这种更加精准、科学、有序的人员出行管理办法省去了许多额外的工作。疫情之下，我深刻地感受到了中国人民为推动国家进步和国际援助所做的一切努力，也感谢中国为全世界所付出的心血。

我与中国的这场美丽的邂逅，将永远刻在我心中。2020 年，我陶醉于乡村之富饶，城市之繁荣，也沉浸在风土人情世间冷暖之中，虽然我

桂林山水 / 勒黑波妮摄

family, but also my teachers, friends, classmates, and even the dentists, who made me deeply feel the love and care from the Chinese people. In addition, the introduction of health code has changed some of my living habits. Travelling in other provinces, at scenic spots or in supermarkets, you only need to show the health code. This more accurate, scientific and orderly personnel travel management method saves a lot of extra work. During the epidemic, I deeply felt all the efforts made by the Chinese people to promote national progress and international assistance, and I also thank China for its painstaking efforts for the world.

My beautiful encounter with China will be engraved in my heart forever. In 2020, I revel in the richness of the countryside, the prosperity of the city, and the care and warmth of the ordinary people. Although there have been some changes in my way of life, it is right because of those changes that I learned that a broader mind could hold more fun. Thanks to China, which gives ordinary me the opportunity to experience an extraordinary life; I am grateful to China, which sheds sunshine upon my body and eternalizes my memories.

桂林山水 / 勒黑波妮摄

的生活方式有了一些改变，但正是因为改变，才让我知道更广阔的胸襟，装得下更多的趣味。感谢中国，让平凡的我体验了不平凡的生活；感恩中国，让阳光照耀我身，让回忆变得永生难忘。

一封来自中国的邀约
An Invitation Letter from China

[南非] 王飒成 深圳大学
[South Africa] Watson Saskia Chan'el, Shenzhen University

Dear young Saskia Chan'el,

Hi! I know you're busy preparing for the college entrance exams in South Africa right now, but I really want to write and talk to you as you'll be flying to China in the near future!

I want to tell you that in a few months you will embark on your first long journey alone, flying 12,000 kilometers to China, your future home. I want to tell you that when you set foot on the land of China, your life will be bound up with the nation and changed forever.

王飒成 / 在广州

You will find a country with a very different culture from your own country, listen to a harmonious and pleasant language that you don't understand at all,

小飒成：

你好！知道你此刻正忙于准备南非的高考，但我很想写封信，告诉在不久的将来要飞抵中国的你！

我想告诉你，几个月后你将独自踏上人生中的第一次远行之旅，飞行一万两千公里来到中国这个你未来的家。我想告诉你，当你踏上中国大地的那一刻，你的生活将与中国心息相依，永远改变。

你会发现一个和自己国家文化迥然不同的国度：倾听一种和谐悦耳而你完全不懂的语言，品尝许多色香味俱全但并不总合自己胃口的食物，

深圳大学 / 王飒成提供

try a lot of food with perfect combination of color, taste and appearance that' you don't always like, and appreciate the charm of a seaside city with long summers. You will come to a city known as "come and then you become a native of Shenzhen," where you will study, live and make friends with students from all over the world! You will listen to the sound of cicadas to spend endless hot summer days. You will sit around with friends to eat barbecue or spicy hot foods, and enjoy happy nights in KTV singing. Before you know it, you'll find yourself immersed in the city and falling in love with the land and its kind, warm and friendly people.

You may go to a city called Chengdu, where you'll experience the boisterous sounds of Kuanzhaixiang (Broad and Narrow Alley), the bustling traffic of Chunxi Road, and the exuberant atmosphere of bring lights at nights. While sipping green tea, you will taste Three Cannon (sticky rice cake, local food that makes the sound of cannon during the production process) and Juntun Pancake (local food made of flour), and marvel at the mystery of the changing faces of Sichuan opera. You will ascend to the golden summit of Mount Emei and be rewarded with the magnificent and heaven-like view in the clouds. The glowing ray of sunrise in the morning will galmorize the entire sky into a majestic landscape painting. When you finally leave, you will find that you enjoy the peace and leisure in the dense fragrance of cover bowl tea. Chengdu, a city in Sichuan, noted as a land of abundance, captures your heart and soul with its prosperity, beauty, leisure and idle life style.

You may also visit a city called Guangzhou, where you'll learn to haggle with vendors in clothing markets and taste typical Cantonese morning tea (local breakfast). When you first taste the chicken feet that are cooked to be so

领略一个有着漫长夏季的海滨城市的风情。你会来到一个被称为“来了就是深圳人”的城市，在那里学习、生活，结交来自世界各地的同学与朋友，你会聆听声声蝉鸣度过无尽的炎炎夏日，你会与友人雅集围坐吃烧烤或麻辣烫，在 KTV 的欢唱中度过一个个愉快的夜晚。不知不觉地，你会发现自己已经融入这座城市，并深深爱上这片土地以及这片土地上亲切、热情、友爱的人民。

你会去一个叫作成都的城市，在那里，你会感受到宽窄巷子的人声鼎沸、春熙路的车水马龙以及华灯初上的盛世氛围，一边喝着绿茶、品尝三大炮和军屯锅盔，一边惊叹川剧变脸瞬息万变的神秘，你将登上峨眉山金顶，获得云中天堂无边风月的奖赏，黎明破晓时的万丈霞光将整个天空渲染成雄浑壮阔的山水画卷。最后离去时你会发现，安逸闲散的时光都融在盖碗茶的氤氲里，这个天府之城的都市，它的繁华与秀丽，它的闲适散淡的风韵让你魂牵梦绕，让你刻骨铭心。

你还将去一个叫作广州的城市，在那里，你学会了在服装市场和

深圳大学 / 王飒成提供

delicious, your surprised look makes friends laugh with a glee. When you take a night cruise on the Pearl River, you will be amazed at the light show with the image of fishes projected on the "slim waist" (nickname of the Canton Tower, a narrow and tall building). The fishes seem to swim around you shuttle, and the Canton Tower is like a guardian angel of the ocean to stand tall in front of you.

Your best Chinese friends may take you on a tour to Huizhou, her hometown. You'll see a historic city with such a deep cultural heritage. It's amazing to observe that the local business miracle was made by young artists. When you see the various cultural creative projects of local enterprises, the innovative and refreshing atmosphere will make you wonder how art and commerce can be so skillfully blended. You will be amazed at how history and modernity can have such perfect fusion. You'll also harbor natural love for the people of Huizhou and even wonder if you'll be able to do your part for Huizhou in the future.

Dear young Saskia Chan'el, I want you to know that you will have many adventures in your life, but studying in China will be a fresh and unique experience that you will never forget! I want to tell you how much you will enjoy learning Chinese language and culture in the future. "A journey of a thousand miles begins with the first step", please accept the invitation from China so as to tell Chinese legendary stories well to the South African people!

商贩们讨价还价，也品尝了地道的广东早茶。当你第一次看见鸡爪这种食材被做成如此美味时，你惊讶的表情让同行的朋友发出欢快的笑声。乘船夜游珠江时，你会惊叹投射在“小蛮腰”上鱼儿的灯光秀，那些鱼儿似乎在你身边穿梭游动，而广州塔楼就像守护海洋的天使似的屹立于眼前。

王飒成在峨眉山

你最好的中国友人会带你参观她的家乡惠州，你会看到一个有着如此深厚文化底蕴的历史名城，当地繁华的商业奇迹竟然由年轻的艺术家们创立。当你看到当地企业的各种文化创意时，扑面而来的创新和清新的氛围会让你对艺术与商业如此巧妙的融合赞叹不已，你会折服于历史和现代完美融合的魅力，你也会对惠州人民产生一种本能的喜爱，甚至想知道自己的将来是否也能为惠州尽一份心力。

小飒成，我想让你知道你的人生要经历很多次冒险，而留学中国的经历对你来说新鲜而独特，会让你终生难忘！我想告诉你，未来的你会多么喜欢学习中国语言和文化，“千里之行，始于足下”，请接受中国的邀约，向南非人民讲好中国的传奇故事！

幸运的选择，美丽的邂逅
Lucky Choices, Beautiful Encounters

［乌克兰］ 狄安娜 重庆大学
[Ukraine] Kulikova Diana, Chongqing University

In the eyes of many people, China is a mysterious and remote country. But in my eyes, China is not mysterious but charming, not remote but reachable. For me, China is my second hometown, which is not a country too difficult to understand as long as you treat it with love.

The writer Svetlana Alexievich said in her novel *Secondhand Time*, "People are always faced with choices: to be free, or to live a prosperous and stable life? Freedom is always accompanied by pain, but happiness often means the loss of freedom. Most people choose to take the second path." I think I'm luckier than most people because my choices combined both; The decision of choosing to learn Chinese and studying in China gave me freedom and happiness.

My first choice came five years ago, when I chose to study Chinese language and literature at the Taras Shevchenko National University of Kyiv. Thus, the major and the country have become an integral part of my life. Of course, I have encountered many problems in my study. A man who has a settled purpose will surely succeed. The great pleasure of learning Chinese surpasses the fear of difficulties, which enables me to break through all the obstacles. My second choice

在很多人眼中，中国是一个非常神秘、遥远的国家。然而在我眼中，中国不只神秘，而且惊艳；中国并不遥远，而是触手可及；中国并不难读懂，只要有心。对我来说，中国是我的第二故乡。

作家阿列克谢耶维奇在小说《二手时间》里曾说过："人总是面临选择：要自由，还是要生活富足安定？自由总是与痛苦相伴，幸福却往往失去自由。大多数人都是选择走第二条路。"我想我比大多数人都幸运，因为我的选择包含了两个方面。选择了学习汉语，选择了到中国留学，这一系列的选择同时给了我自由和幸福。

我的第一次选择发生在五年前，入读基辅国立大学汉语言文学专业。于是，汉语言文学这个专业以及中国这个国家，就成了我生命中不可分割的一部分。当然，在学习过程中我遇到了很多问题。但是心向往之，行必能至。学习汉语带给我的愉悦感远远大于困难带给我的恐惧感，因此我才能勇敢地冲破重重障碍。我的第二次选择发生在基辅国立大学将要毕业之时。大学几年，老师们教会我很多基本的语言知识，我产生了一种强烈的使用汉语去探索中国、去沟通、去交流的冲动，我强烈地感觉到自己需要与中国来一次最真实的邂逅！正如五年前选择汉语言文学

came at the time of my graduation from Taras Shevchenko National University of Kyiv. Teachers had taught me a lot of basic language knowledge, which brings me a strong desire to explore China, to communicate and to exchange with China. I was longing for a real encounter with China. Just as I chose Chinese language and literature five years ago, I heard my inner voice crying: "Go to China, touch and understand China!" Once again, I took my destiny into my own hands and won the opportunity to study at Nankai University for a year. I think it was one of the best times of my life, during which I met lots of new friends, enjoyed a wonderful campus life. Study life in China opened my eyes. It is a pity I only had one year to study in China and good time always flies quickly, which broke my heart.

There must be an echo if you never forget it. Unexpectedly, the door of freedom and happiness opened to me again; My third choice came. I was given another chance to return to China. And this choice, I would like to say, made me feel more fascinated, delighted and excited than previous ones.

To tell you the truth, China is the country I am determined to continue living in. But which city should I choose? I have multiple options and various expectations. As soon as I saw the pictures of Chongqing, I understand that it is! In Chongqing, I was most impressed by the life in Chongqing University. I attended every Chongqing University International Culture Festival with my classmates. We danced the sleeve dance of ancient China. At the

重庆大学 / 狄安娜提供

狄安娜

专业一样，我再次听到自己内心的声音："必须去中国，去触摸中国，去读懂中国！"再一次，我把命运掌握在了自己手中，我获得了去南开大学学习一年的机会。我想，那段时光可以算是我生活中最美好的时光之一。我遇见了很多朋友，享受到了精彩的校园生活，在中国的生活使我眼界大开。很可惜天下没有不散的筵席，一年过去了我必须回国，这使我心碎。

人们都说"念念不忘，必有回响"。没想到，自由和幸福的大门再次向我打开：我的第三次选择来到了。我再一次得到机会回到中国。而这次选择，我想说，比前两次更让我着迷、疯狂、幸福！

说实话，中国，是我笃定要继续生活的国家。可是要在中国的哪座城市生活呢？我其实有很多种选择和期待。但是，重庆，重庆，一看到重庆的照片我就明白了，就是它！在重庆，最让我印象深刻的还是我在重庆大学的生活。我记得跟同学们参加的每一届重庆大学国际文化节。我们跳了古代中国的袖舞，一开始我觉得很难，但经过反复的刻苦练习，慢慢就学会了。在表演那天，学校让美容师来为我们化了特别的妆，那个化妆很像京剧演员，漂亮至极！在表演之前我很紧张，因为来了很多

beginning, I found it very difficult, but after repeated hard practice, we slowly learned how to dance. On the day of the show, the school invited cosmeticians to make special makeups for us, which look like the beautiful facial makeups in the Peking Opera. I felt nervous before the show because there were so many people on the site. But as soon as I got on the stage, I began to relax and the feeling of happiness filled the air.

A local ballad impressed me a lot, saying "The sisters here are virtuous and brothers straight. Food without peppers and chilies is no good to taste."

For me, "The food here is many and varied, hotpot touchable and noodles unforgettable after trying."

For me, "There are also three golden flowers – bean jelly, pig's feet and pig brains. There are also hot and sour rice noodles and cuisines from other parts of the country, which are hot, spicy, fresh and fragrant."

Chongqing is my third-time choice.

I am fascinated by my beautiful encounter with China. Learning Chinese language and knowing China have brought me endless beautiful memories. I am more convinced that every choice I've made related with China is a beautiful encounter with the nation. All my encounters with Chinese language, China, Tianjin and Chongqing are two-way choices between me and the country. I love this beautiful country, love all her beautiful cities. I will never forget the happy fate of meeting with China.

重庆大学 / 狄安娜提供

人，但是一上场我就放松了，快乐的感觉在空气中弥漫。

对我来说，有一首歌最让我印象深刻：“这里的妹儿嘿巴适，这里的男娃儿嘿耿直。东西没得花椒海椒从来不得吃。”

对我来说，“这里的美食嘿么多，这里的火锅随便摸。这里的小面最霸道，一口叫你忘不掉”。

对我来说，“这里还有三金花——豆花、蹄花和脑花儿。这里还有酸辣粉，相因巴适不得水。这里不少江湖菜，麻辣鲜香娄实干”。

这就是我的第三次选择，我的重庆！

我喜欢我与中国的美丽邂逅，学习汉语，认识中国，这场邂逅带给我数不尽的美丽回忆。然而我更加相信，我每一次与中国有关的选择，都是一场与中国的美丽邂逅。我与汉语、中国、天津、重庆的所有邂逅，都是我与中国之间冥冥之中的双向选择。我爱这个美丽的国家，爱她所有美丽的城市！我与中国的这段缘分我永远不会忘记，对这段生活我充满留恋！

重庆江景

生活，一键切换
One-Touch Life

[尼日利亚] 毕夏 长安大学
[Nigeria] Daniel Biosiya, Chang'an University

"Hello, JD Daojia. Your goods have been placed at the fire exit near the south gate, please pick up as quickly as possible."

"Got it. Thanks a lot."

About 10 minutes later, there was a knock at the door. I opened the door without peeping at the cat's eye.

"Your stuff is here."

Seeing her a little hard, I picked up the parcel.

"Thanks you. I would buy less next time, so you won't have to work so hard."

"Haha, thank you for your consideration. We volunteers will carry it for you even if you have purchased a cattle."

"Please come in and have some water."

"Never mind. Still have more goods to dispatch."

"Goodbye." Today's chatting quota has been used up.

I have been one year in China and only visited large-scale supermarkets, such as Wal-Mart and Best-Mart, once. Later crowded wet markets became my favorite and then online markets. The shopping form has changed, but it

"您好，京东到家，您的货物已经放在南门消防通道，请尽快来取！"

"谢谢，知道了。"

十几分钟以后，敲门声响起，我没有从猫眼看就直接打开了门。

"你的东西到了。"

看着她有点儿吃力的样子，我赶紧接过来。

"谢谢你，下次我少买一点儿，你就不会这么辛苦了。"

"哈哈哈，谢谢你。你就是买一头牛，我们志愿者也给你扛上来。"

"进来喝杯水吧。"

"不用了，还有别家要送呢。再见。"

"再见。"

今天的真人聊天份额已经用完了。

我来中国一年了，一开始只去沃尔玛、百福乐这些大超市，后来爱上了人情味儿十足的菜市场，再到现在逛这个"网上市场"，形式变了，但是依旧是那个品类齐全、琳琅满目的中国市场。我想出去，但是我知道中国正处在抗击疫情的关键时刻，隔离是为了我们每个人的安全，我绝不能添乱！

饭后的我懒懒地躺在沙发上，将手机切换到抖音 App。

remains the same prosperous Chinese market. I wanted to go out, I know that the home quarantine is for the safety of everyone. When China is at the critical moment of fighting against the COVID-19 pandemic, I must not mess up.

After lunch, I lay comfortably on the couch, switching my phone to the Tiktok APP.

"Haha..."

Watching the burned cakes made by Chinese netizens, family pretending to travel at home, drones flying in the street, all these funny videos made me laugh. To be precise, it is a kind of laugh in tears. I saw thousands of doctors and nurses rushed to Wuhan; China set up a hospital in 10 days; All the Chinese people did not give up their hope, doing what they can to combat this pandemic.

Though I am in quarantine without leaving the building, I feel that I have not been abandoned by the world. I can still witness the joy and sorrow of the world.

My telephone was ringing, reminding me it is time to practice martial arts. I switched to Youku APP to follow the online master to practice the "drunkard boxing."

I was fascinated by Chinese kung fu long before I came to China and I have

长安大学彩虹女生雕塑 / 毕夏提供

“哈哈哈哈……”

毕夏

看着抖音上的中国网友们分享自己做的黑乎乎的蛋糕，看着一家人假装在自己家里旅游，看着街上的无人机喊话，这些都让我在隔离生活中还能够哈哈一笑。其实准确地说，是有笑有泪。我看到医生护士一批批赶赴武汉，我看到中国10天建起了医院，我看到所有的中国人都没有放弃希望，都做着自己力所能及的事情去抗击这场疫情。

我虽然在隔离，连这栋楼都出不去，但是我却感觉我没有被这个世界抛弃，我依然看得到这个世界的喜怒哀乐。

“丁零零……”我的手机闹钟响了，手机屏幕提示到“武术时间”。我将手机切换到优酷App，打开了醉拳的教学视频，跟着屏幕上的“师父”练习起来。

我来中国以前就对中国功夫很感兴趣，几乎看过中国的所有功夫电影。我最喜欢的就是成龙、李连杰和甄子丹。我来中国以后特意找了一家武术学校学习，可是因为疫情，武术学校暂时不能开门了。我很沮丧，我真的很想继续学习。

直到有一天，我在抖音上看到一个小伙子练习武术的视频，我就灵光一现。对啊，不能在学校学，我在手机上学总可以吧。在中国朋友的推荐下，我下载了优酷App，让我惊喜的是这里面几乎包含了所有我想学习的功夫视频。

seen almost all the Chinese kung fu movies. My favorite stars include Jackie Chan, Jet Li and Donnie Yen. After arriving in China, I found a martial arts school to practice kung fu. The school was shut down temporarily due to the epidemic, I was really depressed because I want to continue my practice.

Until one day, I saw a video of a young man practicing kung fu. It inspired me and I downloaded Youku APP under the recommendation of a Chinese friend. To my surprise, it contains almost all the kung fu videos I wanted to learn.

I was so excited and wasted no time to search the "drunkard boxing." After that, I began to practice martial arts in this online kung fu school at 3:00 pm every day. After the world pressed the pause button, a greater virtual world is waiting for you to explore.

Feeling tired, I took a break and drank some water. But my brain did not stop work. Opening my WeChat, I noticed the online orders from a WeChat group through electric payment. I realized mobile payment has played an important role in meeting the basic needs of 1.4 billion Chinese people.

Home quarantine slowed down my life but gave me more time to ponder. Looking outside of the window, I realized that this vast country has not come to a halt even if everybody is isolated at home. After I came to China, I was not adapted to the new life at first. But later, I became accustomed to the usage of take-out APPs, car-hailing softwares and mobile payment, which are so fast and convenient. I even began to ignore it.

I feel fortunate to choose to study in China and fight together with the Chinese against the pandemic. In the future, I would return to my motherland with the knowledge I learned here. I will recite to the world all the Chinese stories that have made me laugh, cry, touch and think.

长安大学落日风光 / 毕夏提供

我兴奋极了，赶紧搜索了我最喜欢的“醉拳”，跟着视频一招一式学起来。之后的每一天下午三点我都在这所“网络武术学校”学习。当现实世界按下暂停的按钮，还有一个更大的网络世界等你去探索。

练习累了，喝口水休息一下，身体停了可是我的头脑没有停止工作。我打开微信，看到小区日常生活购买群里的一个个订单，一笔笔微信支付，我意识到平时无处不在的移动支付，在这个关键时刻满足着中国 14 亿人口最基本的生活需求。

隔离生活让我闲了下来，也给了我更多思考的时间。我看着窗外，窗外的中国，这个庞大的国家即使人人隔离在家，依旧没有停止运转。当我来到中国以后，从一开始的不适应，到外卖软件、打车软件、移动支付软件的运用自如，我已经习惯了这里的快捷与方便，习惯到忽略了它。

我庆幸选择了来中国留学，我庆幸能与中国人民并肩作战。在未来，我将带着从中国学习到的一切建设自己的祖国，向世界诉说那些让我笑过、哭过、感动过、思考过的中国故事。

印象华夏
My Impression of Huaxia

[马来西亚] 陈嘉扬 武汉大学
[Malaysia] Tan Jia Yang, Wuhan University

"There is a river in the far east, and its name is the Yangtze River.

There is a river in the far east and its name is the Yellow River.

There is a dragon in the ancient east, and its name is China. "

Before I set foot on this divine land, I was bonded with China through Chinese movies and TV dramas, literary works, the quintessence of Chinese culture, etc. For example, since I was a child, I have come into contact with Jin Yong's martial arts novels, the four Chinese classics, Chinese cultural festival celebrations and such classic TV dramas as "Princess Pearl", "Nirvana in Fire" and so on. These elements have planted the seeds of a beautiful yearning for China in my heart. In 2019, I received the admission letter of Wuhan University and came to the country I had been dreaming of for a long time, opening a new chapter in my life. I think my encounter with Wuhan proves that we have an unspeakable fate. In the several months of studying and living in China, how wonderful were my experiences, feelings and understandings! China has a history of 5,000 years, which is impregnated with humanistic wisdom and the quintessence of construction, and bequeaths cultural treasures and patriotism

“遥远的东方有一条江，它的名字就叫长江。遥远的东方有一条河，它的名字就叫黄河。古老的东方有一条龙，它的名字就叫中国。”

未踏入神州大地的国土前，我与中国是通过中国影视剧、文学小说及中国国粹等联系起来的。譬如说，我自小就接触到了金庸先生的武侠小说、中国四大名著、中华文化节日庆典和经典影视剧《还珠格格》《琅琊榜》等。这些元素在我心中埋下了对中国美好向往的种子。2019 年，我收到了武汉大学的录取通知书，来到憧憬已久的国家展开新的人生篇章。我想我能与武汉邂逅证明了我俩有着不可言喻的缘分。在中国学习和生活了数个月后，我的体验、感受和感悟何其丰富！中国上下五千年历史，其中蕴含着人文智慧与建设精髓，并给予一代又一代的中华儿女文化的宝藏

南京夫子庙 / 陈嘉扬摄

to generations of Chinese. At the same time, the rise of high buildings and the development of economy, science and technology in one city after another coincide with the birth of the great Chinese dream – rejuvenation.

At the end of Yihai year, and in the spring of Gengzi year, a sudden epidemic swept China and wreaked havoc all over the world. Even though I had returned home before the winter vacation, I still learned through the news media that the magnificent Chinese nation had launched a smoke-free war against the virus with the determination of "No returning without conquering Loulan" and some deeds have become legends. For example, within ten days, China completed the construction of a hospital, Huoshenshan Hospital, in an uninhabited wasteland, which covers an area of 3,400 square meters and accommodates 1,000 beds. 10 days! It is an unprecedented miracle taking place in present China. In addition to this "epic" project, the construction of Leishenshan Hospital and Fangcang makeshift hospitals all reflects the extraordinary power that belongs to China. At the same time, a series of decisions and arrangements were rapidly implemented, including village closure, district closure, and city closure, and kept on improving the epidemic prevention and control. Nowadays, China's method of "early detection, early reporting, early isolation and early treatment" has been adopted by many countries, which fully reflects the advantages of China's political system. Not only that, Zhong Nanshan, Li Lanjuan, Zhang Dingyu and tens of thousands of heroes in harm's way ran on the frontline, struggling to save all lives attacked by the virus and building a line of defence for lives. These valuable scenes represent the precious spiritual and cultural richness of the Chinese nation.

During my study in China, I experienced China's means of transportation,

和爱国情操。同时，一座座城市的钢筋水泥、经济和科学技术的崛起皆紧跟着中华民族伟大复兴的中国梦。

乙亥末，庚子春，一场突如其来的疫情席卷中国，肆虐全球。即使我已在寒假前回国，还是通过新闻媒体了解到了气势恢宏的中华民族凭着“不破楼兰终不还”的决心向病毒发起无硝烟的战争的种种事迹，而有些事迹也变成了奇迹。譬如说，中国在10天内在空无人烟的荒地建造了一所占地3400平方米且拥有1000个床位的医院——火神山医院。10天是什么概念？就是一种前无古人，后有“中国”的奇迹。除了这项“史诗级”工程，雷神山医院、方舱医院背后皆映射出了属于中国的非凡力量。同时，一系列决策部署迅速落实，从封村到封区直至封城，疫情防控局面渐入佳境。如今，中国的“早发现、早报告、早隔离、早治疗”的手法已被许多国家借鉴，这充分体现了中国制度的优势。不仅如此，钟南山、李兰娟、张定宇和数以万计的逆行者们奔走在一线，拼搏地拯救一条条被病毒攻击的生命，为生命筑起一道防线，这一幕幕珍贵的画面交织出了属于中华民族的宝贵精神文化底蕴。

武汉大学 / 陈嘉扬提供

such as subway and high-speed rail. To me, China is a deserving transport powerhouse, whose transport network and system are very well-planned, whose buses are never late, whose subway is extremely convenient and whose high-speed rail is reputed all over the world. At the same time, the convenience of paying for transportation in China is beyond my imagination, because all I need to do is to open a mobile phone software and scan the QR code, which is an eye-opener to me. In June 2020, China made a major breakthrough in the field of high-speed maglev technology, that is, the successful trial of a 600-kilometer high-speed maglev test vehicle! This means that China has seized the commanding heights of strategy in international competition and demonstrated unassailable speed to the world. On the other hand, due to the impact of the epidemic on physical stores, live streaming goods quickly spread all over China. We can see that live streaming goods derived from influencer economy has become a new business model, and has even affected the world business trend. In addition, China's big data technology, cross-border e-commerce and cashless transactions have become imitated by many countries, and my country, Malaysia, is no exception. In addition, because of the cooperation opportunities brought about by China's "Belt and Road Initiative" policy, Malaysia coexists with China and pursues a common bright future.

Noble Huaxia, an ancient civilization with an age of 5,000 years, has been reborn in the long river of history. In the future, I will keep on feeling the pulse of Chinese civilization, understand the most rotund cry of Chinese culture and experience the weight of this divine country.

在华学习期间，我体验了中国的交通工具，如地铁和高铁等。对我而言，中国不愧为交通强国，除了交通网络和系统规划得颇为完善，再加上公交车从不迟到、地铁极为便利和高铁的速度已闻名全球。同时，中国交通工具的便利程度已超乎我的想象，因为只需打开手机软件扫一扫二维码就可以完成支付手续，这过程让我大开眼界。2020 年 6 月，中国在高速磁浮技术领域实现重大突破，即 600 公里高速磁浮试验车成功试行！这意味着中国在国际竞争中抢占了战略的制高点，并向全世界展示了无懈可击的速度。另一方面，疫情对实体店的冲击，催生直播带货迅速火遍全中国，可以看到网红经济所衍生出来的直播带货已成为新的商业模式，甚至影响了世界的商业潮流。此外，中国的大数据科技、跨境电商和无现金交易等，已成为许多国家模仿的对象，而我的国家——马来西亚也不例外。除此之外，马来西亚因为中国的“一带一路”政策带来的合作机会，彼此共存共荣，且共同追求璀璨的未来。

巍巍华夏，五千年的文明古国在大浪淘沙的历史长河中洗涤与沉淀。未来的我还要继续感受华夏文明跳动的脉搏、感受中华文化最浑厚的呐喊和感受神州大地的厚重！

武汉大学 / 陈嘉扬提供

爱上一座城
The City I Fall in Love with

[印度尼西亚] 黄美香　柳州城市职业学院
[Indonesia] Monica Kristie Kusuma, Liuzhou City Vocational College

From an early age in Indonesia, I often heard people say "go to China to acquire knowledge", so that when I grew up, whenever someone mentioned a high level of education, high level of knowledge, I would think of a word—China. When I had the opportunity to study abroad, I chose China without hesitation.

The city I study in is called Liuzhou, which seems to break the stereotype of industrial city, and is unexpectedly filled with natural beauty. She is not as noisy as Guangzhou, as old as Beijing, as prosperous as Shanghai, but I still love the city's unique beauty.

I love the special beauty of Liuzhou, which combines ancient and modern, natural and humanistic collocation. When you mount the east gate tower with a thousand years of history, you can see the warm green Liujiang River, and behind the towering tall buildings, and green hills dotted in the modern urban forest, simple and modern, natural and intelligent. In April, the city's Bauhinia blossoms opened overnight, and the city's roads, large and small, seemed to be hidden by pink clouds. At this time, I like to take the Liuzhou bus in the streets, stroll all day and don't feel tired at all.

As a student from Jakarta, Indonesia, I fell in love with the smooth traffic

在印度尼西亚，我从小时候起就常常听人们说“到中国寻找知识”，以至于长大后，每当有人提起高水平的教育、高层次的知识，我脑海里就会浮现一个词——中国。当我有机会出国留学时，我毫不犹豫地选择了中国。

我留学的城市叫作柳州，似乎是为了打破人们对工业城市的刻板印象，柳州这个工业城市意外地洋溢着自然之美。她不像广州那样喧嚣，北京那样古老，上海那样繁华，但我还是爱上了这座城市与众不同的美。

我爱柳州特别的美。柳州的美景，古老与现代融合，自然和人文搭配，相得益彰。登上有千年历史的东门城楼，不远处就是温润碧绿的柳江，身后高楼大厦林立，而一座座青翠的小山点缀在城市森林之中，古朴而现代，自然而灵动。到了 4 月，满城的紫荆花一夜之间全都开了，整座城市大大小小的道路像是被粉色的云藏了起来。这时候，我最喜欢乘着柳州的公交车在大街小巷穿行，逛一整天也不腻。

作为一名来自印尼雅加达的留学生，我第一次出行就爱上了柳州顺畅的交通。这里似乎从不堵车，跟我的家乡雅加达这个著名的“堵”城比起来，在柳州出行格外畅快，即使在上下班高峰期，道路上也没有出现过雅加达那种堵得水泄不通的景象。柳州的基础设施非常好，宽阔的

in Liuzhou for the first time. Compared with my hometown of Jakarta, the famous "blocked" city, there seems to be no traffic jam here. Travel in Liuzhou is particularly smooth, even in the rush hour, the road has not appeared that kind of crowded scene as in Jakarta. Liuzhou's infrastructure is very good. Wide roads and perfect public transport system make me feel very convenient to travel. Teachers teach me to use mobile phones to find the location of buses at any time, pay fares with mobile phones, combine bus systems with mobile phone applications, I seem to step into a new world, where you do not waste time to wait for cars, need not prepare change for buying, I often exclaim "how convenient it is."

I often go out with my friends and taste Liuzhou's delicious food after class in Liuzhou. Chinese food is very rich, Liuzhou's most famous food is "snail rice noodles." When I first tried, I sucked the rice flour into my mouth, and I was surprised by the unique aroma of the snail. This taste is very unique, which makes people can't help eating it, until now I cannot describe this feeling in a word, but once you like it, you will never forget it. I often recommend Liuzhou snail rice noodles to my friends studying in other cities. I hope they can experience the charm of snail rice noodles with me. Friends say that since I went to Liuzhou to study, I become fatter, I think the credit must go to snail rice noodles.

I love to study in Liuzhou, and every day is happy and full. Teachers take me step by step to master professional knowledge, to appreciate the beauty of Chinese. I remembered that when I first arrived in China, I did not know how to express "did you have dinner" in Chinese, so I was grateful to the teachers for their patience. The teachers took me to understand the splendid culture of China and the development of today. I often talk with students from other

道路、完善的公共交通系统让我觉得出行非常方便，老师们教我用手机随时查询公交车的位置，用手机支付车费，把公交系统和手机应用结合在一起，我仿佛踏入了一个新世界，不用花时间等车，不用想办法换零钱，我常常感叹“这真是太方便了”。

在柳州留学的闲暇时光里，我常常和朋友们一起外出，品尝柳州的美食。中国的美食很丰富，柳州最知名的美食就是“螺蛳粉”。第一次尝试的时候，我把劲道的米粉一点点吸进嘴里，螺蛳独特的香气让我很是惊讶。这种味道非常独特，让人欲罢不能，直到现在我也没有办法加以形容或比喻，叫人一旦喜欢上它，就再也忘不了它。独乐乐不如众乐乐，我常常向在其他城市留学的朋友们推荐柳州的螺蛳粉，希望他们能与我一同体会螺蛳粉的魅力。朋友们都说我到柳州留学之后变胖了很多，螺蛳粉在这个过程中一定功不可没。

我爱在柳州学习的日子，每一天都快乐而充实。老师们带着我一步步掌握专业知识，一点点领略汉语之美。回想刚到中国时，那个想问问别人吃饭了没有都不知道如何表达的自己，我心里对老师们的耐心教导充满了感激。老师们带着我领略了中国灿烂的文化，了解了中国如今的发展。我常常和其他国家的留学生在一起谈天说地，每当我们说起中国科技的发展、中国智慧生活的便利，大家都希望自己能学到知识，让自己

参加校运会开幕式各国服装展示（左一为黄美香）

柳州城市职业学院 / 黄美香提供

countries. Whenever we talk about the development of Chinese science and technology and the convenience of Chinese intelligent life, we all hope that we can learn knowledge and make our motherland better and better.

Now, my friends and I cannot return to China for the time being because of the COVID-19 pandemic, but the guidance issued by the teachers makes us feel safe and warm from the bottom of our hearts. Whenever I think of the Bauhinia of Liuzhou City, the winding Liujiang River, the spicy aroma of snail rice noodles on the wide road, the good time of learning in Liuzhou, the bottom of my heart is filled with love for this city, I hope to return to this city sooner.

柳州城市职业学院 / 黄美香提供

的祖国也变得越来越好。

如今，我和朋友们因为新冠肺炎疫情的原因暂时还不能回到中国，但老师们发布的防疫指导，让我们觉得既安全又从心底里感到温暖。每当我想起柳州满城粉若云霞的紫荆花，想起蜿蜒的柳江，想起宽阔的道路上螺蛳粉引人垂涎的辛辣香气，想起在柳州学习的美好时光，心底充满了对这座城市的眷恋，希望能早一点回到这座我爱的城市里。

勇者无畏，行者无疆

The Brave Are Fearless and the Doers Are Boundless

［赤道几内亚］ 罗木 中国地质大学（武汉）

[Equatorial Guinea] Nkogo Bindang Romualdo Obama, China University of Geosciences (Wuhan)

Standing at the intersection of graduation farewell, the voice in my mind came back again – "Are you afraid?"

My name is Luo Mu, and I am a fresh graduate from School of Engineering of China University of Geosciences (Wuhan), majoring in geological engineering. I am from Equatorial Guinea, a beautiful island country with a small population but known as the "Kingdom of Forests."

In the summer of five years ago ,when I held the admission notice from China in both hands, I was both excited and nervous. It had always been my dream to study in China, and I was about to embark on a new phase of my life on this journey. Of course, the unknown also made me feel uneasy. What did China look like that was waiting for me on the other side of the world? Would I get through my study successfully ? Would the people there accept me with a different look? At that time, a voice kept buzzing in my head, "Are you afraid?"

I packed my bag and came to China with this worry.

In the first year of being in China,I spent one year studying at Tianjin University as a preparatory student. A year later, I passed the matriculation

站在毕业离别的十字路口，脑海里的那个声音又响起来了："你害怕吗？"

我叫罗木，是中国地质大学（武汉）工程学院地质工程专业的本科应届毕业生。我来自赤道几内亚，一个人口不多，却拥有"森林王国"之称的美丽岛国。

五年前的夏天，当我双手捧着来自中国的入学通知书时，既兴奋又忐忑。去中国学习是我一直以来的梦想，而我马上就要踏上这段寻梦之旅，开启新的人生阶段了。当然，未知的一切也让我觉得不安，地球另一边等待着我的那个中国究竟是什么模样？我能顺利完成学业吗？那里的人会接受我这个不同的面孔吗？那时候，我的脑子里一直嗡嗡地回响着一个声音："你害怕吗？"

收拾好行囊，我带着这份"害怕"来到了中国。

来中国的第一年，我在天津大学学习了一年预科。一年后，我顺利通过了预科结业考试，终于来到了我的大学——中国地质大学（武汉）。在武汉生活的四年，我见证了这个城市的日新月异，真的是"武汉，每天不一样！"。武汉人的大嗓门，香喷喷的热干面，让人流连忘返的江

final exam and finally came to my university, China University of Geosciences (Wuhan). Living in Wuhan for four years, I have witnessed the city's rapid change. It is true that "Every day is different in Wuhan". People's big voice , delicious hot-dry noodles with sesame paste, the captivating night view of the riverbank and fire-like summer, there is always more to say when it comes to Wuhan. I always wonder how I would feel if I have to leave this city one day when I graudated.

However, on the eve of departure, Wuhan left me with an unforgettable memory.

On January 23, Wuhan was locked down. A city with tens of millions of people was battling with COVID-19 epidemic. Some chose to go home, but I decided to stay with Chinese people ,who are my family in my heart. At the beginning of the epidemic, I had numerous phone calls from my family in Equatorial Guinea, who were worried about whether I was safe here and asked if I was afraid. I also asked myself, "Luo Mu, are you afraid?"

I witnessed the efforts made by the Chinese government to fight the epidemic, the sacrifices made by schools and teachers to protect us, and the dedication and commitment of International Student Volunteer Teams, known as "the Iron Man". Since February 16th, the "Iron Man" volunteer team, made up of international students from the School of International Education, has been providing volunteer services to the students. Under the guidance of the school and teachers, they helped clean public areas, set up many service teams to deliver food and supplies to students, and encouraged everyone to work together to fight the epidemic and not to give up on learning at all times. In this winter, even though they were wearing layers of protective suit, glasses and

滩夜景，热情似火的夏天……提到武汉，总有说不完的话。我以前总在想，如果有一天要毕业、要离开这个城市了，我会是怎样的心情呢？

离别前夕的武汉，给我留下了一段刻骨铭心的记忆。

1 月 23 日，武汉关闭离汉通道，这座上千万人口的城市与新冠肺炎疫情展开了封城鏖战。有的人选择了回家，而我决定留下，陪着我的中国家人们共同经历这一切。疫情之初，我在赤道几内亚的家人们给我打了无数电话，他们担心我在这里的安全，问我是否害怕。我也问自己："罗木，你害怕吗？"

我亲眼见证了中国政府为抗疫所付出的努力，见证了学校和老师们为了保护我们而做出的牺牲，也见证了身边"钢铁侠"国际学生志愿服务队的奉献和担当。从 2 月 16 日开始，由我们国际教育学院的各国留学生组成的"钢铁侠"志愿队一直在为同学们提供志愿服务，在学校和老师的指导下，他们帮助打扫公共区域卫生，成立了多个服务小分队，为同学们送菜、送饭、送物资，鼓励大家一起团结抗疫、时刻不要放弃学习。在这个寒冬，即使他们穿着层层防护服、戴着眼镜和口罩，我还是看到了那些阻隔不了的真心和热情。

罗木

当我见证了无数人为这座城市的苏醒而拼命时，我问自己："你害怕吗？"

masks, I could see the sincerity and passion that couldn't be blocked.

As I witnessed millions of people fighting for the reawakening of this city, I asked myself, "Are you afraid?"

No, I am not afraid, not at all.

Within the 76 days since the city was closed, I have seen the campus from raining and snowing winter to flower blooming spring. Although I couldn't get out of the dormitory building, I observed how China "adheres to people-oriented approach; puts their lives in the first position, " in my small cubicle, and observed how Chinese people stick to the principle "the country is in difficulties and everyone has a responsibility". All the Chinese people are great fighters against the epidemic. I am happy for myself because I stand with my fellow Chinese people.

My fellow Chinese people, I hope you will remember that although I have a different look, we once watched the same starry sky on Nanwang Mountain in Wuhan together.

I always remember a saying that a Chinese teacher told me , "The one who knows is not confused, the one who is benevolent is not worried, and the one who is brave is not afraid". The fearlessness of the entire Chinese people in Wuhan I witnessed was one of the best lessons I've ever learned in China. With this heavy spiritual harvest, I will bravely take every step and go forward with my dreams.

Standing at the intersection of graduation farewell, the voice in my mind came back again - "Are you afraid?".

No, the brave are fareless and the doers are boundless.

中国地质大学（武汉）/ 罗木摄

不，我不害怕，一点儿也不。

“封城”的 76 天，我从校园里的冬日雨雪，看到春季繁花盛开。尽管不能出宿舍楼，我却在我的小格子间里看到了“以人为本，生命至上”，看到了“国家有难，匹夫有责”。全体中国人民都是抗击疫情的伟大战士，而我也为自己感到高兴，因为我和我的中国家人们站在了一起。

我的中国家人们，希望你们会记得，虽然我长着不同的面孔，但我们曾一起守望过武汉南望山上的同一片星空。

一直记得中国老师告诉过我的一句话：“知者不惑，仁者不忧，勇者不惧。”在武汉我看到了中国人民的大无畏精神，这也是我在中国上过最精彩的一课。带着这份沉甸甸的精神食粮，我会勇敢迈出每一步，逐梦前行。

站在毕业离别的十字路口，脑海里的那个声音又响起来了：“你害怕吗？”

不，勇者无畏，行者无疆。

我的武汉故事
My Wuhan Story

［越南］ 阮庆玄 中国地质大学（武汉）
[Vietnam] Nguyễn Khánh Huyền, China University of Geosciences (Wuhan)

We experience setbacks and hardships together with the belief that there will be sunshine and flowers at the end of the journey.

The beginning of 2020 was unforgettable for every one. The COVID-19 pandemic quickly swept us like a storm without any early notification. I still remembered how I felt on January 23 when Wuhan announced to lock down the city and fight against the pandemic.

At the first, there was sadness in Wuhan because we were all upset and at a loss about how the pandemic would end. Life at the beginning of the lockdown was nervous and boring. We could stay only at our dormitories and browse latest news online. Seeing that the number of being infected and dead increased every day, we were full of anxiety and fear. The increased number of death and all the pictures in black-and-white made us deeply depressed. We felt like being disconnected to the outside real world because of lockdown.

In Wuhan, there were lots of moving stories. The university staff and teachers took turns to be on duty to keep us safe even in weekends

我们一起经历风吹雨打，路的尽头阳光必定会照耀，花也会盛开。

2020 年之初，对于每个人来说，都有一段难以忘怀的经历。新型冠状病毒像一场风暴一样迅速席卷而来，没有任何预告。我的脑海里仍然记得 1 月 23 日那天，当武汉宣布封锁城市、与病毒做抗争时，我内心浮现的一幕幕情景。

在武汉，有让人悲伤的故事。最初的一段时间，大家都很迷茫，不知道事情会发展成什么样子。刚开始的生活，让人觉得紧张又枯燥。我们只能待在宿舍里，上网浏览着最新消息，看着确诊人数和死亡人数的增加，心里充满了无奈与恐惧。新闻里，激增的数字和黑白图片让人觉得很压抑。由于无法出门，感觉跟外面的世界断了联系，平日里正常的出行活动都变成了奢望。有的时候，半夜醒来，心里怀念的仅仅是亲人的一个拥抱、朋友的一个微笑。多么想一觉醒来，发现这只是一场噩梦，一切都跟以前一样。

在武汉，有催人泪下的故事。学校的老师们顾不上休息，每日都在宿舍楼里守护着大家。周围的留学生们自发组织团队，为我们提供生活服务、排解心理压力。老师和同学们组建了“手拉手”微信群，在群里

and holidays. Foreign students volunteered to help us for daily supplies and psychological relax. Teachers and students were organized into a WeChat "hand-in-hand" group to help each other and share information. Every need even a pen or a book would be addressed by the university. This was the first time on this foreign land that I experienced such warm care from other people in this cold winter and I was deeply moved. On February 14, the Valentine's Day, people in Jilin Province dispatched 500 tons of medical supplies to Hubei, which we called "the Valentine's Day Gift of One Thousand Tons." Doctors at the frontiers were fighting against the pandemic all the time. Every people, no matter how seemingly unimportant, was carrying with them a strong and great will for victory over the pandemic. They were soldiers in peace time and they contributed a lot to the final victory of winning the pandemic. Staying in Wuhan, I witnessed how the whole China and the whole world was extending their hands to help Wuhan. My gratitude and appreciation were beyond words. I could say nothing besides a simple "thank you" and shed tears.

In Wuhan, there were lots of exciting stories. We kept wearing masks, doing infection routines and studying in our apartments. We kept encouraging each other and doing our best to help with the fight until the final victory came. Millions of excellent medical expertise came to Wuhan to keep us safe and healthy. Though confronting with danger and difficulties, they showed no sign of depression. We heard more and more exciting and encouraging stories and news. Makeshift hospitals were closed one by one and more and more infected patients were getting well and discharged from hospitals. Regarding the COVID-19 pandemic, all efforts were joined

互相分享、互相帮助。就连小到缺少一支笔、一本书，老师们都会尽力解决。异国他乡，寒冬之下，这也是我第一次感受到这么真切的关怀，真的让人很感动。2 月 14 日，正好是情人节，吉林人民向湖北送去了 500 吨抗疫的医疗物资，大家称之为“千吨情人节礼物”。抗击疫情的前线医生每一天每一刻都在战斗，每一个小人物都带着一份坚强而伟大的意志，他们就是和平时期的士兵，他们的功劳确实一点都不小。身处武汉，看到全中国、全世界都在向武汉伸出援手，除了流泪和一声简单的“感谢”，我不知道还能说什么。

在武汉，有激动人心的故事。我们坚持戴口罩、消毒，在宿舍里继续学习，鼓励周围的同伴们，用自己力所能及的努力等待着这场战斗的最终胜利。成千上万的优秀医护人员来到武汉，面对一重又一重新的难关，所有人没有一丝丝气馁。我们听到了越来越多激动人心的故事。方舱医院一个又一个关闭，一批又一批病人痊愈出院。在疫情问题上，我们看不到隔阂，唯有携手共进，没有地理、种族、宗教、肤色、语言等一系列的问题，全世界都在朝着同一个方向前行。听到这里，你是否和

中国地质大学（武汉）/ 阮庆玄提供

together and there was no differentiation between geographic regions, nationalities, religions, skin colors or languages. The whole world was marching toward the same destination, that is, to win the pandemic. After hearing this, are you as excited as I am?

Now Wuhan has passed its darkest hours and is welcoming its warm spring. This reminds me of a famous Vietnam saying, "Today is hard, so is tomorrow. However, the day after tomorrow must be beautiful." Such confidence in the future supports everyone. No matter what difficulties and hardships we are facing, we will sure believe the dawn is coming and the first sign of light will break the darkness of the night.

Let me end my writing with a Chinese song written by one of my Vietnamese fellows for each of you who read my writing.

Keep going Wuhan
You are the most beautiful flower
In full blossom in the world
Those who love you are concerned about you

Remember to smile
The love from Spring is sprouting
Finally into all savors of life, sour, sweet, bitter and spicy
The sunshine will shine through the shade

Millions of stars will light up the sky
Millions of love will brighten the world
One star breaking through the sky

中国地质大学（武汉）/ 阮庆玄提供

我一样激情澎湃？

现在，武汉已经度过了最艰难的时期，也再次迎来了温暖的春天。这让我想到越南的一句名言：“今天是困难的，明天也没有什么容易，但后天一定会美好。”这样的信念，支撑着我们每一个人，无论遇到什么痛苦，我们都要相信，黎明终将到来，这一线光亮定会消除夜晚的黑暗。

想送上越南同胞们写的一首中文歌，给听我这段故事的每一个你。

武汉加油吧
你是一朵最美的花
在世界中绽放
爱你的人为你牵挂

记得微笑啊
春天的爱已经发芽
终将化作酸甜苦辣
阳光会穿过这层纱

Cannot block the light though very beautiful

Friends and families in Wuhan, close to each other, we never fear hardships

Shoulder by shoulder, hand in hand, say good-bye to this episode

Heroes are coming, with full love

Wait until spring when it is warm and flowers are blossoming, let's toast to thank for all the care we have been receiving

——Keep Going Wuhan

群星才能铺满夜空
众爱才能照亮人间
一颗划破天空的星
再美也阻挡不住光明

武汉家人都在身边，从来不畏惧艰险
万众齐心地，肩并肩，向这页插曲说再见
英雄都纷纷到来，他们带着满满的爱
等到春暖和花开，把酒感谢所有的关怀
和这世界的美。

——《武汉加油吧》

方块字里读中国
Read China through Chinese Characters

［泰国］ 陈文辉　桂林电子科技大学
[Thailand] Kunarak MR.Anon, Guilin University of Electronic Technology

I begin to understand China, an oriental civilization with a history of 5,000 years, from the "Chinese characters", especially various Chinese strokes in my Chinese reading and writing classes. With continuous deepening of my study of Chinese characters, I begin to learn that Chinese is the most beautiful language in the world. Each character conveys its own unique profound and subtle meanings. Three-Character Classics, Five-Character Quatrains and Seven-Character Verses, with combination of different numbers of characters, are parts of eastern rhythmic poems of Tang and Song dynasties.

"Raising my head, I see the moon so bright; withdrawing my eyes, my nostalgia comes around", this is how Chinese write about their missing of the hometowns with sincerity and passion. When I first came to China, as a total stranger, I could not communicate well. Deeply lost in depression, I missed my hometown a lot. However, recalling why I chose to study in China, I made up my mind to study hard despite of all the hardships and difficulties. I studied in the Guilin University of Electronic Technology, which had excellent facilities and environment for learning languages. The university had a brilliant curriculum,

右二为陈文辉

中国，一个具有五千年悠久历史的东方文明古国，对于它的认识始于一个个不重样的方块字。点、横、撇、竖、捺是我在汉语读写课上对汉字构成的基本认识，随着学习持续不断深入，我认为中文是世界上最完美的一种语言，每一个汉字都非常之深奥，所表达的意义深刻而微妙，三字经、五言绝句、七言律诗，不同个数的汉字排列组合成为富有东方韵律的唐诗和宋词。

“举头望明月，低头思故乡。”这是我读到的中国人对于思念家乡的简单告白，情真意切。初到中国留学的时候，人生地不熟的我，语言无法沟通，我听不懂他人在讲什么，他人也不懂我在讲什么，我深陷在沮丧和迷茫中，无比思念家乡，可是回想我为什么选择来到中国留学，我就下定决心不论遇到任何困难，都要坚持努力学习。在桂林电子科技大学学习中文期间，我拥有了一个非常好的语言环境，学校安排的课程非常合理，教学的内容很贴近日常生活，我们都能学以致用。我一个字一个字地去认识，然后理解每个汉字背后的含义，每天进步一点点，让我越来越爱上了中文，渐渐体验到了“书中自有黄金屋，书中自有颜如玉”这句中国俗语的意思。

very close to daily life. We found it easy to apply what we had learned to daily life. I learned Chinese characters one by one, trying to understand their meanings. Each day I made some progress until I began to fall in love with Chinese and gradually understand the meaning of an old Chinese saying, "Within books, one can find houses of gold. Within books, one can find beauties as fair as jade."

Another Chinese saying, "Mountains multiply and streams double back, I doubt if there is even a road. Willows cluster darkly and blossoms shine, oh, another village is ahead! "enables me to understand the optimism of Chinese who believes that a beautiful tomorrow is ahead if we are courageous to face up to challenges. This displays itself even more clearly in 2020 when Chinese are fighting against COVID-19 pandemic. The pandemic seized Wuhan like a storm. The anxiety and fear kept spreading. Confronting with this unprecedented pandemic, our university staff devoted themselves fully in keeping us safe and healthy. They kept themselves very busy in measuring temperatures for the students, handing out prevention and control supplies such as face masks and disinfectants etc. Some medical experts lost their lives for saving those infected. Seeing what they had done to keep others safe and healthy, I admired deeply from my heart their devotion, united spirits and sacrifice they had made to protect common people safe and healthy. The Chinese government had tried its utmost to protect their people, showing great administrative capability and responsibility. I found myself understand China more comprehensively. I fully appreciate and was grateful for what our university and Chinese government had been doing for us. I felt safe, happy and lucky to study in China. Now the pandemic has been under full control in China, which cannot be achieved

“山重水复疑无路，柳暗花明又一村。”这是我读到的中国人关于直面苦难、勇于开拓终将迎来美好明天的乐观精神。一方面，2020 年的中国遭遇了罕见的流行传染病，人们心里的惶恐和不安在一天天地增加。另一方面，学校和老师也很繁忙，在疫情期间为保障留学生们的健康安全做了各种工作，为学生们测量体温，免费为同学们发放口罩、消毒液等防疫物资等，坚守在工作岗位的医护工作者为抗击疫情不幸牺牲，我从心里佩服中国人在灾难面前的团结一心以及中国政府为人民生命安全所做出的努力。从此，我更全面地认识了中国，体会到了在中国学习的安全感、幸福感，十分感谢学校对我们的关心和中国政府的努力。现在中国的疫情已经基本控制住了，然而国外的疫情不容乐观，十分严峻，情况与疫情开始发生在中国时来了个大反转。中国抗击疫情的成效当然离不开中国人民和中国政府的齐心协力，奋勇拼搏，责任担当在这个国家和人民身上留下了深刻的烙印。

我相信每一个人都拥有自己的梦想，每个不同的梦想交加起来就形成了国家的大梦想。而没有梦想的人，就像在广阔无垠的大海上，迷失

桂林电子科技大学图书馆 / 陈文辉提供

without the united efforts of both Chinese people and the Chinese government. However, the situation is worse in countries outside China. The sharp turn of situations in China and countries outside China leaves deep impression on me about how responsible and arduous Chinese people are.

I believe everyone has dreams. Dreams of individuals lead to the bigger dream of a country. A person without dreams is like sailing in the vast sea without directions. Dreams are compasses, pointing correct directions for those having dreams; dreams are also like a light house, glistening and lighting up roads for those having dreams. Everyone who has dreams has to fulfill their beautiful dreams through hard working step by step. The experience in China strengthens my dreams, that is, learn Chinese to become a cultural envoy between China and Thailand.

Finally, I am very grateful to Chinese government for providing us the opportunity of studying Chinese in China. And also many thanks for the care, help and teaching of the staff, management and teachers of my university. My dreams are coming closer and next year I will be flying towards my dreams. I wish the relationship between China and Thailand are becoming more sustainable with enhanced cooperation in politics, trade and economic and cultural fields. I wish I would devote my talents and efforts into the progressive development of relationships between China and Thailand.

桂林电子科技大学 / 陈文辉提供

方向；梦想像是一个指南针，给拥有梦想的人指引了正确的方向；梦想也像一个灯塔，闪烁着光芒，照亮了追梦者前进的道路。每个拥有梦想的人，都需要通过自己的努力来实现心中美好的梦想。而实现梦想需要脚踏实地、一步一个脚印、坚持不懈，直到成功。在中国留学的经历让我更加坚定了我的梦想，那就是学好中文，成为中国和泰国的文化交流使者。

最后，非常感谢中国政府为我们留学生提供来中国学习中文的机会，同时也非常感谢桂林电子科技大学领导和教师给予留学生的关心、帮助和教学，使我梦想的翅膀羽毛渐渐丰满，待到学业有成之时飞翔，明年我将展翅飞向我的梦想。中泰两国友好关系历史悠久，源远流长，政治、经贸、人文领域的交流与合作不断增强。希望我学好中文，能够为中泰友好关系不断向前发展贡献出自己的一份微薄之力。

重新出发看中国
Rediscover China

［巴基斯坦］ 高兴　中国科学技术大学
[Pakistan] M Shujah Islam Sameem, University of Science and Technology of China

When I was young, one of my teachers told me that there was a nation called China and it was our best brother. My father, who loves China so much, kept telling me that China and Pakistan are best friends. I still remembered how excited my father was when we saw a Chinese people. He always dragged me and pointed to me, "Look, that's a Chinese." This was the primitive impression I had on China. I had never dreamed that one day I would come to my legendary nation.

I still remembered how timid I was when I first came to China. Though I knew that Chinese people were very friendly, I was still quite nervously because there were a lot of challenges. Time flies and three years have passed. I have become a half-an-expert on China from knowing nothing about this country. Many foreigners speak highly of China's highways, express deliveries, high-speed railways and electronic payment. However, I am not going to talk about these obvious achievements China has made but to tell you my true feelings toward China.

The year 2020 is destined to be unusual. I made a trip to Malaysia during my

从小我的老师就告诉我们，这个世界上有个国家叫中国，它是我们最好的兄弟。我的父亲特别喜欢中国，他告诉我，中国和巴基斯坦是最好的朋友。还记得每当我们外出时，我父亲看到中国人，总是又激动又兴奋地拉着我说："快看，那个人是中国人。"这是我对中国最原始的印象。谁也不知道我会来到"传说"中的中国。

还记得刚来中国时的胆怯，虽然知道中国人非常友好，但是来一个陌生的国度学习对我来说仍有很多挑战。我怀着忐忑不安的心情来到这里求学，不知不觉已经过去 3 年了，时间过得真快啊，我也从最初的懵懂变成了现在的半个"中国通"。很多外国人总说中国的高速公路发达，中国的快递发达，中国的铁路发达，中国的无现金支付发达，这些都是全世界有目共睹的，而我今天要抛开这些，谈谈我对中国的真实感受。

2020 年注定是不平凡的一年，我在寒假到来前已经定好去马来西亚的旅行计划。当我离开中国时，那个时候我还不知道有个病毒叫新冠病毒，它已悄悄蔓延。关于病毒的大部分信息主要来源于我的同学和朋友，在中国的朋友告诉我病毒蔓延的速度，告诉我武汉封城，告诉我每天新增的病例，告诉我商场关闭了，告诉我人们都躲在家里避难。我在零零

winter vacation as planned. When I left China, I had no idea that the pandemic COVID-19 was spreading slyly. Most of the information about the virus came from my Chinese friends, who told me the lockdown of Wuhan and the number of newly-infected cases. They also told me that shopping malls were shut down and people were restricted at home to prevent from being infected. I gradually learned this and felt like terrors in some disaster movies. The return date of my trip was approaching, and I did not know what I should do. My family in Pakistan were much concerned about me and asked me to return to Pakistan, keeping away from the pandemic. Some of my friends also suggested me to stay in Malaysia. I was in great panic, not knowing what to do. After one-night's struggling, I decided to follow my original plan and return to China. My family and friends did not understand my decision. I was confident that Chinese government would do their best to fight against the pandemic and protect their people. I chose to have confidence in China and Chinese government and I would not run away when China was in trouble. Therefore, wearing two layers of masks and gloves, I returned to China as per my original plan. The airport was almost empty. This was the first time in the last three years that I saw an empty airport. At that moment, I realized for the first time how serious the situation was.

After returning to China, I immediately completed registration procedures and temperature check, and then followed instructions about fighting against the COVID-19 from the Chinese government: Wash hands more, go out less; wear mouth masks, no social gathering and keep 2-meter social distance. I stayed at home like all other Chinese people. During the period, I saw all functional departments of Chinese government were on duty every day; supermarkets were open as usual; community service staff set up virus-

碎碎的片段中仿佛看到灾难电影里才会呈现出来的恐怖景象，眼看返程日期临近，我不知道如何是好。远在巴基斯坦的家人担心我，希望我回国避难；我的朋友建议我留在马来西亚暂时不要回去；一时我也慌了神，但经过一夜的思想斗争后，我仍然决定坚持原计划不变，我要按时返程。我的家人和朋友非常不理解我，但我心里非常清楚明白中国政府不会袖手旁观，我选择相信中国，我不能在中国有困难的时候选择逃跑。于是我做好防护，戴上两层口罩和手套，按时前往机场，准备回到中国。那个时候机场空无一人，这是我三年来第一次见到机场萧条的景象，也是我第一次感受到事情的严重性。

回中国后我第一时间办理相关登记手续，并且接受体温检查，然后响应中国政府“勤洗手、少外出、戴口罩、不聚集、保持 2 米距离”的号召，并和所有中国人一样乖乖待在家里。疫情期间我看到中国职能部门坚持每天在岗；大型超市正常营业；社区街道工作人员在大街上成立大

高兴在呼伦贝尔

prevention stations to spread scientific virus prevention and control measures; even community guards were joining the fight and they helped measure temperatures for their community residents and register those going in and out of their communities; delivery people were delivering food supplies in a well-organized way door to door. The terror scenes in disaster movies did not occur at all and everyone was having their normal daily life. The sun still rises from the east and sets to the west every day, everyone was peaceful, without panic or crying and no one gave up.

Actually, Chinese people had been making greatest efforts to fight against this pandemic. They built Huoshenshan Hospital within 10 days; they dispatched national military forces and doctors in the quickest way to help fight the pandemic in Wuhan; and they quickly and scientifically scheduled the supply of pandemic prevention resources. I saw a greatly united nation and people fighting against the pandemic bravely with joint efforts. I saw the brave and selfless sacrifice the Chinese people who had devoted in this fight; I saw that the Chinese government put the safety and health of their people at the first priority and I experienced the strictest and most comprehensive pandemic prevention measures in China. I was greatly moved by the bravery and tenacity of China as a nation when I learned that some doctors lost their lives in the fighting frontier just for saving others' lives. I was greatly touched by all these I had experienced and wondered what I could do for them. I contacted my family in Pakistan, asked them to buy mouth masks as many as possible and delivered to me to dispatch to my friends around me. I also donated 500 yuan, which was the only cash I had with me, to Chinese government. I also wrote a letter to the government, saying "I come from Pakistan. Pakistan and China

中国科学技术大学 / 高兴提供

大小小的防疫站，向人们循环科普新型冠状病毒的防范措施；小区保安也加入抗疫的战斗中，每天坚持给小区居民测量体温并做好登记工作；外卖小哥更是有条不紊地给每个家庭送食物。而我以为的电影场景却并没有发生，每个人都在正常生活不被打扰，太阳照常升起，夕阳照常西下，一切看上去都是那么平静，没有慌张、没有哭泣，更没有放弃。

事实上中国正在为这场疫情做巨大努力，他们用 10 天的时间建成了火神山医院，他们快速调用国家部队和全国的医护力量前往武汉抗疫，他们迅速调度防疫物资，这场战役中我看到全国人民上下齐心，与病毒做着顽强斗争。在这场无硝烟的战争中，我看到中国人民勇敢无私的奉献，看到中国政府将人民群众生命安全和身体健康放在第一位，看到中国最全面、最严格、最彻底的防控举措，看到为疫情牺牲在第一线的医生时，我真的不禁感叹这个国家的勇敢坚韧的品质。这一切都深深地触动了我，我想我也应该做点什么了。我联系远在巴基斯坦的家人，让他们动用一切关系购买口罩寄到中国并分给身边的朋友；我将口袋中仅有的 500 元钱捐给中国政府，并配上了一封信。我在信中写道：“我来自巴

are good friends. I'm a student and I do not have much money. However, I want to help China go through this hardship, therefore, please accept my donation to help others." This is my heartfelt and sincere blessings to China. Later I read from the press that my 500 yuan had been donated as the pandemic prevention resources and I was very happy.

Under the joint efforts of Chinese government and Chinese people, China put the epidemic under control at the highest speed. As an eyewitness of this fight, I cannot describe my feeling with words how great efforts and dedication had been put in this fight. Now China is doing their best to help other countries in the world, and with no doubt it is a big winner of this fight against the pandemic and has won the respect of the whole world. How can you not love such a great nation and people?

Thanks to the teachers of my childhood and my father, who had taught me to know this great nation when I was still a child. It was so lucky to have the opportunity to study in China. I am grateful to this hardship of experiencing the pandemic, which made me be surer that coming to China for study was my wisest decision in my life.

Finally I want to express my blessings to China: Wish you all the best, China. I will always pray for you!

中国科学技术大学 / 高兴提供

基斯坦，巴基斯坦和中国是好朋友，我是学生，我没有很多钱，但我想帮助中国一起渡过难关，请帮我捐献出去。”这是我心里最诚挚的祝福。后来我在媒体上看到，这500元钱已经为防疫捐献出去了，我非常开心。

最后在中国政府和中国人民团结一致的努力下，中国以最快的速度控制了疫情。作为整个事件的目睹者、亲历者，我无法用语言去描述这场战役背后付出的心血和努力。现在中国正在尽自己最大的努力去帮助世界人民，中国无疑是这场战役中的大赢家，取得了世界人民的尊重和赞扬。你说这样的国家和民族有什么理由不被热爱呢？

谢谢从小教我的老师和我的父亲，在我很小的时候就让我认识这个伟大的国家；谢谢我有幸能来到这里，也感谢经历的这场磨难，使我更加确信我来到中国是人生中做出的最伟大的决定。

最后我想说：“祝福你伟大的中国，我永远为你祈祷！”

从上网课到当主播，我们把中国歌声带给世界

——难忘的 2020 年故事

Singing Chinese Songs to the World

［土库曼斯坦］ 李米娜 方洁 西北工业大学

[Turkmenistan] Astanova Elmira and Kurbanova Govher, Northwestern Polytechnic University

We are from Turkmenistan, a Central Asian country along the Belt and Road. Each of us has a beautiful Chinese name, Li Mina and Fang Jie. By today, we have just been studying in a Chinese university for one whole year. During the past year, we had many heart touching moments and stories, especially in this unforgettable year of 2020.

Becoming online broadcasters. During the pandemic, students take online courses to continue their study. Online courses kicked off on February 24. It was our first time to take online courses. We never had such experience, and were not sure of the effect. We got the computer and textbook ready. We got up in the morning, read the books, made the preparations before the course started, just as we did in the classroom before. When we completed one day of online courses, we found the effect was rather good. We took down some questions

我们来自“一带一路”沿线的土库曼斯坦，我们各有一个美丽的中文名字——“李米娜”“方洁”。今天，是我们在中国大学学习整整一年的日子。在中国，我们一起经历了点点滴滴的故事和难忘的2020年。

从第一次上网课到成为“网红”主播。特殊的时期，“上网课”成为保障正常学习的方式。2月24日开课的第一天，也是我们第一次网络上课。每个人都有一些紧张，因为以前没有这样的经历，也不知道效果会怎么样。因此，我们提前准备好电脑和课本，和在教室上课一样早起读书，做好预习。一天的课程结束，效果还是很好的，我们把听不懂的问题记录下来，课下再去问老师。老师鼓励我们说：“万事开头难。坚持下来，慢慢适应后就简单了。”于是我们每天坚持努力学习，受到了很多老师的表扬。老师们不仅讲课，还告诉我们很多像“愚公移山”“闻鸡起舞”的成语故事，让我们学习中国文化，体会中国精神。受电脑屏

of what we failed to understand, and then asked our teachers afterwards. Our teachers encouraged us: "Everything is difficult at the beginning. Hang in there, you will gradually get used to it, then it will be easier." So every day, we studied hard, and we received praises from our teachers. In addition to giving us online courses, they also told us lots of Chinese idiom stories such as *"Mr. Fool Moves the Mountain" and "Start Practicing at the First Crow of the Rooster."* Through these stories, we learned Chinese culture and got to know the Chinese mindset. Although we could not see each other face to face, we were connected via the computer screen and we felt warm and close to each other nevertheless. However for students stranded in their home countries, the online courses were a challenge. The internet conditions in Turkmenistan lag behind China, and there is time zone difference as well. So the online courses did not have the same good effect as in China. Encouraged by our teachers, we became online broadcasters. Every day, we digested the courses and took the notes and then we live-broadcast to classmates in our country. We also sent reference books and homework assignments to them. Thus we "acquired" and then "spoke out" the knowledge. On the one hand we digested the knowledge and enhanced our study effect; On the other hand, we helped others. We became "messengers" to pass on knowledge and spirit. Currently every day there are around 50 students all over the world tuning in to take our online courses. We have literally become online broadcasters bringing the world together.

As volunteers, we sing the song of China to the world. We found a most meaningful thing during the pandemic was our new roles as volunteers on campus. When the university was shut down due to safety concerns, foreign students could not go out for shopping. Apartment janitors were not allowed to work on campus.

校园俯瞰 / 西北工业大学提供

幕阻隔，虽然我们不能见面，但大家仍然能感受到开心与温暖。然而，对于身处在我们国家的学生来说就存在很大困难，因为土库曼斯坦的网络条件不如中国，而且存在时差，同学们上课效果并不好。在老师的支持下，我们便当起了“网络主播”，每天将上课内容整理，然后再通过网络直播讲授给本国同学。我们也会把参考书、课堂作业发送给他们。这样把知识“学进去”再“讲出来”，一方面能巩固自己学习的效果，另一方面还能帮助他人，作为传递知识与精神的“信使”，我们感到十分自豪。目前，每天大约有 50 名全球学生会听我们讲课，我们已经成了连接世界的“网红主播”。

当志愿者，让我们把中国之歌唱给世界。这段时间里，我们觉得最有意义的事情就是担任疫情期间在校的志愿者了。当时学校封闭管理，为了确保安全，在学校的留学生不能外出购买物品，公寓管理员也不能进入校园继续工作。于是我们就自发成立了“志愿者服务小队”，来自

So we voluntarily set up a "Volunteers Team" which consisted of more than 30 students from over 10 countries. We purchased daily necessities for our peers, maintained and clean the public spaces in the capacity of the apartment janitors, and helped teachers with their anti-virus self protection publicity. Although we felt lonely and scared during the period, we were confident that China would finally surmount the pandemic. At the end of January, we wrote down our inner wishes for all Chinese people. On Lantern Festival, we recorded a Chinese seasonal greeting video to extend our hope for a happy reunion of all Northwestern Polytechnic University students. In March, we learned a Chinese song *Great China*, the song that sings out the great power of China and its unwavering spirit of perseverance and hard work. As the powerful lyric goes, "Braving all storms, we will always protect her... Bless you, China! You are always in my heart. Bless you, China! My blessing is more than tens of thousands of words."We believe this song reflects the China spirit and Chinese people's mentality and determination. We will learn more Chinese songs and bring them to my home country and sing them all over the world. We are now learning the song *Dare to Ask Where is the Road,* the ending song of the blockbuster Chinese TV series *Journey to the West.* And we are eager to present it to our friends and teachers.

As an old Chinese proverb says, "one cannot travel 1,000 miles without taking a succession of solid steps, like a broad river cannot take shape without admitting numerous small streams." This one year experience in China has made us grow and given us touching enlightenments. We are now gradually accustomed to life here and the Chinese mindset. However there is a long way ahead for us. We have bigger and farther dreams to pursue and we are ready to embrace a hopeful tomorrow.

10余个国家的30多名学生积极参加，帮助学生购买生活必需物品，帮助宿舍管理人员维护公共区域卫生，帮助老师宣传防控防疫知识。虽然那时我们也会感到孤独和恐惧，但是我们坚信中国一定能够战胜疫情，迎来春暖花开的一天。1月底，我们写下心中的祈愿，献给所有中国的人们；元宵节，我们录制祝福的视频，希望工大学子再相聚；3月里，我们学会了中国歌曲，一首《大中国》唱出了中国的底蕴，也唱响了不屈不挠、顽强奋斗的精神。正如铿锵有力的歌词中写道：“经过那个多少，那个风吹和雨打……中国，祝福你，你永远在我心里；中国，祝福你，不用千言和万语。”我们想：一首简单的歌曲，其实却反映着这个国家的气质，凸显着中国人民的精神。我们要学习更多的中国歌曲，把这些歌声带回我们国家，甚至唱到世界的每个角落，这样才更有意义。现在，我们已开始学习《西游记》的歌曲《敢问路在何方》了，期待以后精彩的表演。

李米娜在宽窄巷子

古语说：“不积跬步，无以至千里；不积小流，无以成江海。”这一年在中国的经历，让我们成长很多，感动很多。我们也渐渐地熟悉了这里的生活，这里的精神。但是，我们还有更长的路要走，有更远的梦要去实现，拥抱充满希望的明天。

我与北京
Beijing and I

[缅甸] 段兆嘉 中国政法大学

[Myanmar] Phone Myint oo, China University of Political Science and Law

On September 20, 2018, I finally received the long-awaited letter of admission to a Chinese university. On October 3, I boarded on the plane to Beijing with full expectation and set foot on the journey of studying abroad. It was my first time to take a flight and leave Irrawaddy River in Myanmar, my hometown. I thought in the air that I would never fail to live up to the expectations of my family. I must strive for progress and success in a foreign land.

I remember one day shortly after my arrival in Beijing, I put forward a suggestion to three Burmese friends in my class that we should go to the Great Wall together, "How about being a hero together?" They agreed immediately. In two hours, we got to the Great Wall that I have been longing for. When I stepped on it in reality, I am overwhelmed by a tidal surge of emotions and mixed feelings. The scene of building the Great Wall by people in ancient time appeared in my mind when I touched the old and strong walls. Without trucks and machines, how much blood and sweat the working people had spread to complete this endless great wall in a time when there was no advanced science

2018 年 9 月 20 日我终于收到了期待已久的中国大学录取通知书。10 月 3 日，我满怀期待地坐上了飞往北京的飞机，踏上了出国留学之路。这是我第一次坐飞机，也是第一次离开家乡，离开缅甸的伊洛瓦底江。我在飞机上想着，我绝不能辜负家人的期望，到了异国他乡我一定要发愤图强。

记得刚到北京不久的一天，我建议班里的三位缅甸小伙伴一起去长城："一起当好汉怎么样？"他们二话不说就同意了。两个小时后，终于到达了我一直梦想要去的长城。此前我读过很多关于长城历史的书，所以当真正登上长城之后，我不禁心潮起伏，百感交集。站在长城上面，摸着古老又坚固的城墙，就好像看到了古代人民修建长城的那一幕。在没有车没有机器、科技也不发达的古代，劳动人民付出了多少鲜血和汗水才修建成了这一望无际的万里长城啊！我心里不由得为这世界奇迹和它背后的中国古代劳动人民点了个大大的赞。

在学校的组织下，我们还参观了不少北京的特色文化景点。在中国古代最高学府国子监，我们欣赏了原汁原味的古代礼乐表演；在雍和宫萦绕的淡淡烟雾中，我们和老师们讨论了很多关于佛教的话题；在网红

and technology. I cannot help giving the thumbs up in my heart to the world wonder and the Chinese labors behind it.

Organized by the school, we also paid visits to several cultural attractions of Beijing. We were treated to an authentic performance of ancient rituals and music at Guozijian, the imperial college and the highest education institution in ancient China. Amidst the lingering pale smoke of the Yonghe Lama Temple, we had discussions with our teachers about Buddhism. We saw hutong with charm of old Beijing and shops with trends of new Beijing at internet-famous spot Nanluoguxiang Street, and ate raisin-filled candy canes, a traditional snack of Beijing. We went to Sanshao Cultural Center of Miyun county to learn how to make pancakes, visited Cuandixia village and Tanzhe Temple, and made thread bound books in the National Collection Museum. These cultural activities greatly enriched my extracurricular life in Beijing. I also visited Sanlitun, Wangfujing, Xidan, the Bird's Nest and the Water Cube, where I enjoyed specialties such as roast duck and noodles served with bean sauce, and even drank old Beijing bean juice. As the saying goes, "He who travels much will learn much." I have learned a lot from all these activities and gotten a three-dimensional view of Beijing!

Most notably, on October 1, 2019, I had the privilege of being part of the expat formation in Beijing for the grand parade celebrating the 70th anniversary of the founding of the People's Republic of China! On the evening of September 30, we entered the prescribed place in an orderly fashion and waited. We were all ready and waiting to go! When the official parade took place on October 1, I was particularly excited and so focused on the instructions that I didn't dare let up. We followed the float themed as "a Community of Shared Future for

中国政法大学昌平校区 / 段兆嘉提供

打卡地——南锣鼓巷，我们看到了老北京风韵的胡同和新北京潮流的店铺，还吃上了传统小吃葡萄干冰糖葫芦。去密云三烧文化馆学做烧饼，到爨底下村和潭柘寺参观游学，还有在国家典藏博物馆制作线装书，这些中国文化体验活动极大地丰富了我在北京的课余生活。我自己也去了三里屯、王府井、西单、鸟巢、水立方等地游玩，品尝了北京烤鸭、炸酱面等特色美食，甚至还喝了老北京豆汁儿。都说“行路多者见识多”，所有这些活动让我学到了很多，也认识了一个立体的北京。

最值得一提的是，2019 年 10 月 1 日，我有幸作为在京外籍人士方阵的一员，参加了庆祝中华人民共和国成立 70 周年的盛大游行。9 月 30 日晚上我们就井然有序地进入规定地点等候，一切准备就绪，只待出发。10 月 1 日正式游行时，我心情特别激动，全神贯注地听着指挥，不敢有一丝松懈。我们紧跟着“人类命运共同体”彩车游行，前进了一段

Mankind." After a while I saw the most amazing large aircraft, the echelon of these aircrafts pulling out a rainbow of colored smoke in the sky and then whizzing by! We waved bouquets of flowers and shouted "China, China! Happy Birthday!" It is no exaggeration to say that this is the biggest and most memorable celebration I have ever attended in my life. Through this parade, I felt the strength of China and the unity of the Chinese people. After decades of hard work, China is not what it used to be!

After returning home for the winter break in January 2020, I thought I would be able to go back to school at the end of February as usual. Unfortunately, the emergence and ravages of the novel coronavirus forced schools in Beijing to delay the start of the new term. We have to study online for a semester and missed our school days very much. I sincerely hope that the heroes in white will overcome the virus as soon as possible, and that we will be back in the classroom next semester to study, discuss, progress and graduate together with my lovely classmates.

拓荒牛 / 段兆嘉提供

之后我看到了最震撼人心的大飞机，飞机梯队在空中拉出像彩虹一样绚烂的彩烟，然后呼啸而过！我们挥动着花束，齐声高呼：“中国，中国！生日快乐！”毫不夸张地说，这是我这辈子参加过的最大最难忘的庆典。通过这次游行，我感受到了中国的强大和中国人的团结，经过他们数十年的奋斗，中国已今非昔比！

2020 年 1 月放寒假回国之后，本以为 2 月底就能如往常一样重返法大上课了，不料新冠病毒的出现和肆虐让北京的学校不得不延迟开学，我们也只能在线上学习了一个学期，这让我很怀念在学校上课的日子。衷心祈祷白衣英雄们早日战胜病毒，希望我们下个学期能重返法大的课堂，与可爱的同学们一起学习，一起讨论，一起进步，一起毕业。

跟你谈场最"烧脑"的恋爱

A Brain-Burning Love with You

[塔吉克斯坦] 苏逸 北京交通大学

[Tajikistan] Saidov Saidshohzod, Beijing Jiaotong University

I first met you in history class. In the textbook of our country, the history of ancient China is divided into three aspects: the national system, the spiritual culture and the achievements of Chinese civilization. I vaguely remember some of the Chinese words in the textbook "world," "imperial examination system," "small," "big," "Silk Road," "four great inventions." China has vast territory and abundant products. What attracted me most was the Silk Road, and through which, the Han Dynasty sold silk, tea and porcelain to Western Asia to earn gold and silver. The ancient Silk Road matches perfectly with the modern Belt and Road Initiative, which is the main reason why I come to China to study economic management. There are also the four great inventions of ancient times, papermaking, printing, compass, gunpowder all come from China, these brilliance and civilization promoted the progress of history. China is a mysterious ancient civilization, just like a veiled girl, let you want to uncover her veil. The heart tickles, maybe that is the so-called love at first sight.

Passion is the best mentor and impetus, so I began to learn Chinese through self-study. A few months later, although I only learned some simple

与你初见是在历史课上。在我国家的历史教科书上，讲古代中国分了三个方面，古代中国的国家制度、古代中国的精神文化、中华文明的成就。我依稀记得课本中出现的一些中国词语："天下""科举制度""小""大""丝绸之路""四大发明"。中国疆域广阔，物产丰富。最为吸引我的是中国历史通商甬道丝绸之路，汉朝把丝绸、茶叶、瓷器卖往西亚，赚取金银。古代的"丝绸之路"与现代的"一带一路"完美契合，这就是吸引我来中国留学学习经济管理的主要原因。还有古代的四大发明，造纸术、印刷术、指南针、火药都来源于中国，中国这些辉煌和文明，对促进历史的进步具有深远影响，中国是一个神秘的文明古国，就犹如一个戴着面纱的姑娘，让你想去揭开她的面纱。心里痒痒的，这就是所谓的一见钟情吧。

"钟情"是最好的老师和动力，于是我开始自学汉语。几个月后，虽然我只学习了一些简单的汉语，但就是因为如此，我得到了在众多角逐者中脱颖而出来中国留学的机会。兴奋的我在想，我终于有和你亲密接触的机会了，等待我的一定是一个非常浪漫的故事。原来故事的开端并非浪漫，而是不停地"烧脑"。之所以说是烧脑，是因为越是学习汉

Chinese, I got the opportunity to study in China among many competitors. How excited I was that I finally have a close contact with you, what waiting for me must be a very romantic story. It turns out that the beginning of the story is not romantic at all, but constantly "brain burning." The reason is that the more you learn Chinese, the more you feel that your knowledge is limited and not enough. There are too many things to learn. Fortunately, there are painstaking Chinese teachers who have been encouraging me. Let me lay the foundation of Chinese steadfastly. From the beginning of writing Chinese characters like paintings, now I can use the vocabulary I have learned to express my ideas, which is really amazing. The process of learning Chinese in China at the beginning is like a brainstorming, constantly storing and turning, and making me more familiar with it.

My major is economic management, so I am interested in economic news. Besides, I come from a country along Belt and Road Initiative. There were four great inventions in ancient China. Living in China today, we can enjoy the "new four great inventions" – high-speed railway, shared bicycles, Alipay and online shopping. I took a high-speed train to Xi'an, Luoyang, Wuhan, Taiyuan; I shuttle between dormitory, teaching buildings, canteens by shared bikes, and by the way to the supermarket to sweep the mobile phone to buy a carton of milk; and when I am lacking in something in life, I can order by clicking on the mobile phone, and the goods may reach in two days. How convenient it is here. These are the topics I often talk to my domestic friends on the internet. They all envy me and shout that I should be their tour guide. If they come to China, I will naturally say yes, because it seems to be my responsibility. I can't wait to introduce you to all my friends.

北京交通大学 / 苏逸提供

语，越觉得自己知道的知识很有限，很不够，要学习的东西实在太多太多，好在有不辞辛苦、不厌其烦的汉语老师们，一直在鼓励我，让我踏踏实实地打好了汉语的地基。从起初写汉字像画画儿，到现在我已经可以用所学的词汇把自己的想法写出来，用文字来表达自己的想法真是让人无比兴奋。初来中国学习汉语的过程，现在回忆起来就像一场头脑风暴，不停储存转动，也让我与你更加熟识起来。

苏逸（左一）与同学们

The year of 2020 is so extraordinary that the COVID-19 pandemic spread around the world. When I first returned home, I was worried to death and paid daily attention to the growth number of patients from WeChat. I looked at the color on the map changed from shallow to deep, and then slowly from deep to shallow, which was the result of the efforts of the Chinese people. Even now I am thousands of miles away, but my heart will always be with you and cheer up for you. Because I fall in love you with you at the first sight, and I will go through with you till the end of my life. Now you and I just walked through the first sight, familiar, know each other, and a long way is waiting for us, even if sometimes a little "brain burning," but I would like to forge ahead with you for all my life.

我的专业是经济管理，所以有关促进经济发展的所有事情我都非常关注，尤其我是一个来自“一带一路”国家的留学生。前面我提到了中国古代的四大发明，住在当今中国必须要好好享受“新四大发明”，那就是高铁、共享单车、支付宝和网购了。我坐高铁去了西安、洛阳、武汉、太原；骑着共享单车穿梭在宿舍楼、教学楼、食堂之间，顺便去超市刷下手机购买一盒牛奶；享受着缺什么生活、学习用品，在手机上一点击下单，慢则两天就到的生活便捷。这些都是我在网上跟我国内朋友常聊的话题，他们个个羡慕不已，都嚷嚷着让我当他们的导游，要来中国看看，我自然都会爽快答应，因为这仿佛变成我的责任，我迫不及待要把与我相知的你，介绍给所有我的朋友们。

2020 年是不平凡的一年，新冠肺炎疫情在全球蔓延。刚回国的时候我简直担心死了，每天都关注来自微信里关于新冠肺炎感染者的增长数字。我看着地图上的颜色从浅到深，再由深到浅，这背后是所有中国人的努力付出换来的结果。即使现在我远在几千里之外，但是我的心永远和你在一起，和你一起加油。因为我在和你谈一场初见、相识、相知、相爱、相伴、相守一生的恋爱。现在我与你才走过初见、相识、相知，等待我们的路还有很长很长，即使有时有点儿“烧脑”，但我愿一生与你砥砺前行。

少年游
Journey of a Youth

[马来西亚] 陈俐晴　南京信息工程大学
[Malaysia] Tan Li Qing, Nanjing University of Information Science and Technology

"The Xipu Road in Chengdu ("Nanjing") used to be my home, I came here in April when the plum had ripened. The clear water of the Yangtze River is flowing down, and the fine drizzle is going on." Nanjing was the first Chinese city I knew in my junior high school. The teacher recited Du Fu's poems and described the city's long history to me. The thoughts of mine gradually floated out of the classroom, as if they had come to the drizzling and magnificent ancient city.

Youth dream dwellt in my heart deeply. And six months ago, I finally set foot on this land.

Just arrived, I was surprised by China's convenient transportation and fast consumption mode. But the most shocking thing I feel is the Chinese character ads everywhere, so ostentatious, so lively, as if they were saying welcome you to China. For a time, the sense of achievement swept away my uneasiness and hesitation about the future.

The logistic efficiency here is even more astonishing. Online-ordered items can be received in up to three days, return/refund service is perfect so

“南京西浦道，四月熟黄梅。湛湛长江去，冥冥细雨来。”南京，是我在初中的时候第一个知道的中国城市。老师朗诵着杜甫的诗句，向年少的我绘声绘色地描述着南京的悠久历史，少年的思绪渐渐飘出了课堂，仿佛来到了那个细雨蒙蒙而又波澜壮阔的古老城市。

年少时的向往来势汹汹，在我心底埋下了深深的憧憬。半年前，我终于如愿以偿踏上了这片土地。

初来乍到，我惊讶于中国便利的交通、快捷的消费模式。可最让我感觉震撼的却是遍地可见的汉字广告，那么招摇，那么热闹，争先恐后地冲我欢呼着，像是在告诉我：“恭贺你，终于来到了中国！”一时间，满满的成就感扫去了我对未来的不安和彷徨。

这里的物流更是让人眼前一亮，今天订购的物品至多三天就能收到，退货退款服务更是完善得让我能十分安心地在网上购物。当然，最令我感动的当数中国人的热情善良。当我一时沉迷于网购不能自拔时，取货点里一堆小山似的快递给了我当头一棒。正当我决定一趟趟慢慢将快递搬回自己宿舍时，也许是因为看到我为难的表情，一位中国学姐跑来主动施以援手。得知我是留学生，她更是热情地向我介绍南京当地的美食

that you can go shopping online without any worry. Of course, what moved me most was the enthusiasm and kindness of the Chinese people. When I was addicted to online shopping, a pile of mountain-like express delivery gave me a blow. Just as I decided to slowly move the express back to my dormitory one by one. Perhaps seeing my embarrassed expression, a senior student came to help. Knowing that I am a foreign student, she is more enthusiastic to introduce to me the local cuisine in Nanjing and the scenic spots worth visiting. I was infected by her and put down the restraint in my heart, and began to talk freely with her. In this way, I made my first Chinese friend.

In the process of communicating with Chinese students, I not only got a lot of correction in Chinese pronunciation, but also changed my thinking mode to some extent. They tend to be mature and independent. After exchanging opinions with each other, I began to get fascinated by the feeling of communicating with them, and my perspective gradually got widened. The resonance of thought has brought me closer to my Chinese friends. In order to let me know more about China, they often take me to visit some famous scenic spots to experience local culture and customs.

The Memorial Hall of the Victims of the Nanjing Massacre by Japanese Invaders was the first stop for me to know Nanjing. Never will I forget the feeling of visiting, which is a shock from the heart and soul. The interview in the shadow room made me cry, and at that moment I knew that the peace we used to take for granted was not a matter of course. It deserves us to maintain and fight for. So far, the four characters inlaid on the memorial wall, "Remember history, Cherish peace" is still vividly kept in my mind.

That day, I carried a heavy heart back to the dormitory, I thought a lot.

和值得一去的景点，而我也受到学姐的感染，放下心中的拘谨，开始与她谈天说地。就这样，我交到了第一个中国朋友。

在与中国学生的交流过程中，我不只在中文发音上得到了很多纠正，更多的是一定程度上改变了我的思维模式。中国学生的思想多偏向于成熟独立，在我们彼此交换自己的阅历后，我开始迷上了和他们交流的感觉，我的很多想法也潜移默化地逐渐开阔起来。思想上的共鸣，更加拉近了我和中国朋友们的距离。为了让我更深入地了解中国，他们常常带着我去参观一些著名景点的文化与风情。

侵华日军南京大屠杀遇难同胞纪念馆是我认识南京的第一站。我永远忘不了参观时的感觉，那是一种来自心灵的震撼。暗影室内播放的访谈内容更是让我泪如雨下，那一刻我才知道，我们习以为常的和平并不是理所当然，它是需要我们去维护、去争取的。至今，纪念馆墙壁上镶嵌的八个大字“铭记历史，珍爱和平”仍历历在目。

南京牛首山 / 陈俐晴提供

陈俐晴在桂林

I hope I have enough ability to protect everything I want to protect, and only when I have enough ability can I do so. I like one of the words in "Youth China Say" most, "Youth is strong, then country is strong." When the country is strong enough, it can protect the hearts of young people, and so does a generation of young people. "Don't be idle until you get white hair." As a young generation, we should do our best to help build the world and fight for our endeavor.

I think I get ready.

南京信息工程大学图书馆 / 陈俐晴提供

那天，我揣着一颗沉重的心回到了宿舍，我思考了很多。我希望我有足够的能力保护我想要保护的一切，也只有拥有足够的能力才可以做到如此。我很喜欢《少年中国说》里的一句话：“少年强，则国强。”当国家足够强大，才可以庇佑少年的心之向往；而作为青年的一代足够强大，才有能力保护自己的心之所向。“莫等闲，白了少年头。”济世破壁，务实拼搏，才是我辈青年的应有之态。我想，我准备好了。

破晓之春

——记 2020 年春校园生活

Dawn of Spring

—My Campus Life in the Spring of 2020

［缅甸］ 叶林特　扬州大学

[Myanmar] Ye Linn Htet, Yangzhou University

The exams for which we nervously expected finally came to an end. I went to Guandong Street with my friends. It is a street we keep thinking of. The moment I stepped out of the bus, a familiar smell of the stinky Toufu blew against my face. However, the street was not as noisy as it was before, with only several people on the street. It had been bustling and hustling with large crowds. Time seemed to stop now and I became little bit melancholy. I knew it was caused by the COVID-19. To memorize the special period, we used our mobile phones to take shot of what happened around us so that we could keep the memory of history.

Due to the pandemic, many international students around me were hesitating whether go back to their homelands or stay in China. I decided to stay on campus because I had confidence in the capability of my university and China in handling of the public health crisis. Meanwhile I cherished at my heart the hope from my home country, that is, to accomplish my university

让大家既期待又忐忑的考试终于结束了，我跟朋友又去了那条让我们心心念念的“东关街”。刚下车，扑面而来的依然是熟悉的臭豆腐的味道。然而，现在的东关街和以往不太一样，马路上只有零星的几个人，没有往日熙熙攘攘热闹的人群。时间好像停止了似的，不免让人有点感伤，这都是疫情带来的变化啊。为了记录这段特殊的时期，我们用手机将这一刻定格，收藏到历史的长河里。

受疫情影响，很多同学拿不定主意到底是回国还是留校。我毫不犹豫地选择留在学校，因为我相信中国的力量，相信学校的力量。同时，我还肩负着祖国母亲的殷切希望：学有所成，为祖国做贡献。应对疫情，学校贴心地为我们安排了志愿者，教我们如何防范新型冠状病毒，为我们的衣食住行提供方便。学校还特别关注我们的心理情况，组织了“宅健康”活动来帮助我们缓解情绪，释放压力。在学习中文知识，了解中国文化的同时，我们也体会到了学校老师的良苦用心。

我不禁开始怀念以前自由自在的日子。日复一日的生活真正让我体

study and make due contribution to my country in the future. To fight against the pandemic, the university volunteers trained us how to prevent from the coronavirus and provide help in daily life. The university also pays much attention to our psychological health, and organizes "Home Health" activities to help us release stress and emotions. We fully understood and were grateful for what the university had done for us. We also learned Chinese culture from these activities.

I cannot help missing those carefree days before the pandemic. The current life of repetitions made me understand the old saying "Live in the present and cherish what you have at the moment." Seeing those who were fighting against the pandemic on the forefront, we truly understood why freedom is relative, not definite. These heroes sacrificed everything they had to make us enjoy the freedom. They were facing with infection risks and kept fighting the virus and some of them even had to wear "adult diapers" while on duty. Some nurses cut their cherished long hairs to save time for work. We were grateful to their indomitable devotion in keeping us away from the virus. The winter was no longer unbearably long because of their devotion and love. Chinese President Xi Jinping said, "As long as we had strong confidence in winning the virus and in working indomitably together, we could win this anti-pandemic fight through scientific prevention and concise decision making." President Xi's words strengthened our confidence and determination in wining this anti-pandemic fight.

Knowing that my home country Myanmar had the first infection case, I immediately sent the summarized prevention measures, symptoms and cautions in China to friends and relatives back home. Many of my friends in Myanmar said they were very boring staying at home all day, so I made a homepage in social media,

会到了那句“活在当下，且行且珍惜”的含义。但想到那些在灾难面前逆行而上奋斗在一线的英雄，我们也真正明白了为什么“自由是相对的”。他们牺牲了自己的一切，只为早日换取我们的自由。这些英雄冒着被感染的风险，坚守在一线，为了全身心投入工作还穿上了“纸尿裤”，有的护士为了节省时间剃光了她们珍爱的美丽长发……感谢他们大无畏的付出，这个冬天因为有他们不再漫长！“只要坚定信心、同舟共济、科学防治、精准施策，我们就一定能打赢疫情防控阻击战。”习大大的话坚定了我们打赢这场战役的信心和决心。

得知我的祖国缅甸发现了第一个病例，我立马把自己在中国总结好的新冠病毒症状、预防措施和注意事项告诉了祖国的亲人们。在缅甸，我的很多朋友说在家很无聊，所以我在社交网站做了一个主页，然后从抖音App里找出一些比较搞笑的中文视频，把它们翻译成缅甸语，发布在我的

扬州大学扬子津花海 / 叶林特提供

found some funny Chinese videos, translated them into Burmese and then posted them at my home page. Around 3 million people watched the videos I posted and 1 million people liked them. I suddenly realized that I could make so many people laugh wholeheartedly though I deemed myself not funny at all, which I attributed to the teaching of my teachers. In Myanmar, safe and hygiene masks were not available to some people, so I donated part of my scholarship granted by Jiangsu Provincial Government to my fellow citizens in Myanmar on behalf of Jiangsu people to make my contribution.

Under the risks of the pandemic, we could still study safely in China, first I was thankful to my motherland, who gave us a good opportunity to come in China; then I was thankful to the concerns and caring that the Chinese government had paid to international students. Also we were thankful to our universities and teachers, who had been very devoted in protecting us in the anti-virus days. They cared not only our personal safety but also our psychological health.

Thanks to China, thanks to Myanmar, thanks to my parents, thanks to my teachers and thanks to all my friends. Without their selfless devotion and sacrifice, we could not go through this period safely. Wish my home country Myanmar and my second homeland China would win the pandemic as soon as possible. I believe that we will welcome our spring as long as we stick together and fight whole-heartedly. I will also study diligently to make myself grow into a person who contributes to both China and Myanmar.

主页，竟然有300万人观看，100万人点赞！我突然发现平时一点儿都不幽默的我也可以让很多人笑得很开心，这些都是老师们的功劳！在家乡，因为种种原因，有些人不能戴上安全卫生的口罩。我主动把自己获得的江苏省政府奖学金的一部分以江苏省的名义捐赠给远在缅甸的同胞们，尽我的一份绵薄之力。

叶林特

我们之所以能够安全地在中国学习，首先要感谢的就是我的祖国，为我们提供了这样一个好的求学机遇。同时也非常感谢中国政府对我们留学生安全的高度重视和关注。还要感谢学校，感谢老师们的付出，他们为了我们能够安全度过这段被新冠病毒侵袭的日子操碎了心，不仅照顾了我们的人身安全还细致地考虑到了心理健康。

感恩中国、感恩祖国、感恩父母、感恩老师、感恩朋友。没有他们的无私奉献我们就不可能平平安安度过这段特殊的日子。祝愿我的祖国和我的第二个故乡中国都早日顺利战胜新冠恶魔。我相信只要大家齐心协力，一定会等到我们期待的“春天”！我也会努力学习，将来做一个对中缅两国有贡献的人。

我与中国的美丽邂逅
My Beautiful Encounter with China

[土库曼斯坦] 张小龙　中国石油大学（北京）
[Turkmenistan] Sogundik Shohratjanov, China University of Petroleum (Beijing)

In the years of studying in China, I have been impressed by the peacefulness, stability and liveliness of this country. People had been pursuing their dreams in earnest and with ease up until December 2019, when China announced a major epidemic outbreak. A new type of epidemic called COVID-19 was spreading amongst people, and the infected were facing life threats all the time. What was even more desperate is that there had been no record of this virus in the medical history of mankind, leaving people at a loss as to what to do about it. In order not to risk more lives, the whole country entered a state of strict vigilance. All units including companies and schools were shut down one after another, which changed people's life completely. Plenty of pessimistic thoughts came into my mind at that moment – worrying that the number of the infected would increase endlessly, since, after all, China has a population of 1.4 billion ; worrying that people would not have access to timely supplies of food and water, since restaurants and markets were all closed; worrying that the economy would have a downturn, since people were staying at home and many companies were out of normal functioning. But then I found that the Chinese people had

在中国求学数年，这个国家带给我的印象是平和安定的，也是热气腾腾的。人们怀揣着梦想，在属于各自的轨道上有条不紊地奔忙着，直到 2019 年的 12 月，中国宣布遭遇重大疫情，一种叫“COVID-19”的新型冠状病毒在人群中肆虐地传播着，感染它的人时时刻刻面临着生命威胁，而更令人绝望的是，全人类的医学史中并没有关于这种病毒的记载，这令人们束手无策。为了不使更多的生命遭到威胁，整个国家进入了严格的警备状态，各个单位陆续宣布停工停学，人们的生活也因此完全变了样……那一刻我的脑海中出现了很多悲观的念头：担心感染人数会永无休止地增长下去，毕竟中国有 14 亿人口；担心人们会得不到及时的食物供应，断水断粮，因为餐馆和市场统统关闭，不再营业了；担心经济下行，因为人们都待在家中，很多公司将不能正常运转……但是后来我发现，中国人利用智慧和他们的凝聚力战胜了这一切的问题，让我惊讶也令我敬佩。

待在家中！在新闻媒体的倡议声中，我和亿万中国人一起开启了“宅家”模式——在家吃饭，在家学习，在家锻炼，在家娱乐。最初的几天真的有些不习惯，但是后来慢慢发现除了不能和朋友相聚外也并没有

overcome all these difficulties with their wisdom and cohesion, which surprised me and made me admire.

Stay at home! Following the advice of the news media, Together with hundreds of millions of Chinese, I switched to the "stay at home" mode – eat, study, exercise and entertain at home. I was really not used to it during the first few days, but later I gradually found that there was nothing inconvenient except for not being able to get together with friends, all of which actually owed greatly to the rapid development of China's internet. Some food delivery platforms like Meituan, ele.me and Baidu worked stably, and I had my favorite roast duck, steak and even Chongqing hot pot during the epidemic. As an old Chinese saying goes, " be prepared in advance." In my opinion, the development of internet industry is a kind of preparation in advance for this special period. It is the existence of those delivery platforms that maintained us at home and easily got us what we want with just one mobile phone.

The convenience of internet was felt not only in life but also in our work and study. The "Ding Talk" which, encountering complaints from Chinese high school students on the internet though, dispelled the worries of my top-student friends for their learning progress did not fall much behind because of the epidemic. Using this application, teachers were able to provide online classes, and also to call the roll, ask questions, ask students to raise their hands and speak as they did in class. In addition, I learned from some friends who had already been using that app before, many enterprises were also using similar applications in their management, such as daily clocking in, checking attendance, reporting, meetings and making reimbursement. The development of these functions may seem very simple, but it is very difficult in practice. Fortunately, there are

什么不方便的地方，这要得益于中国互联网行业的飞速发展。一些类似于美团、饿了么这样的送餐平台一直在有条不紊地运转着，我在疫情期间吃到了最喜欢的烤鸭、牛排，甚至还有重庆火锅。中国有句古话叫作“未雨绸缪”，在我看来，互联网行业在这个特殊时期就是一种未雨绸缪的存在。是那些外送平台的存在让我们足不出户，只用一部手机就可以轻松得到我们想要的东西。

不只是生活，在工作学习中我们也切实感受到了互联网给予的便利。钉钉——消除了我和朋友们心中的担忧，通过钉钉直播，我们的学习进度并没有因为疫情而落下太多。在这个应用中，老师可以在线为学生们提供教学，还可以像在课堂上一样进行点名、提问、举手发言等。另外我通过一些已经工作了的朋友了解到，很多企业在这之前也在利用类似钉钉的应用来实现企业管理，像一些日常的打卡、考勤、报告、会议、报销等，在这类应用中一应俱全。开发这些功能看似很简单，但是实际

中国石油大学（北京）/ 张小龙摄

中国石油大学（北京）/ 张小龙提供

some "top notch" figures in science and engineering in China, who are fast and accurate in developing applications, which in my opinion is very remarkable.

The year of 2020 is destined to be an extraordinary one. The outbreak of this pandemic makes us reflect on our insufficiency in disease prevention and control and disaster response. It also allows us to feel the warmth of human nature and enjoy the benefits of scientific and technological innovation. I sincerely pray for mankind that such an epidemic will never happen again, and if it does, I hope everyone would have learnt enough from this crisis. It's amazing that next month I will be able to study in the bright classrooms again. I will work harder in the hope that human beings will have enough strength to save themselves at a critical moment like this. Such is my 2020.

中国石油大学（北京）/张小龙提供

开发起来是很难的，幸好中国有一些理工科很厉害的“学霸”级人物，他们做起应用来快速、精准，这在我看来也是非常了不起的事情。

2020年注定是不平凡的一年，这场突如其来的疫情让我们对疾病防控和灾难响应的不足产生了反思，同时也让我们感受到了人性的温暖和科技创新带来的益处。在这里虔诚地为人类祈祷，希望这样的疫情不再发生，如果发生了，希望所有人都从这次的经历中汲取了足够多的经验，以便更好地应对。下个月我就能重新坐在明亮的课堂中学习知识了，我会更加努力，希望在类似这样的关键时刻中，人类能有足够的实力脱离险境。这就是我的2020。

中国是我强大的后盾
A Strong China Stands Behind Me

[保加利亚] 李明涛 华东师范大学
[Bulgaria] Dimitrov Dimitar Iliev, East China Normal University

The year 2020 is just like a book called *Cherish*, which tells the catastrophe that the human being faces –the rampant pandemic. This outbreak reminds us to think deeply a question: What is the most precious thing in a person's life? The answer is neither fortune nor fame, but health and safety. Everyone should cherish the current life, which is plain but priceless. So please cherish the people who love you and those you love in your life.

Before the epidemic, I returned to my home country on winter vacation and had planned to return to China at the end of January. But the sudden outbreak disturbed my schedule, I had to stay at home for quarantine. I decided to grasp this opportunity to accompany my family, recharge myself through study and absorb as much knowledge as possible.

During my six-month-long home isolation, the first thing I got up every day is to surf the real-time big data report on the WeChat and Baidu on China's progress in fighting against the epidemic, which has become a new habit of mine. Some Chinese friends and classmates and I would greet each other online, brief the outbreak situation in their hometown. I also remind them not

2020 年就像一本书，书名叫作《珍惜》，书中讲述了一个关于巨大灾难的故事——人类正面临着严重的疫情危机。这场疫情让大家重新回归冷静的思考：人的一生最珍贵的是什么？答案既不是金钱，也不是名利，而是健康平安。所以我们要珍惜当下，此时此刻平淡的生活变得弥足珍贵，同时请珍惜身边爱你的人和你爱的人。

在疫情来临前，我放寒假回到自己的国家，原计划 1 月底返回中国。但是疫情的到来阻挡了我的脚步，我不得不待在家里进行居家隔离，利用这段时间好好陪伴家人，充电学习，尽可能多地储备知识并培养新技能。

在我进行居家隔离的这半年中，每天起床的第一件事就是打开微信和百度疫情实时大数据报告，关注中国的抗疫进展，这似乎已经成了我的习惯。每天和一些中国朋友同学通过云端彼此问候，我会关心他们家乡的疫情，也会提醒他们不要放松警惕，出门一定做好防护。此外，我时常回忆起我在中国度过的美好时光，我会想念我的中国朋友们；我会想念华东师大美丽的校园和校园内如梦境般纯净的丽娃河；我也会想念学校门口美味的手抓饼、南京东路和外滩美丽的夜景、方便我们出行的

to relax their vigilance and to do a good protection when going out. In addition, I often recalled the good times I spent in China, I missed my Chinese friends. I missed the beautiful campus of East China Normal University and the dream-like Liwa River. I also missed the delicious shredded pancakes at the school gate, the bustling Nanjing East Road and beautiful night view of the Bund. The convenient traffic, shared bikes, roadside barbecue and warm services of the subway staff are all good memories in my heart.

While missing China, I also keep an eye on the news in China. China's preventive and control measures during the outbreak are very reasonable. Many of the decisions and measures are unprecedented, such as the cancelation the Spring Festival gathering celebrations, delayed start of primary and secondary schools, closure of the assembly venues. At the beginning of the outbreak China had taken effective preventive and control measures, I shared them with my family and friends, and everyone gave a thumbs-up. It only took China 10

华东师范大学 / 李明涛提供

李明涛参加华东师范大学新年师生同乐会

共享单车、路边飘散着香味的烧烤店；我更会想念便捷的轨道交通和地铁工作人员的贴心服务。

我在想念中国的同时，也一直关注中国的新闻。我觉得疫情期间，中国采取的防控措施非常合理，许多决策和措施都是前所未有的，比如政府取消了春节的聚集性庆祝活动，推迟大中小学的开学时间，关闭了所有地区的集会场所等。当我看到中国在疫情刚开始时就采取了高效的防控措施后，我就将这些与我的家人朋友们分享，大家纷纷表示称赞。中国只用了 10 天时间就在武汉建成了火神山医院，震惊世界。中国的信息技术也非常发达，在疫情期间我的大多数中国朋友都在家办公，学生在家上网课，信息时代给很多人带来了方便。严格的防控措施不仅使中国抗疫工作取得了第一阶段的成功，而且也为世界抗疫工作提供了经验参考并做出表率。在欧洲疫情暴发后，有一些国家也借鉴中国的防控经验开展工作。但是在我看来，虽然很多国家的防控措施相对严格，但并不能达到中国的效果。究其原因，我觉得主要是人民的思想和习惯不同。欧美人本身就不习惯戴口罩，疫情初期也并没有意识到新冠病毒有

days to build the Huoshenshan Hospital in Wuhan, which surprised the world. China's information technology is also very developed, bringing convenience to many people. During the outbreak, most of my Chinese friends worked at home, students attended online classes at home. Strict prevention and control measures have not only made China's anti-epidemic work a success in the first phase, but also provided an empirical reference for the rest of the world. After the outbreak in Europe, some countries learned from China's experience in pandemic prevention and control. But in my opinion, although many countries' prevention and control measures are strict, they do not achieve China's effect. The major reason, I think, is because people's thoughts and habits are different. Europeans are not used to wearing masks and they failed to realize how terrible the COVID-19 is at the beginning, just treated it as ordinary influenza. Nor did the governments remind their people to keep social distancing and to wear of masks. In China, everyone started to wear masks and stay at home as much as possible after the breakout. I think this reflects Chinese people's self-discipline and willingness to protect others, which is why China has been able to quickly resume production and gained world's admiration.

I believe that China has the ability to tame this epidemic, and China is the country I want to stay in. People often say that the motherland is our most powerful backing and safest harbor, and I would like to say that a strong China is also standing behind me. Living in China makes me feel safe and happy. My body beats a Chinese heart and my dream is to settle in China for life and work. I would like to share China's prosperity to the whole world!

China, I love you.

华东师范大学 / 李明涛提供

多么可怕，仅仅当作普通的流感对待，政府方面也没有及时提醒大家社交隔离和佩戴口罩的重要性。反观中国，遭遇疫情后，所有人都开始戴口罩，尽可能不出门。我认为这充分体现了中国人民的自律和保护他人的意识，这正是中国得以迅速复工复产的原因，也使世界为之钦佩。

我相信中国有能力彻底战胜这场疫情，我发现中国就是我想要留下来的国家。我们常常说，祖国是我们最强大的后盾，是我们最安全的港湾，而我想说中国也是我强大的后盾，在中国我感觉到安全和幸福，我的身体里跳动着一颗中国心。我的梦想就是定居中国，在中国生活工作，将中国的繁荣昌盛告诉全世界！

我爱你，中国！

中国，我梦起航的地方
China, the Place Where My Dream Sets Sail

［韩国］ 申文燮　深圳大学
[Republic of Korea] Shin Moonsub, Shenzhen University

My mother once told me that my musical journey started since I was still in her womb – she had me listening to all kinds of music every day. Though I couldn't recall whether it is Beethoven or Mozart, I have had a seed of "music dream" planted in my heart since then.

At the age of four, my mom introduced me to a new "friend" – piano. At the first sight, I thought it was nothing but a noise-making toy, but gradually it became my closest friend. I enjoyed the happiness it brought to me. Besides playing piano, I also liked singing. At the age of 11, I joined in Korean Haeundae Boys and Girls Chorus, and found my love in choir since then. Whenever the chorus sang, I always felt that all of us seemed to merge into one, and the resonance that we together made was so natural and moving.

In 2010, I came to China with my family and started to study here. What surprised me were the diversity and openness of China. I made a lot of like-minded friends here.

Then in 2016, I founded in Shenzhen an "International Chorus" formed by young people from all over the world. Unexpectedly, I had to learn everything

前排右四为申文燮

听母亲说，当我还在她肚子里的时候，我就开始了音乐之旅。母亲每天坚持给我听各种音乐，虽然我不记得听的是贝多芬还是莫扎特，但在这些音乐名家的熏陶之下，一颗叫作“音乐梦”的种子悄然在我心中种下。

四岁那年，妈妈给我介绍了一个新“伙伴”——钢琴。当我第一次见到它时，觉得它只是一个制造噪声的玩具，但随着时间的推移，它渐渐变成了最亲密的朋友。我喜欢它带给我的快乐，喜欢它带给我的幸福。除了演奏钢琴，我还喜欢唱歌。11 岁那年，我加入了韩国海云台少年少女合唱团，从那时起，我爱上了合唱。每当所有成员一齐歌唱时，我总觉得大家融成了一个整体，那种共鸣，浑然天成，令我感动。

2010 年，我随家人来到了中国，也开启了中国的留学生活。令我意外的是中国的多元和开放。我在这里结识了很多志同道合的朋友。

于是，在 2016 年，我在深圳创办了一个由来自世界各地的青年人组成的“国际合唱团”。没想到，合唱团从成立到经营，处处都需要我学习。一开始的时候后，合唱团的成员并不多。从人选到排练、演出和语言翻译，都需要和大家一起相互配合包容。虽然每一个人都有弱项，

from the establishment to the management of the band. The chorus was not big at first, and we need to support and tolerate each other on everything such as member recruitment, rehearsals, performing and translation. No one was perfect, while being together we could learn from each other and make ourselves better. In my opinion, this is exactly the charm of chorus.

However, the journey to dream is never smooth. I still remember our first performance in 2017. While being happy for more new members on board, I had a lot of difficulties, too. For example, I tried my best to borrow costumes for the performance. In the end we still had one suit short so an Iranian member had to perform in a white shirt, and I really felt ashamed at that time. In the face of difficulties, I had to confront them bravely rather than escaping from them cowardly.

During the past years, many people joined the chorus and many left. Nevertheless, I would remember every one of them. I still remember Martin, one of our first chorus members. At the interview, many interviewers were

深圳大学图书馆 / 申文燮 提供

深圳大学国际合唱团（中间为申文燮）

但是很多人在一起，我们可以互相弥补，可以完善自己的不足。我想，这就是合唱的魅力。

可是，实现梦想的旅途并非一帆风顺。我还记得，2017 年第一次演出时候的情景。那学期突然增加了很多团员，我非常开心，但与此同时也增添了不少烦恼。因为，我要到处去借演出服。一番努力过后，还是缺了一套服装，有个伊朗团员只能穿着白色衬衫演出。当时我真的感到十分愧疚。在很多事情面前我只能勇敢地面对，没有时间去懦弱。

这几年很多人加入合唱团，同时也有很多人离开。不过我都会记得合唱团的每一个朋友。我还记得第一批团员中的 Martin。刚面试他的时候，很多面试官反对他加入合唱团，因为当时他性格太内向了，不善于表达自己，唱歌也一般般。不过我觉得这个并不是大问题，因为以前的我也和他一样。我相信音乐可以改变一个人，相信音乐带来的力量。

加入合唱团后他一直没有什么存在感，不过他慢慢习惯了在合唱团

against of having him onboard since he was very introverted then, not good at expressing himself and his singing was just so-so. While I thought these weren't problems since I was exactly the same before, and I believed that music could change and bring power to every music lover.

After participating, he didn't have any sense of existence in the chorus at first, but gradually he got used to life here. As time went by, he made many friends. Whenever a chorus member met him, they always called out his name "Martin"! He was shy at these moments. However, I could feel the power, which was encouragement.

In his senior year, I recommended him to be a deputy leader of the band. Though others were not sure whether he was fit or not, I believed that he could make it, since he had been with the chorus for three years.

Time flies fast. He really made it that year. Introverted as he was, he handled all kinds of things perfectly, and chorus members were all very cooperative. At his graduation, he sincerely said to everyone, "Thank you everyone, thank you my leader for your company and guidance these years. I have grown up a lot and learned a lot in our chorus. Thank you all for the encouragement that you have given to me. I am really very happy that I have met so many good friends here, and I cannot bear to leave." Hearing his words and recalling all the good memories and his changes in the chorus, I almost burst into tears.

A few years passed quickly, and the chorus has experienced a lot of changes. In recent years, our chorus has traveled to many places in Shenzhen, Guangzhou and even Beijing. We have performed in different stages, won lots of awards, been interviewed by many media, and been on TV shows, too. But I

深圳大学文山湖 / 申文燮提供

的生活，随着时间推移，他在合唱团里认识了很多朋友。团员每次碰到他，就大声喊他的名字“Martin！”。每次别人喊他的时候，他都很害羞。不过，我感觉到了一分力量，那就是鼓励。

他大四的那年，我推荐他担任副团长。当时其他人不太确定他合不合适这个岗位。不过，我很坚定地相信他能做好，毕竟他在合唱团待了三年。

时间一转眼就过去了。那一年他真的做到了，虽然他很内向，但各种事情处理得特别好，团员们也很配合他的工作。在他毕业的时候，他真诚地对大家说：“谢谢你们，谢谢团长多年的陪伴和指导。我在合唱团成长了不少，学了不少。感谢你们给我的鼓励和勇气，我真的很幸福，在这里认识了很多好朋友，我真的舍不得离开。”当他说这句话时，我真的舍不得。重温我们在合唱团这几年一起做的事情，还有他的变化，我差点

still enjoy most the moments of singing with my chorus.

Since last year, I started to learn to compose and arrange. At the university graduation ceremony of 2019, my chorus sang the song "I like it", which was arranged by my chorus members and me. Many graduated members also came back to the university to rehearse and perform especially for this event. I was particularly moved by the power that this journey and music has brought to me. It seems that my dream has been setting sail, and my music dream has been realized.

I think this is exactly the charm of music, irrelevant to languages or countries. A dream would become true as long as you love and persist it. Love knows no country borders, and so does music. Being proud of myself, I am also deeply grateful to this land where I have grown for 10 years – China, the place where my dream sets sail.

哭了。

白驹过隙，几年的时光一转眼就过去了，合唱团发生了很大的改变。这几年，我们合唱团慢慢走遍了深圳、广州甚至也到了北京。我们到处表演，上了无数个舞台，拿过很多大奖，接受了无数次媒体的采访，也上过电视台节目。但是我依然享受和团员们一起唱歌的瞬间。

去年开始，我尝试作曲编曲。2019 年，在学校的毕业典礼上我们唱了我和团员一起改编的歌曲《我喜欢》。很多已经毕业的团员也为了这次演出回来一起排练，重新登上了舞台。这次的旅程、音乐带来的力量让我特别感动。似乎看到了我的梦已经在起航，我的梦被诠释了。

我想这就是音乐的魅力，无关语言，无关国家，因为热爱，因为坚持，梦想就会变成现实。爱无国界，音乐同样如此。我为自己感到骄傲和自豪的同时，也深深地感激这片我成长了十年的土地，中国，我梦起航的地方。

我与中国人在特殊时期共同战疫
Fighting Pandemic Together with Chinese People

［柬埔寨］ 索克兰 清华大学
[Cambodia] Louy Sokleang, Tsinghua University

I chose to stay in China during the COVID-19 pandemic.

Amid the chirping of birds at Tsinghua University in the morning, I wake up to check up the real time data of the pandemic. Epidemic is the enemy of human being. People around me never discussed who or which country should be responsible for the disaster. Instead, our attentions focus on China's efforts in fighting against the epidemic. Our discussions are more about the development of science and technology of China and related topics, such as epidemic prevention and control of schools and how the 1.4 billion Chinese people combat epidemic hands in hands. Since the outbreak of the epidemic for the last four months, I observed that the most crucial reason for China to make great breakthrough in this fight lies in two elements, the Chinese people and the Chinese technology.

After finishing the fall semester, I went back to Fuzhou to visit my old friends. In the mid of January, the virus stuck suddenly. Being on a trip outside school, I was deeply worried. At that time, I received phone call from a teacher in the International Student and Scholar Center of Tsinghua University. What

疫情期间，我留在中国。

清华园早晨鸟叫声优美动听，我每天起来都要看一眼疫情实时数据。疫情是人类的敌人，我身边的人从未谈论这次疫情该由谁来负责，该由哪国来承担，我们都把目光聚焦在中国的抗疫过程中。我们讨论的话题往往围绕中国科学技术的发展，学校的疫情防控以及 14 亿中国人如何共同战疫，等等。遭遇疫情这四个月以来，我发现中国抗疫之所以取得巨大突破，最重要的原因就在于“中国人”和“中国科技”这两个因素。

秋季学期课程结束后，我回到福州市看望老朋友。1 月中旬，病毒突然来袭。在校外旅游的我对此深感担忧。那时，我收到了清华大学国际学生学者中心老师的电话，我印象最深刻的是老师的那句叮嘱：“一定要时刻与学校保持联系！”学校的牵挂顿时让我倍感温暖。两天后，我买不到口罩了，迫不得已向一家饭店老板求助，想从他那里买一些口罩，老板爽快地从抽屉里拿出了 5 只一次性口罩给我，摇头对我说：“小伙子拿着吧，不要钱。”曾经频繁出现在我脑海里的一句话，在那一刻又冒了出来：“我是中国人！让我来吧！”后来，我顺利从福州坐高铁回到了北京。归途中，我随处可见忙碌工作的警察叔叔和志愿者，他们特别辛苦，但一点儿也没

impressed me most was the advice from the teacher: "Please keep in touch with the school all the time." The concern of the school made me feel warm instantly. Two days later, I failed to get a mask from the market. I had no choice but asked for help from a restaurant owner and wish he could sell me some masks. He immediately took out five disposable masks from a drawer and told me: "Take them. No charge." The sentence coming to my mind frequently jumped out again at that moment: "I am Chinese, let me do it." Later I went back to Beijing from Fuzhou by high-speed rail without hinderance. On the way back, I noticed that there were busy policemen and volunteers everywhere. They worked very hard but didn't show any impatience on the face at all. Many seats on the train were not occupied. Temperature measurement was strictly required on many customs barriers. I felt the efforts and determination of the Chinese people in fighting against the epidemic. Back in Tsinghua University, I was put in quarantine in a single dormitory room. After that, I forgot to wear the mask when going out one day. The warden met me and reminded me responsibly: "Remember to wear a mask whenever going out, so to protect yourself well." The teachers caring about students, the restaurant owner willing to help others, the policemen and volunteers being courageous to contribute are the best portrayal of the Chinese people who were making concerted efforts to fight the epidemic. In difficult times, these qualities are more prominent. I find that China is the strongest nation in the world that recognized the problems and took actions right away.

It is worth noting that everyone was worried about the epidemic situation in China in early 2020. At present the whole world is learning from China. In addition to the efforts of the Chinese people have made, I think the second

清华大学二校门 / 索克兰提供

把这种辛苦流露在脸上。列车上很多座位都空着，多个关卡严格要求测量体温。我感受到中国人民抗击疫情付出的努力和决心。回到清华，我被安排到单人宿舍隔离。隔离结束后，有一天我出门忘记了戴口罩，走到楼下，宿管员碰见了便负责地提醒我："同学，出门记得戴口罩，做好个人防护哦。"心系学生的学校老师、乐于助人的饭店老板、甘于奉献的警察和志愿者，这些就是我亲眼看到中国人齐心战疫的最好写照。在艰难时刻，这些品质更加凸显出来，我发现，中华民族是世界上问题意识最强的民族。

值得思考的是，2020 年年初人人都为中国的疫情担忧，现在，全世界都在向中国学习。这背后的原因除了中国人的努力，我想第二根源是来自"中国科技"的力量，中国背后有"千万个中国科学家"在给予着强大的支持。

疫情期间，我见证了中国科学家如何在国家处于危难时刻仍然坚持科研。以清华大学单思思学姐为例，5 月 3 日央视《新闻联播》以"用

impetus is the power of "technology of China". Tens of millions of Chinese scientists" are giving strong support in China.

During the epidemic, I witnessed how Chinese scientists persist in scientific research when the homeland was in crisis. Take Shan Sisi of Tsinghua University as an example. On May 3, CCTV news reported her story with the theme "Devoting to the Motherland with Striving Youth." Since the outbreak of epidemic, Shan had no rest for continuous 104 days. Fighting against time and overcoming difficulties on the forefront of scientific researches, she did research in the lab during the May Day holidays. Why do Chinese scientists work so hard? The answer is "to contribute to humanity." It took 10 days for China to build Huoshenshan Hospital with 1,000 beds, took several days to solve the nationwide shortage of masks and brought innovative teaching mode for internet education. As President Xi Jinping said: "Science and technology are the most powerful weapons for human beings to fight diseases. Human beings cannot overcome major disasters and epidemics without scientific development and technological innovation." Besides, when the domestic epidemic situation is relatively stable, China has sent medical expert groups to many countries, donated medical supplies and shared China's experience in fighting the epidemic. This also reflects the image of China as a great power.

I will always bear in my mind of those stories how I fight the epidemic with the Chinese people together at a particular time. I will try my best to spread these wonderful stories and let the world know what the real China is. At last, I would like to use a sentence to sing high of China I deeply love: "With diligence and wisdom, you have more brilliant break-through again!".

"The haze will disperse. The light will come."

清华大学新学堂 / 索克兰提供

奋斗的青春告白祖国”为主题报道了她的故事。遭遇疫情以来，单思思学姐 104 天无休息，在科研战疫一线争分夺秒、攻坚克难，五一假期时，她仍天天泡在实验室做科研。中国科学家为何如此拼命呢？答案是“为人类做贡献”。我们见证了中国在 10 天内建成了能容纳 1000 张床位的火神山医院，短短几天时间解决了全国性的口罩紧缺问题，互联网教育带来创新教学模式，等等。正如习主席所说：“人类同疾病较量最有力的武器就是科学技术，人类战胜大灾大疫离不开科学发展和技术创新。”此外，在国内疫情比较稳定后，中国还向许多国家派遣医疗专家组、赠送医疗物资、传授中国抗疫经验等。这也体现了中国的大国风范。

这些我与中国人在特殊时期共同战疫的点滴故事，我会永远铭记在心。我也会力所能及地把这些美好的故事传播下去，让世界知道这才是真正的中国。最后，我想用一句话赞美我深深热爱着的中国：“你用勤劳，你用智慧，进行了又一次更加辉煌的开拓！”

“阴霾总会散去，光明终将到来！”

我用手机做公益

——留学生活中的特别收获

Charity with Mobile Phone

—A Special Gain of Studying in China

[泰国] 叶子琪 北京师范大学

[Thailand] Jinnakrit Natlada, Beijing Normal University

Mobile phones have become an indispensable tool in our daily life nowadays. You can almost do anything you want with your phone – browsing the news, shopping online and searching information. My lifestyle has changed a lot after coming to China. I have never used electronic payment before in Thailand but began to use it in China. Moreover, I have fulfilled a long-time dream with my phone in China.

I saw a quite moving commercial when I was a kid. In it, some kids with cancer or disabilities smiled and sang "Qué Será Será, whatever will be, will be..." on the stage, and their parents and the commercial director all burst into tears. I couldn't help crying after seeing it. Although they couldn't see, hear, or even take care of themselves, they didn't give up or were discouraged by these difficulties. Since then I made up my mind to help the disabled and started to pay attention to public welfare issues. Although I really wanted to help those children, I didn't know what to do. After arriving in China, one day when I was

手机已成为人们生活中不可或缺的东西，用一部手机就可以完成你想做的所有事情，人们用手机看新闻、网上购物、查看各种资料。来中国之后，我的生活方式也发生了很大的改变，天知道我这个在泰国从来没有使用过电子支付的人，却在中国第一次用电子支付，更让我没有想到的是，在中国，我用手机还完成了一个很久以来一直在心底的愿望。

我小时候看过一部特别感人的广告。得癌症的小朋友、残疾的小孩子们在台上合唱“Qué Será Será，Whatever will be，will be…”，台下的家长们、广告的导演都热泪盈眶，但小孩子们在唱歌时脸上充满微笑，我看完之后禁不住哭了。虽然他们看不见、听不到，甚至生活都不能自理，但是他们从没有对遇到的困难退缩，也没有气馁。我暗下决心，我要帮助那些残疾人，从那时起，公益的事开始引起我的关注，我很想帮助那些小孩子，可是不知道该怎么做。到中国后，有一次我偶然间在刷手机的时候看到支付宝上的项目“爱心捐赠”，我发现可以随时用支付宝做公益，虽然不是大笔钱，但是我一直充满公益心。

using my mobile phone, I happened to see the "Love Donation" project at Alipay, in which I could do my contribution for charity at any time. Not a big sum though, I was always happy to contribute my share of charity.

At Apps such as Alipay and WeChat, I noticed and was attracted by charity projects such as "Love Donation", "Ant Manor" and "Tencent Charity". I have experienced difficulties before and understand that not everyone's difficulties are the same. Many people in this world just lack opportunities and need help. When I was in Thailand, I always wished to act as a volunteer to find and help those in difficulties, but I didn't realize it until I was in China, quite unexpectedly, with the help of my mobile phone. I could feel that these charity projects are helping my charity dream become true. Every time I make a donation, from my phone I could hear the kids' voices whom I've helped, sometimes receive thank-you messages and paintings with grateful words such as "Thank you brothers

北京师范大学 / 叶子琪提供

北京师范大学 / 叶子琪提供

在支付宝、微信等 App 上，我看到“爱心捐赠、蚂蚁庄园、腾讯公益”等公益项目，这些项目中的活动引起我的关注。不是自己以前没有经历过困难，可是每个人的困难不一样，反过来让我联想到这个世界上缺失机会的人不在少数，他们需要他人帮助。我在泰国时一直有个心愿，想帮助那些生活困难的人，想当志愿者去找他们，但是我的愿望一直没有实现。我没有想到，在中国，手机竟然帮助我完成了这样的心愿。我从心底里感到，这些手机里的公益项目，令我这个愿望渐渐成真。每次我进行捐赠后，手机上会显示小孩子们的录音，有时收到他们的感谢信，还有他们的画儿，写上了“谢谢哥哥姐姐们给我们温暖和勇气”。这些都令我非常感动。

除了捐助儿童，我还参与了一起守护环境、为乡村种树、救助流浪动物等项目，这样一来，这些项目令我感到自己虽然在远方，但是我们

and sisters for the kindness and encouragement." I'm really touched.

In addition to the donation for children, I've also participated in projects such as environmental protection, countryside tree-planting and stray animals rescue. These projects allow me to help others even though I am far away from them. Now that the environmental problems are getting serious and excessive loggings are making the environment worse, I hope that my donation to these projects could help grow a few more trees, and my donation to the stray animals could give them an extra meal so that they could live on. I'm not really sure whether my donation could be of any help, but I carefully arrange my living expenses every month so that I am able to save and donate a little money. I have donated for more than half a year now and I'm very happy. The reason of my donation is that I feel that I already have a lot of opportunities such as having enough food, being able to attend good schools, study abroad and pursue my dream. Maybe I don't have much money, but I still want to help those in need with my humble charity. Our small donation could be a huge encouragement to them, like a beacon in the darkness.

I have never expected that my mobile phone has enriched my study-abroad life in such a way. As we use the modern science and technology, we not only enjoy the convenience it brings, but also gain mental fulfillment and happiness.

A Chinese proverb says, "Trickling currents converge into the sea;" and there is a similar saying in Thailand, "Big results always start from small things." I believe that everyone can make their own contribution, and gain happiness from helping others. I hope your beacon will shine in other's heart, too.

也可以帮助到别人。现在环境问题日益严重，伐木越来越多，破坏了环境，捐助环保项目我就能多种几棵树，捐助流浪动物就能多给它们一顿饱饭而让它们活下去。我不知道自己是否真的能够帮助他们，我每个月合理安排自己的生活费，根据我的安排，我愿意捐助一笔钱。我参与各种捐助项目已经半年多了，我心里充满幸福。之所以我有这样的想法，是因为我觉得自己已经拥有了不少机会，如在好学校上课、有饭吃、出国留学，也有机会追求自己的理想。我也许不是拥有那么多钱的人，但是想用我们一点一滴的公益心来帮助他们，我们的小笔钱对他们来说可能是巨大的鼓励，令他们勇敢地坚持下去，如指路明灯。

叶子琪

我没想到，手机使我的留学生活多了这样一项特别的内容，我们在利用现代科学技术的时候，不仅在享受它的便捷，而且也得到心灵的充实与快乐。

我听过中国有这样一句话："涓涓细流汇聚成海。"泰国也有这样一句话："大结果总是从小事做起。"我相信每个人都能贡献一份自己的力量，在帮助别人的同时也得到快乐，希望大家的指路明灯一直到每一个人心里。

我的中国梦

——我想成为“中国通”

My Chinese Dream

—*To Become a Mr China*

［美国］ 张博 沈阳大学

[The United States] Paul McLellan Alexander III, Shenyang University

After I came to China, completed my university studies, got married and had children, I knew that I must have saved the Galaxy in my last life. I feel so lucky to choose to live in China and gradually realize my Chinese dream - to become a "Mr China."

In the summer of 2005, I first came to China at the age of 18. I remember clearly that my uncle and I arrived at the hotel in Hong Kong in the small hours of the morning. Although the long journey made me very tired, I did not feel drowsy but excited and curious. For me, unlike the United States, everything in China is brand new! So I begged my uncle to take me around the hotel. My uncle ordered me a plate of smelly black fried tofu on the Snack Street. He told me it was a super delicious gift from God! It doesn't look delicious and smells bad, but my uncle gave me the first lesson about China. "Don't judge from the appearance and rush to conclusions, taste it first, then say how you feel," he said. I pinched my nose and ate a mouthful. Although not so good-looking, it

当我来到中国，完成了我的大学学业，娶妻生子以后，我才知道我一定上辈子拯救了银河系，才能这么幸运地过上了在中国的生活，逐渐在实现我的中国梦——成为一个“中国通”！

2005 年的夏天，18 岁的我第一次来到了中国。我清晰地记得，我和叔叔到达香港的酒店，已经是凌晨了。虽然长途旅行让我非常劳累，可我却没有一丝困意，更多的是感到兴奋和好奇。对我来说，不同于美国，中国的一切都是崭新的！于是我求叔叔带我到酒店附近转转。叔叔在小吃街给我点了一盘臭臭黑黑的炸豆腐。他告诉我这是上帝赐给我们的超级美味！说真的，它看起来并不好吃，也非常难闻！但对这盘臭豆腐，叔叔给我上了来中国以后关于中国的第一堂课。他说：“不要看外表，先尝尝，之后再说你的感觉，不要着急下结论。”我捏着鼻子皱着眉头吃了一口，虽然不是那么好看的食物，但是居然越吃越香，直到我几乎一个人吃光了一盘臭豆腐！我似乎明白了些叔叔告诉我的话，从此，我的中国梦就此开始了。

我选择了在华东师范大学学习汉语，了解这个神秘的国家和文化。

tastes delicious after eating more. I almost ate a plate of stinky tofu. I seem to understand my uncle's words, and from then on, my Chinese dream kicked off.

I chose to study Chinese language at East China Normal University and to learn about this mysterious country and culture. Time passed quickly, and the year of study language came to an end. During this period, I fell in love with the people of China, the food, and the comfortable and harmonious atmosphere I couldn't experience in the US. Everything makes me feel so pleasant and unforgettable.

Back in the United States, I can't stop my longing for China. Whenever someone asks me about my life in Shanghai, my memories revived. I tried to continue my studies of Chinese and in the US made a lot of friends from China. They gave me a Chinese nickname, "Egg Zhang." The reason is that I am like the structure of an egg, the outside is protein (white people), but the core is egg yolks (yellow people). I like this nickname very much – this is me, there is a passion of China under the white skin. However, without the environment of Chinese language, I still can neither master this language nor know China better.

Three years ago, things I never dared to think about happened. With the strong support of my family and my own efforts, I got the chance to study in China again. To better understand Chinese and learn Chinese culture in different regions, I chose Shenyang, a northern city with a long history. It turns out this is a most intelligent decision I have made in my life. While studying at Shenyang University, I fell in love and met my beautiful and charming wife. She took me to many places of interest, taught me to speak a lot of Northeast dialect and let me experience the warm affection between her family and relatives. And my command of Chinese has improved unknowingly. I still remember a very interesting episode. When I first met my wife's grandfather's brother, he asked

时间过得很快，一年的学习时间很快就结束了。在这短暂的一年里，我爱上了中国的人们，这里的美食，以及我在美国无法体会的那种安逸和谐的氛围。一切都让我感觉那么舒服，难以忘怀。

回到美国后，我无法停止对中国的想念。每当有人问我在上海生活的种种，我的回忆就会被勾起来。我试着在美国继续学中文，还交了很多中国的朋友。他们给我起了一个中国的昵称——“张鸡蛋”。原因就是我如同鸡蛋的结构一般，外面是蛋白（白种人），可是里面核心是蛋黄（黄种人）。我非常喜欢这个昵称，也觉得形容得非常贴切，这就是我，白色皮肤下的一颗热爱中国的“心”。但是，毕竟没有中国的语言环境，我还是无法更好地学习汉语和更深地了解中国。

直到三年前，我做梦也没敢想的事情发生了！在家人的大力支持和我的努力下，我又可以去中国了！为了让我更好地学习中文以及了解不同地区的中国文化，我选择了一个历史悠久的北方城市——沈阳。现在看来，来到沈阳学习是我一生中做的最明智的决定！在沈阳大学学习期间，我恋

沈阳大学图书馆 / 张博提供

沈阳大学 / 张博提供

me in Northeast dialect, "How many brothers do you have? " I was in a fog; I never sang a single song, why did he ask me how many songs? I didn't understand until my wife explained it to me. What an interesting language Northeast dialect is, what a kind relative he is! I really love this big family so much.

After holding a traditional Chinese wedding, my wife and I lived a real Chinese life in Shenyang. My Chinese dream has been fulfilled so far. In May 2020, our son came into this world, which is a precious gift to me once again. One night, I chatted with my wife about my life in China and said, "I must have saved the Galaxy in my previous life, so I can come to China in this life to have such a wonderful wife and such a handsome son."

China is becoming stronger. I will continue my study of Chinese language and culture, so as to realize my Chinese dream – to become a "Mr China." I want to tell more foreigners what I have seen and heard in China, so that they can learn about and fall in love with the real China as I do.

爱了。我认识了我美丽迷人的妻子，她带我去了很多名胜古迹，教会我说很多东北话，让我体会到了她一大家子亲戚之间的温暖亲情。而我的汉语水平也在这种氛围中不知不觉地提高了。我还清晰记得一件非常有趣的事情。当我第一次见到我妻子爷爷的弟弟时，他用东北话问我：“你哥儿几个哪？”听得我一头雾水，我没给他们唱过一首歌，他为什么问我几个歌曲呢？直到我妻子给我解释后我才明白。是在问我的家庭哥弟有几个人啊！多么可爱的东北话，多么和蔼的亲戚！我太喜欢这一大家子人了！

我和妻子举行了中国的传统婚礼，在沈阳过上了真正的中国日子。要说我的中国梦，到这里已经是非常圆满了。2020 年 5 月，我们的儿子来到了这个世界，这是上天再一次给我的珍贵的礼物。有一天晚上，我跟妻子聊天回忆我的中国生活时说：“我前世一定是拯救了银河系，这辈子才能来到中国，完成梦想，有你这么棒的妻子和这么帅的儿子。”

中国正在变得更加强大，我会继续努力学习中文，了解更多的中国文化，只有这样我才能完美地实现我的中国梦——成为一名“中国通”。我想把在中国的所见所闻所学所感讲述给更多的外国人，让他们也可以和我一样了解到真正的中国，和我一样爱上现在的中国！

在金茂大厦看大上海 / 张博摄

中国，我把你藏在心里
China, I Cherish You in My Heart

［菲律宾］ 黄雯芳 对外经济贸易大学

[Philippines] Señor Joanna Chen, University of International Business and Economics

It is so lucky for me to step out of my motherland to a strange and familiar country– China–at the prime time of my life. It all started a year ago. To apply to study in China was a choice by chance until I received that text message. It was a sunny afternoon, when I took a taxi to go home. My mobile phone dinged to inform me receiving a message, "Joanna, you are going to study in China!" I felt widely awake. Later I came to Beijing to start my pre-university program at the University of International Business and Economics (UIBE).

Because the flight was delayed, I arrived at the Beijing Capital International Airport at 1 am. But the first impression of the Chinese capital was unforgettable. Despite the small hours in the morning, the city is still full of lights and neons. I still remember the first time I got lost in Beijing. I rode my bicycle, shuttled through the streets and hutongs of Beijing and lamented that the capital's greening is so good. The retired people's living conditions are really good. Because I haven't been riding a bike for a long time, my legs are sore and numb in less than an hour. As I was about to return to school, I found that I couldn't find my way back to school. Finally, I decided to take a taxi back. The

我是幸运的，在自己花儿一样的年纪，迈出国门来到一个既陌生又熟悉的国家——中国。这一切要从一年前说起。申请去中国留学本是无心插柳之事，直到那个短信的出现。还记得那是一个明媚的下午，一切像往常一样，放学后的我坐在计程车上准备回家，手机突然“叮”的一声，我漫不经心地拿起手机，看着发来的信息，瞬间困意全无，瞪大了双眼：“Joanna，你要去中国留学了！”就这样我来到了北京，来到了我的预科学校——对外经济贸易大学。

因为飞机晚点，凌晨一点多我才抵达首都机场，而北京给我的第一印象却很深刻。尽管是凌晨，但这个城市依旧处处灯火阑珊、流光溢彩。我至今还记得在北京第一次迷路，我骑着自行车，穿梭在北京的大街小巷里，一路上感叹着北京的绿化真好，还有，这里的退休老人的生活状态真不错。久不骑自行车的我，还没到一小时双腿就已经酸痛无力了。在准备返回学校时我发现自己竟然找不到回学校的路了，无奈的我最后只好坐计程车返回了。司机是一位地道的北京大爷，特别善谈，我们聊了一路，最后才知道司机师傅一直以为我是台湾人，有意思的一段经历让我离北京更近了。

driver is a middle-aged Pekingese, who is very talkative. We chatted all the way, he thought I was from Taiwan – an interesting experience driving me closer to Beijing.

Time flies. I also met international students from all over the world and found many fellow Filipinos. Gradually I have adapted to the weather in Beijing, the accent of Beijing and the food in Beijing. Every day I stick with my Vietnamese roommate after class because our relationship is really good. After returning home I have been looking forward to return to school, back to Beijing. A Chinese saying goes "God's way is higher than men's." China experienced a sudden epidemic outbreak.

No one could predict that this year would be so special. When the Chinese New Year bell was about to ring, a novel coronavirus had sneaked into the nation and waged a battle without smoke with Chinese people. People say that life is so fragile that it can be destroyed by some microorganisms. In my opinion, life is tenacious. In the face of such a disaster, I see that no one in this country has given up, no one retreated. China stands strong thanks to the endeavor made by their bravest people. The so-called heroes are those brave ordinary people. During the pandemic, I

黄雯芳 / 对外经济贸易大学提供

对外经济贸易大学 / 黄雯芳提供

随着时间的推移，我也结识了来自世界各地的留学生，同时也找到了许多菲律宾同胞。慢慢地我也适应了北京的天气、北京的口音和北京的饮食。我每天除了上课的时间，都会和越南室友黏在一起。我们俩关系实在太好了，回国后的我一直期待着回到学校，回到北京，但中国人常说“人算不如天算”，谁能想到我们这一回国，中国就经历了一场突如其来的疫情。

谁也不曾想到这一年竟是如此不平凡，当中国新年的钟声将要敲响的一刻，一种新型冠状病毒也加快了蔓延的脚步，和中国人拉开了一场没有硝烟的战斗。都说生命是脆弱的，只需要一些微生物就可以毁灭；我却说生命是顽强的，在这样的灾难面前，我看到的是这个国家没有人要放弃，没有人要逃跑，我眼中的中国总是被他们最勇敢的人保护得更好。其实那些所谓的英雄，不过是拥有勇敢的平凡人而已。身在国外的我，每每看到手机里播放关于中国疫情的视频时都会不争气地默默流下眼泪，气自己无能为力，也不知能为我的第二个故乡做些什么。当我看

stayed in the Philippines. I burst into tears every time I watched a video of the outbreak in China on my cell phone. I feel regret for nothing I could do for my second hometown. I saw those doctors and nurses, whose faces were covered with streaks of blood for wearing masks for so long. When they raised the hands with the operating knives, needles and potions, sweat has been soaked in their heavy protective clothing. People use the gesture of hugs to express their encouragement. Residents were called to "Stay at home, which is to make contributions." I think at the moment Chinese people are of one mind and unite as one. Once again, I feel fortunate that I have got the chance to come to this great country, and although I cannot fight alongside you, I will always pray for you.

Nowadays, I am looking forward to return to China to continue of my study of Chinese. I miss the teachers, my classmates and all the delicacies in Beijing. Photos will be yellowed weathered by the passage of time, letters will be lost after years. But my memory will be like wine, the longer the more mellow. Beijing, you will be the city that will always be cherished in my heart.

China, I love you.

Beijing, I love you.

UIBE, I love you.

到那些医生护士为了救治病人，脸上被口罩勒出的一道道血痕，举起手中的手术刀、针管、药剂，汗水早已浸湿了他们厚重的防护服时，当我看到那些隔空给人的拥抱，隔空给予的鼓励时，当我听到“宅在家，不出门就是做贡献”时，我想此刻的他们都拥有同一颗心，叫“万众一心”，他们的样子，就是中国的样子，就是常说的那个词“众志成城”。我再次庆幸我来到了这个伟大的国家，虽然我不能与你们并肩战斗，但我永远会为你们祈祷。

对外经济贸易大学 / 黄雯芳提供

直到现在，我没有一天不在期待，学校通知中国国门已打开的好消息，欢迎我回去继续学习汉语。我想念老师们、同学们和北京的各种各样的美食。照片会因为时间的流逝而泛黄，信件会因为岁月的脚步而丢失，只有心头的记忆会像美酒一样越久越醇厚浓郁。北京，你将会是那个永远藏在我心里最深处的城市。

我爱你，中国！

我爱你，北京！

我爱你，对外经济贸易大学！

给爸爸妈妈的一封信
A Letter to My Parents

[喀麦隆] 李睿阳　青岛大学
[Cameroon] Kamgue Idris Arnold, Qingdao University

Dear Dad and Mum:

How are things going these days? The novel coronavirus pneumonia is rampant all over the world, and I'm worried about your health. Through the news reports, I saw the current spread of the COVID-19 in Cameroon.Thouth it is not as serious as that in European countries and the United States, you should not relax your vigilance, please take careful protective measures, keep good hygiene habits and go out as little as possible. Please wear a mask whenever you have to leave home. Try not to step to a place with crowded people.

I am really sorry for seldomly writing letters to you after leaving home to study in China. You must have imagined many times my study life in China. I stay with my teachers and classmates in the classroom when having class; After class, my friends and I go to the gyms for fitness, participate activities together and visit bookstores on weekends.

Alas, I can only recall it now. starting from this winter vacation, the university has adopted full close management in order to protect our health and safety. However, during the "anti-epidemic" period, our closed life is not as boring as

亲爱的爸爸妈妈：

你们最近还好吗？当前新型冠状病毒在全球范围内蔓延，我非常担心你们的健康。在新闻里我看到了目前病毒在喀麦隆传播的情况，虽没有像欧洲国家及美国那么严重，但你们也不能放松警惕，应该坚持做好防护措施，养成良好的卫生习惯，尽量少出门。如果出门一定要戴好口罩，千万别去人多的地方。

我真是不好意思，从离开家来到中国留学，一直疏于和你们联系。你们肯定想象过很多次我在中国的留学生活吧？平时和老师同学一起在教室里上课，课下和朋友结伴健身、一起活动、周末去书店看书，等等。

唉，这些我现在也只能是想想了。因为从这个寒假开始，学校为了保护我们的安全，采取了校园封闭管理政策。不过在抗疫期间，我们的封闭生活并没有如想象中那么无聊，对我来说，这段时间我的学习、运动从未停止，厨艺也在不断提高。现在我要向你们汇报一下我这段时间的生活啦，有图有真相，你们快坐好慢慢欣赏吧！

首先，是我的学习情况。在疫情防控期间，学校要求我们上网课。一般，周一到周五的上午 10 点就开始签到，10 点 10 分开始上课，上完两节

imagined. For me, I never stopped my study and fitness and my cooking skill has got improved during this period of time. Now I would like to report to you on my campus life in detail with a picture. Please sit down and enjoy it!

First of all, my study continues. During the pandemic prevention and control, the university asked us to take classes online. Generally speaking, check-in starts at 10 am from Monday to Friday and classes start at 10:10 am. After two sessions in the morning, we will have more than one hour for lunch and rest. The afternoon session is from 1:30 to 3:20 pm. At the beginning, it was not easy for me to use online study software. Gradually, I was able to master the use of DingTalk, Fanya platform, Rain Classroom and Duifene software. The teachers are very strict with us and give us a lot of homework every day, because they don't allow us to be lazy at all. I think I have made some progress in my thesis writing recently, but the comprehensive Chinese is still a little difficult for me. Although I can get more than 94 points per quiz, my teacher still set higher requirements for me.

青岛大学 / 李睿阳提供

Study life is busy, but I still take time to do exercise every day. I have made a very strict training plan for myself every week. At the beginning, I ran alone on campus

课休息一个多小时，下午从 1 点 30 分到 3 点 20 分。刚开始的时候，用学习软件对我来说很困难，但慢慢地我已经可以熟练使用钉钉、泛雅学习平台、雨课堂、对分易等网课软件了。老师们每天都会给我们布置很多作业，而且他们对作业的要求很严格，一点儿也不允许我们偷懒放松。我觉得我最近写作水平有点儿进步了，但汉语综合课还是学得很费劲，虽然我每次小测验都能考到 94 分以上，可我的老师会一直对我提出更高的要求。

学习生活忙忙碌碌，但我每天仍会抽时间锻炼，而且我每周都会给自己制订一个很严格的训练计划。刚开始的时候，我一个人在校园里跑步，在宿舍里健身。后来一个朋友建议我带动其他留校的同学一起锻炼，所以我现在每天都会根据他们的情况帮他们制订不同的训练计划——有氧训练和力量训练。一开始同学们都觉得我的训练太难了，有的同学刚开始跑步时连两公里都坚持不了，但在大家的鼓励下，现在一次就能跑上七八公里，甚至偶尔还可以跑到十公里。不知不觉，漫长的冬天已经走远了，我们每天坚持锻炼，就这样“跑”进了百花盛开的季节，每天跑步的路上都能发现学校里的变化，也欣赏着不同的美景。

青岛大学 / 李睿阳提供

and conducted exercise in my dorm room. Later, a friend suggested that I lead other students to practice together. So I decided to help them draft training plans every day according to their situation - aerobic training and strength training. At first my classmates thought my training schedule was too tough for them because some of them can hardly run 2 kilometers. We kept encouraging each other. Now we can run on 7-8 kilometers at a time, and even 10 kilometers. The long winter has passed before we knew it. We do exercise every day and have "run" into the blooming season. We not only witness the changes on campus, but also enjoy the different scenery.

Netizens said an outbreak of pandemic has turned doctors and nurses into soldiers, teachers into internet anchors, all Chinese people into chefs. As a Cameroonian student in China, I successfully transfer myself into a "fitness instructor & physical education teacher." Besides, my cooling skill got improved rapidly. Recently, I have learned a variety of dishes through the internet, especially baking. I would like to show you the bread and cakes I baked. Haha, I think I'm going to be a qualified cook. Next time when I go home, I'll show up my new skill.

It turns out this special lockdown period has sped up my rapid growth. Many of us began to pay attention to their own health. When participating practice, I have discovered the unique charm of our campus of the Qingdao University. During the fight against the pandemic, we learned to cherish every day and everything in life.

I will end my letter here. Wish you all the best! Next time when I return home, I will bring back my good grades,health and cooking skills. I hope this day will come soon.

Truly yours

青岛大学 / 李睿阳提供

网上都说一场疫情让医生护士成了战士，老师成了主播，全中国人民成了厨子。而我这个在中国的喀麦隆留学生在完成“健身教练 + 体育老师”这一身份的转变之余，也入乡随俗，大大提高了自己的厨艺。最近，我在网上学会了各种各样的菜的做法，特别是学会了烘焙，给你们看看我做的面包、蛋糕吧。哈哈，我觉得我就要成为一名合格的厨师了。下次回家，我一定要做给你们尝尝。

说到这里，突然觉得这场意外的“禁闭期”也成了我的快速成长期。我们很多人开始关注自己的身体健康，在校园里健身的时候也发现了我们青大校园独特的魅力。抗疫路上，我们学会了珍惜时间，也明白了在活着的每一天都应该珍惜自己拥有的一切。

先写到这里吧，祝你们一切都好！下次回国的时候，我一定会带上我的好成绩、好身体和好厨艺。希望这一天快点儿到来。

深爱你们的儿子！

我的 2020
My 2020

［哈萨克斯坦］ 安迪　华东师范大学
[Kazakhstan] Tursynzhan Pariza, East China Normal University

Everyone lives a unique life in the world, but all of us have suffered same epidemic, worry, memory, gratitude and expectation since January 2020.

On the eve of the year of 2020, my friends and I had mapped out various plans for the upcoming new year. Meanwhile, it turns out the year of 2020 has its own plan that differs from ours.

In January, my parents urged me to return home after the outbreak of COVID-19 pandemic. After careful consideration, I decided to stay in China. On the one hand, I thought it was too dangerous to travel at that time. On the other hand, I have learned all the measures taken by the Chinese government and the university authorities, which made me believe that China has the determination, ability, medical resources to control the epidemic. I decided to stay in China to fight against the pandemic.

After the lockdown of the university, teachers in the international student office have kept a close contact with everyone of us. Although the campus is kind of deserted, but the WeChat groups are bustling with life every day. To help solve the problems caused by closure of the university, the university established an "online

我们每个人都拥有独一无二的生活，可是自 2020 年 1 月以来大家又何尝不是拥有了一模一样的 2020 呢？我们所有人都在经历着同样的疫情、担忧、刻骨铭心、感动与期待。

2019 年跨年夜，我和小伙伴做着各种 2020 年的计划，把即将到来的 2020 安排得明明白白。可不到一个月时间，我们却被 2020“安排”了。

一月，武汉突然遭遇疫情，父母催促我赶紧回国，经过深思熟虑，我还是选择了留下。一方面，我觉得那时出门风险实在太高，不如就待在原地安全。另一方面，我也认真了解了当时中国政府的行动，以及学校采取的各项措施，最终我和同学得出的结论是：中国有决心有能力也有医疗水平控制住疫情，而学校也会把我们保护得很好。就这样，我们留在中国开始了我们的抗疫生活。

学校实行了封闭管理，但留学生办公室的老师们和大家保持着密切联系。虽然校园里有些“荒凉”，但各个微信群里每天都热热闹闹的。因为担心大家不能出校园造成生活不便，学校为大家建立了“网络超市”——大家可以在微信小程序里选择自己需要的食物和日用品，然后校外超市会将物资统一配送到学校。

supermarket." We can choose what we want through WeChat program, then the supermarket delivers the commodities to our campus.

It turns out the initiative decision we have made is correct. At first, we worried a lot and surfed daily news to check out the latest data of confirmed cases, the actual situation in Wuhan, the recent medical teams that have arrived to help and the countries who have made donations to China. It's untrue to say that I did not feel worried when seeing the rising data every day. It's untrue to say that I was not distressed when seeing people are going through life and death struggles. It's untrue to say that I was not happy when seeing recovered patients were discharged from hospital. It's untrue to say that I was not moved by the doctors who risked their lives to save people. During that period of time, my face was always covered with tears caused by worries, gratitude and torment.

After entering June, the epidemic situation in China has been controlled. In early May, the campus began to revive. At the same time, there remained strict

华东师范大学 / 安迪提供

华东师范大学 / 安迪提供

回想起我们当初的决定——留在中国，绝对是正确的。但最初那段时间我们也真的感到害怕，每天早上起床第一件事就是打开新闻，看看今天又确诊了多少病例；看看今天的武汉实况如何；看看又有哪些驰援医疗队到达了武汉；看看哪些国家的捐赠物资抵达了中国。看着每天上升的数据说不害怕是假的；看到经历着生离死别的人们说不心疼是假的；看着康复出院的患者说不欣慰是假的；看着前线的医生舍身忘我地救助说不感动也是假的。那段时间觉得自己总是在哭，有害怕的泪水，有感动的泪水，也有心疼的泪水。

如今已是6月，中国的疫情已得到了控制。5月初，学校里渐渐恢复了“烟火气”。但同时，各项防控措施依然严格：大家依然坚持上网课；出校依然只能是一周一次；图书馆就座需要保持距离；食堂里吃饭必须按规定隔一个座位；宿舍进出依然要量体温，大家也依然要每天两次自测并上报自己的体温给老师。虽然规定严格，但大家都默默遵守，因为我们知道这一切都是在为自己和他人的生命安全负责。

现在全世界依然受到疫情的影响，许多国家仍处于抗疫的艰难阶段，

anti-epidemic measures; We had to attend online lessons and were permitted to leave the campus once in a week. Social distancing should be maintained when visiting to the library. Students are asked to sit seperate from each other while having dinner. Body temperatures were measured every day and we were asked to report twice a day. All of us have followed the strict measures simultaneously, which we believe were good for us and others.

The pandemic is still rampant around the world and many countries are fighting arduously with the virus. I have not returned my home country for a year. I miss my parents and hometown very much and I pray that they can be safe and sound. I also hope the people suffering from the epidemic on earth will recover as soon as possible. The COVID-19 virus is a disaster for mankind in the 21st century. No matter what countries we come from, what colors we are, what languages we speak,in the face of such a havoc of human history, all these differences no longer matter. To solve the problems, the most valuable and most needed is the unity of all of us through cooperation and mutual support. For younger generations like us, we should be brave in facing the challenges in such a great era of change in human history and exploring new opportunities and development.

The year 2020 is unprecedented for the mankind. We are all siblings of the Earth and heroes for each other. Let us pray for human kind's peace and unity. Wish you and I be brave and strong.

华东师范大学 / 安迪提供

我已经有一年的时间没回国了，我非常想念我的父母和家乡，每一天我都祈祷他们能够健康平安，也希望地球上饱受疫情折磨的人们都能早日康复。新冠肺炎疫情是21世纪全人类的一场劫，无论我们来自哪个国家、是什么肤色、说着什么语言，在这样一场人类历史的灾难面前，这些差异已经不再重要。在这样的困难面前，最可贵和最需要的是我们全人类的团结一致、合作共赢，是我们的互相帮助、互相支持。而像我们这样的青年一代，更应该在这样人类历史的大变革时代中，学会勇敢、迎难而上，善于在巨大的苦难和挑战中发掘新的机遇，不断发展，自强不息！

这是每个人独一无二的2020，也是全人类共同的2020，我们都是地球的孩子，也是彼此的英雄。愿人类平安、团结，愿你我勇敢、坚强！

疫情与希望
Pandemic and Hope

[哈萨克斯坦] 卡米拉 北京科技大学
[Kazakhstan] Usmanova Kamila, University of Science and Technology Beijing

We tend to feel boring during the COVID-19 pandemic period. However, we are also embracing hopes...

During the COVID-19 pandemic period, what brought joy and hopes to me and my families was the active thinking and resolution about "doing something from tomorrow." Besides study at home every day, I helped my cousins with their homework, paid close attention to news, browsing over old pictures and contacted some old friends and relatives who we had not seen for long. Sometimes I also watched science fiction movies to experience different life, did some physical exercises to build up my body and release pressures. I planned to accomplish many tasks, such as learning

卡米拉在北京国际鲜花港

疫情期间很容易感到无聊，但，无聊的我们反而满怀希望……

疫情这一段时间，给我和我家人带来快乐和希望的就是积极的想法和“从明天起，做一个……”的决心。每天除了学习以外，我还陪表弟做作业，关注新闻，翻翻老照片，联系好久没联系过的亲戚朋友，有时候看科幻电影体验一下不一样的人生经历，锻炼身体，释放压力。我计划要完成的事情也不少，比如，学习新软件的应用，阅读好书提升自己，学习做新的巧克力蛋糕，找出培养个性彩虹玫瑰花的方法等，让长长的宅家时间变得丰富而充实。这样一来，我在慢慢地实现很多平时觉得没时间做或者懒得去做的事。疫情这段时间也让我明白多陪家人多关注周围环境的重要性。当我开窗看到春暖花开的风景却无法接近慢慢品赏花香时，我才领悟到我们平时多么需要珍惜大自然短暂的美景，并与大自然交流。

疫情让宅在家里的我们掌握新的应用软件进行线上学习或工作，快速适应新环境，培养新的习惯，接受自我挑战。疫情总会过去，而它的脚印已经记载着全球的新变化。由于这场疫情而不知所措的人们对机器人服务有了紧急的需求，很多落后的习惯与不合时宜的观念都将慢慢地

to use new Apps, reading books to improve myself, learning to cook chocolate cakes and finding a method to cultivate unique rainbow roses. All these activities made my long period of staying at home not boring. Gradually I was slowly accomplishing many tasks which I did not have time to do in the past. I also came to understand the importance of accompanying family members and caring those around you. When I opened windows, saw the beautiful flowers and felt the warm breeze outside, I realized that I could not enjoy them freely as before due to the COVID-19 virus. I missed and began to cherish all those moments when I could enjoy the beauty of the nature and communicate the nature whenever I wanted to.

The pandemic enabled us learn new Apps for study or work, quickly adjust ourselves for new environment, cultivate new habits and be ready for new challenges. It will finally be bygones and its footprints carry new changes of the world. People who were at a loss by the pandemic began to have urgent demands for robot service. Habits and ideology that won't develop with the time will gradually phase out. A gift brought to us by the pandemic was to shake hands with modern technologies. We won't need to take risks personally for many tasks since we will be having robots to help us in the near future. New jobs will be created to adjust ourselves to new life.

During the pandemic period, the technology development of China, including the contribution of robots into medical industry, the application of virtual reality, disinfection and food delivery accomplished by unmanned drones, showed China's future-oriented insights. Actually, the interconnection of "Belt and Road" had already showed us the advanced technology of China's high-speed railways and the development of China's logistic industry was really

被淘汰。疫情带来的礼物就是让我们和现代科技“握握手”，将来我们再也不需要费时费力冒风险亲自完成多项工作了，因为有了机器人服务生活就会更便捷，人们将会随之而创造新的岗位以适应新的生活。

疫情期间，中国的科技发展，包括机器人服务对医学领域的贡献，虚拟现实的应用，无人机消毒、送餐的实现等，都让我们看到了中国面向未来的眼光。其实“一带一路”的联通早已让我们感知中国高铁技术的先进，而中国物流的发展更是让人叹为观止。当您走进京东物流时，可以看到多少可爱的小机器在物流管理全过程中的自决策、自诊断、自控制并相互配合的画面，这一瞬间惊艳了您！也不难想象，未来会有小巧玲珑的飞机敲您窗户将您的快递配送到家。中国的科技太给力了！因为我们就幸运地处于非常精彩的一段当代历史。中国人的创新精神让我

参加国庆大游行之前和同学们校内彩排（右四为卡米拉）

amazing. When you go into JD Logistics, you can see the self-decision, self-diagnosis, self-control and cooperation scenarios of quite a number of robots in the logistics management process. It is amazing. We cannot help imagining that in the future unmanned drones will knock at your window and deliver parcels to your house. China's technologies are amazing! We are very lucky to experience such an amazing history. The innovation of Chinese enabled me to see the greatness of China.

The warmth is in the air of China now. The advanced technology of China brings us comfort as well as warmth and consideration, which makes us feel like home. Chinese are very tolerant to different cultures and the modernization of China has always been progressing with the introduction of traditional cultures, which displays the beautiful wishes and hopes of Chinese people. During the pandemic, we are deeply moved by the help and care China has been giving to us foreigners. This is the manifesto of China's development ideology for global health and peace. Wish the world support China and cheer for China! The wisdom of Chinese helps us achieve a beautiful life and a promising future. There is an old Arabic saying that says "Go to seek for wisdom even it is far away in China." That means, everyone knows earlier the importance of China to the world and the future.

China, you are our lighthouse and we are waiting for your instruction. Your lamp is shining and leads us to our "home". The world needs you, China!

卡米拉在排练舞蹈

们感悟中国的伟大。

中国的天空充满着温暖的气息：正是因为先进科技带来的舒适感，在中国我们能感受到亲切体贴的气氛和如家一般的温馨。中国的土地孕育着包容，中国现代化发展总离不开传统文化的引入，这让我们看到了中国人民对美好生活的愿望和理想。抗疫期间中国对你和我的帮助令人感动泪目，这"一颗中国心"展现了中国的全球健康和平的发展观，让世界更加支持中国，为中国加油！中国的智慧帮助人们实现着美好的人生和满载希望的未来。怪不得阿拉伯语有句俗话说："去求知吧，哪怕远在中国！"原来人们早已知道中国对全世界和未来的重要性。

中国，我们等待你的指路，你的明灯照耀着我们的"家"，世界需要你！

疫情无情人有情
Fighting Ruthless Pandemic with Love

[越南] 阮春海　华南理工大学
[Vietnam] Nguyễn Xuân Hải, South China University of Technology

At the end of 2019, when the whole world was ready to welcome the spring, a sad thing happened in Wuhan, China. Many people in the city suffered a terrible virus, which was later named COVID-19. What scares people most is that the virus is highly contagious – children, youngsters and aged people may get infected. It spread very fast, and patients with severe symptoms may lose their lives. China is fully aware of the danger of the virus. To curb the further spread of the virus, the Chinese government has made an unprecedented decision in history to lock down the city of Wuhan and ask people not to go out as far as possible and prohibit all crowd gathering activities. Residents stay at home willingly for the health of themselves, their families and friends.

The pandemic has caused numerous companies, factories, shops and schools to temporarily or completely shut down. It turns out that the "epidemic" is really merciless. The COVID-19 virus has brought remendous loss to human beings, but it has not stopped its rampant pace.

Although the epidemic situation is severe, there are groups of angels in

在2019年年底，当整个世界都在准备迎接春天的到来时，中国的武汉却遭遇了令我们难过的事。很多人生病了，他们感染了一种可怕的病毒，这种病毒被称为“新型冠状病毒”，英文名字叫“COVID-19”。让人们觉得恐慌的是，这种病毒传染性极强，无论是儿童、年轻人还是老年人，都有可能得病，它的传播速度也非常快，而且具有严重症状的人很可能因此失去生命。中国意识到了这种病毒的危险性，为了避免病毒的进一步传播，中国政府做出了历史上前所未有的决定——封锁武汉这一座大城市，并要求人们尽量不要外出，禁止一切人群聚集活动。人们为了自己和家人、朋友的健康，都自觉、主动地待在家里。

疫情导致许多公司、工厂、商店和学校等暂时停止或者关闭。这样看来疫情真是没有感情，病毒给人类带来了巨大的伤害，但它还没有停止肆虐的脚步。

虽然疫情无情，但在疫情的中心——许许多多的医院里却出现了一群群的白衣天使，他们不管面临多大困难，不管工作多么艰苦，都愿意逆行进入危险的地方去拯救那些濒临死亡的病人。他们不得不离开自己的家人去工作，他们把所有的时间都花在工作上，从早到晚都在忙着拯

华南理工大学 / 阮春海提供

white in the center of the epidemic – hospitals. No matter how many challenges they are facing and how hard their work is, they are ready to enter dangerous places to save the dying patients. They had to leave their families and spent all their time at work. They took care of patients from morning to night. Having been wearing masks for a long time, many doctors and nurses' faces have been left red marks. Despite this, they continued to work endure despite of the pain and trauma they suffered. Many retired medical workers chose to return to work and joined the fight against the epidemic.

During this time, we have seen and heard many moving stories. A couple of doctor lovers delayed their wedding ceremony because they have been combating in the front line. A woman doctor mother can only see her children from a distance to avoid the risk of infecting her family. A retired doctor, who are determined to return to work to save patients, died of the virus. A volunteer offered to send food to isolated people. An entrepreneur donated medical

救和照顾病人。因为一直戴着口罩，许多医生和护士的脸上被口罩勒出了深深的伤痕。尽管这样，他们还是会忍着这些疼痛和创伤，坚持工作。也有很多医生虽然已经退休了，但还是会选择申请返回工作岗位，加入抗疫战斗中。

这段时间里，我们看到了也听到了许多让我们感动的故事：一对医生恋人因为一直奋斗在前线，选择推迟了他们的婚礼；一位医生妈妈为了不给家人带来感染风险，只能从远处看看自己的孩子；一位已经退休的医生，毅然选择重返岗位拯救病人，自己却因感染病毒而离世；一位志愿者主动给被隔离的人送食物；一位企业家自愿转产医疗设备，缓解医院物资短缺的燃眉之急……他们都是抗疫的英雄！

在此次疫情中，人们不仅会帮助本国人民，还会帮助其他国家和地区的人，比如，中国政府把口罩和医疗设备捐送给别的国家，以帮助它们对抗疫情。还有很多的好人好事，我没办法全部说完。但你会发现，

华南理工大学 / 阮春海提供

equipment to help hospitals ease the shortage of medical supplies... They're all the anti-epidemic heroes!

In this outbreak, people will not only help their own people but also assist other countries and regions. For example, the Chinese government donated masks and medical equipment to other countries. There are a lot of warm-hearted people who have done good deeds. But you'll find people are helping each other to the best of their ability no matter how different their nationalities are, no matter what their colors are. Assistance comes not just from individuals, but also from businesses and government departments, whose selfless love and passion help fill our world with warmth.

Living in the global village, the fate of mankind is linked. Although the pandemic may last a long time, but as long as we work together, we will defeat the virus. After the outbreak is curbed, I hope one day in the near future you can invite me, a Vietnamese, to Wuhan to eat a bowl of hot dry noodles!

华南理工大学 / 阮春海提供

不论我们的国籍有何不同，不论我们的肤色有何差别，人们都在提供力所能及的帮助，这些帮助不仅来自个人，也来自企业，还来自政府，无私的帮助让我们的世界充满温情。

我们同住地球村，人类的命运是连在一起的。尽管疫情可能会持续很长时间，但只要我们一起努力，万众一心，病毒一定会被打败！我希望疫情能尽快结束，在未来的某天你们可以邀请我，一位越南人，去武汉吃一碗热干面！

生与死
Life and Death

［韩国］ 崔志佑　北京外国语大学
[Republic of Korea] Choi Jiwoo, Beijing Foreign Studies University

When I studied in Beijing, I rented an off-campus apartment that was very far from our school. I usually rode an electric bike and wasted two hours a day commuting to and from school.

After toiling and moiling like this for a semester, I finally returned hometown for my winter vacation. Before long, the novel coronavirus epidemic occurred first in Wuhan, Central China's Hubei Province. Soon, more and more patients were diagnosed in Republic of Korea. The government of Republic of Korea has implemented a policy of "social distancing," which demands to stay at home and to get gathering as little as possible. I had to stay at home without going out and interact with anyone but my family.

At first, it was quite comfortable to stay at home alone like this. It seems I was set free as the busy study and laborious commute to school in Beijing were all over. I watched all TV dramas I didn't have time in the past, played all kinds of computer games, and ate Korean food I've been missing in China. However, the epidemic is not over.

Schools have decided to start online classes. More and more people

左一为崔志佑

我在北京上学的时候，在校外租房，我租的房子离我们学校非常远；我平时自己骑电动车来回，每天两个小时的时间浪费在上下学的路上。

这么辛辛苦苦地上了一个学期，终于放寒假回国了。没有多久，新冠肺炎疫情突然袭来，韩国也有了越来越多的确诊患者。韩国政府实行了“保持社交距离”，即尽量不出家门，尽量不聚集的政策，我只好待在家里，不出门，除了家人以外不跟任何人接触。

刚开始这样一个人待在家里挺舒服的，在北京繁忙的学业、辛苦的上学路都结束了，好像被释放了。我看完了以前没时间看的电视剧，玩够了各种电脑游戏，吃完了在中国一直很想念的韩国菜。可是，新冠肺炎疫情并没有结束。

学校决定以线上上课的方式来开学，全世界有越来越多的人失去了生命，以前只能在电视新闻里看到的确诊患者，不再是陌生人了，爸爸职场上的、朋友认识的、住我们小区的……新冠肺炎疫情不再是“别人的事”了。

独自一人待在家里的时间越来越长了，休闲变成了无聊，无聊的感觉开始让我沉淀，沉淀的底部有我的老朋友——恐惧。

北京外国语大学 / 崔志佑提供

around the world are losing their lives. The diagnosed patients, who could only be seen on the news before, are no longer strangers. They are from the work circle of my father, the social network of my friends and even our community... The epidemic is no longer "other people's business."

All alone at home for more and more time, I feel bored from leisure. At the bottom of the depression I sank into, I came across my old friend, fear.

I saw people dying of the novel coronavirus infection and imperceptibly pondering over life and death. Once there is life, there is death. Death is not a thing you have to be old to face. No matter how wealthy you are and even if you've done a thousand charities, you'll lose your life unjustly.

I came to the realization that it wasn't death at all I was thinking about, but the life I now had. Death is out of my control, but my life is up to me.

I made up my mind to change my life, not to remain so powerless and pessimistic, but to spend every moment of my life to the fullest.

What exactly can I can do during this time period? Compared with my stay in Beijing, I had two hours of "spare time," which I can make use of doing a lot of things.

我看到被新冠病毒感染失去生命的人，不知不觉地深思生死。一旦有了生命，就有死亡。死亡，不一定你老了才面临它，你多么富裕也无所谓，即使你做了一千个慈善事业，也会冤枉地失去生命。

我顿时醒悟，我思考的根本不是死亡，而是我现在拥有的生命。死亡，是没法控制的，而我的人生，是由我决定的。

我下定决心要改变我的生活，不要一直这么无力、悲观，而要充实地度过我人生的每一刻。

我在这个时段可以做的事情到底有什么呢？跟我在北京的时候做比较，我有两个小时的“业余时间”，我可以用这个时间做很多事情。

首先，我开始养成了读书的习惯，不管每天读的页数有多少，可是每天都坚持下去，让我再次爱上读书。

然后，我定好了早上起床和晚上睡觉的时间。以前的生活就是为了上学才起床，生活没有规律。定好了起床和睡觉的时间之后，有规律的新生活让我更加有活力。

北京外国语大学 / 崔志佑提供

作为一个留学生，虽然这次疫情和线上上课并不是一件好事，但是从积极的方面来看，这段时间内可以跟家人一起生活了。我经常拜访姥姥，经常跟表哥表妹们见面，为每天上班的爸爸妈妈做晚饭，虽然我做的菜不能跟妈妈做的比较，可是家人一起吃饭的时刻非常

I started to get into the habit of reading. No matter how many pages I read each day, but the daily perseverance made me fall in love with reading again.

Then, I set the time to get up in the morning and go to bed at night. In the past, the only motivation for me to get up early was going to school and there was no routine for other occasions. A regular new life made me more energetic after being more disciplined.

As an international student, though the pandemic and online study are not good things, on the positive side, I get more time to be with my family. I visited my grandma and gathered with my cousins more frequently. I help prepare dinner for my parents who work every day. Although the dishes I cooked are not as good as those my mum did, the happiness are the same as long as we eat together.

I can only manage such trifles, but my life has a brand-new look. The epidemic has not come to an end so far and there are still a lot of people living miserably. I still cannot go out at ease and the final exam had to be conducted online. However, I can say with confidence that my life changed, for the changes are from the heart rather than circumstances.

Life is short and long. Many people said life is too short to hesitate. And life is not that short because It takes time to prepare for a better future by making money and other undertakings.

Before I was always wondering which saying is right or wrong. Now I stopped wasting time on these meaningless issues, because I have an awareness that as long as I handle each day to the fullest without self-delusion, cherish the time by overcoming laziness, love people around me and have no regret when I look back the whole day before sleeping every night, my life is successful.

北京外国语大学 / 崔志佑提供

幸福。

我仅仅做到这些小事情而已，可是我的生活完全改变了。虽然新冠肺炎疫情，到现在为止并没有结束，还有很多过着痛苦生活的人，我还是不能安安心心地出门，连期末考试都要在网上进行，但是我还是能有信心地说我的生活改变了，是因为改变的不是我的环境，而是我的内心。

人生既短暂，又长远。很多人说，人生太短暂，想做什么事情就不能犹豫。可是人生又不是那么短暂的，需要为了更好的未来做赚钱等准备。

我以前也总是思考这两个没有一个对一个错的问题，但是现在再也不会思考这种无意义的问题。因为我知道，只要是我充实地对待每一天，不要骗自己，不要懒惰，珍惜光阴，爱我周边的人，晚上睡觉前回顾一天而没有后悔的人生，就是成功的人生。

我与中国美好的相遇

——千里之行，始于足下

My Beautiful Encounter with China

—The Journey of a Thousand Miles Begins with a Single Step

［俄罗斯］ 塔蒂阿娜 哈尔滨工业大学

[Russia] Sitnikova Tatiana, Harbin Institute of Technology

My first Chinese tour started from September 2020, but I learned about the nation earlier than this trip. First of all, the city where I live is not far from China and has a close contact with China. Chinese is taught at school, which always organizes various cultural exchanges between Russia and China. One could see Chinese logos in the street. In the summer, you can meet a lot of Chinese tourists, who are happy to talk to us. When I was 11, I first encountered Chinese in middle school. From then on, I had fallen in love with Chinese. I am fascinated by China's unique culture. I began to learn Chinese knowledge every day and took part in various speech and calligraphy competitions about Chinese, which brought me honors.

Time flies. My dream to study in China came into reality seven years later. I decided to go to Harbin, which is known as Moscow in the East. The climate of Harbin is very similar to my city, and more importantly, it has a long history with Russia, which makes me to open her mysterious veil. Because of my excellent

我的中国之行始于 2019 年 9 月，但是我对它的了解却早于我的中国之行。首先，我住的城市离中国不远，因此，与中国的联系特别亲密：在学校里会有人教授汉语，在俄罗斯和中国之间的文化交流中经常举办各种各样的主题活动，大街上有中文标志，尤其到了夏天，您可以遇到很多中国游客，他们很高兴跟我们交谈。我 11 岁那年，在中学第一次认识了汉语，从那一刻起，我和汉语如影相随。我对中国独一无二的文化着迷。于是，我每天都会学习中国知识并一有机会就去参加各种关于汉语的语言和书法比赛，我也获得了荣誉。

时间飞逝，七年之后，我的梦想实现了——我获得了去中国学习的机会。我决定去具有东方莫斯科之称的哈尔滨，哈尔滨不仅气候跟我的城市非常相似，更重要的是它还有着跟俄罗斯悠久的历史，这使我更加向往，更想去揭开令我觉得神秘的面纱。因为我的成绩优秀，我可以上中国最知名的学府之一——哈尔滨工业大学。

初来乍到，我对这里却一点也不陌生，感觉像自己久别重逢的家，

grades, I can go to Harbin Institute of Technology, one of the top universities in China.

After the arrival, I found the city far from alien. There was kind of intimacy just like returning to my family after a long separation. My life in China is very colorful and not dull at all. From the first day, we began to have Chinese classes, during which teachers seldom use English. Because I had learned some Chinese, I could catch what the teacher said. But most of the students had never studied Chinese, so we began to help each other after class. I though I can only learn Chinese, but this was a wrong idea because there are foreigner students from all over the world in my class. Besidess of English we all speak, I can learn other languages. This is a truly rare and valuable opportunity – one can learn the cultures and languages of different countries. We tried to speak our country's language, because it was not only fun but also very useful. Study in China has brought us a better understanding of different cultures.

Out of campus, people I talked to were surprised to see I could speak Chinese fluently. In fact, after more than six months' study in China, my Chinese level has been significantly improved. I remember the first time I took the subway (there is no subway in my hometown city). I missed several times because I didn't know the station's name. I remember the beautiful sunset seeing from the window of the dormitory every night. I remember that I stayed up with my roommates all night to do homework or prepare for the exam. I remember the day when the heating was made. I remember the first time I was in the cheerleading team, which was a gala held by the university – "World Hands in Hand." I remember that I was strolling in Harbin streets with my friends. I remember we went to the Ice and Snow World. I remember eating a

哈尔滨工业大学 / 塔蒂阿娜提供

有种亲切感。我在中国的生活非常丰富，一点儿也不单调。从第一天开始，我们开始上汉语课，课堂上老师们很少使用英语。由于我有一定的汉语基础，所以，老师说的话，我能知道个大概，但是大部分同学没有接触过汉语，所以课下我们开始互相帮助，互相学习。我以为我只会学习汉语，但这是一个非常错误的想法，因为我的班里有来自世界各地的外国人，因此，除了我们大家都说的英语以外，我还可以学习其他语言。这是一个真正难得和宝贵的机会。可以学习到不同国家的文化和语言。我们在一起努力地尝试了说我们国家的语言，因为不但很有趣，而且特别有用，这让我们更好地了解彼此之间完全不同的文化。

我记得大学校园外面，与我交谈过的中国人都对我能说一口流利的汉语感到非常吃惊。实际上，在中国学习了六个多月之后，我的汉语水平已经有了显著的提高。另外，我记得第一次坐地铁（因为我家乡的城市没有地铁）时的样子，由于不知道站名，坐错过好几次。我记得每天

bunch of delicious sugar-coated haws in the cold winter. I remember walking with friends in the campus at night, watching the beautiful scenery and listening to the rustling of trees, the ripples of water. I remember my classmates' first sight of snowflakes, sharing their joy and excitement. I remember when I went out from the dormitory in the morning, the wind pushed the snow into a snowpile. My classmates and I threw snowballs happily and they were almost late for class. I remember many new things, which seemed strange at first; The first time I used WeChat, shopped on Taobao and paied bill through swiping QR codes.

After living in China for six months, I realize how strong the country is and feel proud to have an opportunity to study here. For me, China is one of most developed countries in economics, with tremendous potential of scientific development. People live comfortably thanks to the rapid development. It seeks advanced science and technology and maintains historical relics. You can feel no arrogance from the country but the steadiness stemmed from its 5,000 years of history. It is really an admirable country.

哈尔滨工业大学 / 塔蒂阿娜提供

Finally, I want to express my deep love toward this land, people and culture. Only nine

晚上从宿舍房间的窗户看美丽的日落；我记得我和室友熬夜开通宵在一起做作业或准备考试；我记得供暖的那一天；我记得第一次参加啦啦队，那是在大学里举办的一个大型活动——“世界手牵手”晚会；我记得和朋友一起在哈尔滨的大街小巷逛街；我记得去冰雪大世界游玩；我记得在寒冷的冬天吃一串可口的糖葫芦；我记得晚上在校园里跟朋友散步，看着无限美丽的风光，听着树木沙沙作响，听着流水潺潺，特别美好！我记得我的同学第一次看到飘落雪花的神情，跟他们分享着喜悦和激动。我记得早上从宿舍出门时，风把雪推成了雪堆，我的同学们快乐地打雪仗，上课差点儿迟到。我记得一开始所有的东西看起来都很陌生，记得第一次学习怎么用微信，怎么在淘宝上购物，怎么用二维码付款。

在中国生活了六个月之后，我意识到这个国家多么强大，我为在这儿学习而感到自豪！对我而言，中国是当今经济最发达的大国之一，拥有巨大的科技潜力。经济发达，人们的生活简单而舒适；科技先进的同时又保留了历史遗产级的文化，但却感受不到她的骄傲，你能感受到的是她具有五千多年文化的沉稳，这是一个独具风格让人钦佩的国度。

哈尔滨工业大学 / 塔蒂阿娜提供

最后，我想再表达一下，我热爱这片土地，爱上了这里的文化和人民。大约九个月前，我无法想象我会跟中国人自由地用汉语交

months ago, I had no idea how to exchange with Chinese people. Things that seemed complicated and incomprehensible began to change into familiar ones. I can't wait to return to China again and continue my academic career, to discover this amazing country from different perspectives. China is a vast country with many fascinating places. Here you can enjoy the culture to keep pace with the times and appreciate the comfortable rhythm of life. I believe that studying in China is the best decision in my life. After only six months' study in China, I have gained invaluable experiences. I am very grateful to have this opportunity to "grow up" in China, to spend my youthood happily in Harbin and to witness the rapid development of this country and become a part of it.

哈尔滨平山 / 塔蒂阿娜摄

流，看起来很复杂和不可理解的东西慢慢地变了，变成了完全熟悉的样子。我等不及要再次回到中国，继续我的伟大前程，从不同的角度认识并发现这个神奇的国家。中国幅员辽阔，拥有众多让人神往的地方。在这里你可以一边感受与时俱进的文化，一边享受着舒适的生活节奏。我相信去中国留学是我一生中最好的决定，因为在中国住了仅六个月以后，我获得了无比宝贵的经验。我非常感谢有这个机会在中国“成长”，在哈尔滨幸福地度过青年时代，看着这个国家的快速发展，成为她的一部分。

唇齿留香，情暖心田
Delicious Food, Warm Love

［马来西亚］ 吕纯晶 北京中医药大学
[Malaysia] Lee Chun Ging, Beijing University of Chinese Medicine

What do you think of when somebody mention China? Is it the majestic Great Wall, or kebabs, pancakes, dumplings and other mouth-watering cuisine? For foreigners who arrived in China, they must be moved by the hospitable Chinese people, such as the amiable teachers, warm-hearted and friendly Chinese friends. Having studied at Beijing University of Chinese Medicine for eight years, I am no exception. In addition to the above-mentioned people, a number of vegetable vendors working at the Yuan Dynasty Capital City Relics Wall Park, Litianhong Market, which is north of the school, have gradually integrated into my life.

In the dormitories of international students, there is a shared space dedicated to students' cooking in spare time, which enables foreign students to showcase their cooking skills, enjoy home food to ease their homesickness. A female schoolmate from Malaysia introduced me the Litianhong Market, which has everything I wanted in cooking. During the past eight years, I became a regular visitor and made friends to many of these vegetable vendors. Many heart-warming stories have taken place at the market.

提到中国大家一般会联想到什么呢？是雄伟的长城，还是烤串、煎饼、饺子等令人垂涎三尺的美食呢？而身为外国友人来到异国他乡，想必会被热情好客的中国人感动，这些人可能包括和蔼可亲的老师、热心友善的中国朋友等。作为自 2011 年在北京中医药大学留学 8 年的我也不例外。除上述的人物外，在学校北面元大都遗址公园里有个利天弘市场，里面有一群可爱的菜商们在不知不觉中，融入了我在北京的生活。

在我们学校国际学院的宿舍里，有着专门供学生烹饪美食的共享空间，这让留学生们在闲暇时能一展厨艺，享用家乡美食，排解思乡之情。起初利天弘市场是一位马来西亚学姐介绍我去的，对于日常做饭的我来说，我甚是喜欢这百货齐全的菜市场。在北京的八年时间里，我也成为这里的常客，隔三岔五地出现在集市中，并在一来二往中与这些菜商们成了朋友，当中也发生不少温馨的故事。

“姑娘，来了呀！想吃什么随便挑啊。”这是我每次进入市场里面时，听到各档老板吆喝最多的“开场白”。当中有位专卖豆腐的大姐特别友善，经常会附送她自制的豆浆给我。品尝着无食品添加剂和糖类加工成的原味豆浆，除了满口香醇外，心里也甚是温暖。

吕纯晶在奥林匹克森林公园

"Girl, welcome! Whatever you want to eat, pick it." This are the opening remarks that I heard every time I entered the market. One of the vendors is an elder sister who sells tofu. She is very friendly, always gives me a cup of her homemade soy milk as a gift. Tasting the fragrant original-flavor soy milk without any food additives and sugar, my heart was melt.

The auntie who sells eggs also has her daughter, son-in-law and daughter-in-law working in the market. There are a wide variety of eggs sold here, from white to black, raw to pickled, small to large. Every time she will carefully check and clean the eggs, allow the customers to choose. I would like to pick a big one, hoping to get one with "double yolks." On a winter day, I bought a cart of vegetables, auntie's son-in-law rode a tricyle to take me to the dormitory. This is my first and only "special" experience.

Another time I wanted to cook Hot and Sour Soup, then went to the market to buy ingredients. Because it was the first time I made it, I asked advice from vendors, who were very warmhearted and gave me all kinds of vegetables. After returning to dormitory, I put different peppers into the pot to cook. Unfortunately, it turned out the soup was so strong that I caught a cold

北京中医药大学岐黄殿下晨读的中医学子 / 吕纯晶提供

卖鸡蛋的阿姨带着她的女儿、女婿和儿媳在市场里营业。这里卖的鸡蛋种类丰富，从白的到黑的、生的到腌的、个儿小的到大的，应有尽有。阿姨每次都会认真检查并清理鸡蛋，任顾客们自由挑选，像我就喜欢挑个儿大的来看是否有“双黄”的惊喜。记得在一个冬天，我买了满满的一车菜，阿姨的女婿就用三轮车送我到宿舍楼下。这是我第一次，也是唯一一次“特别”的体验。

还记得有一次我想煮酸辣汤，便到市场买食材。由于是初次做，便向各档的阿姨们请教具体做法及所需食材，没想到大家都没做过，但她们都非常热心，硬是把各种菜塞给我拿去煮，其中辣椒也送了好几种，红的、绿的、短的、长的皆有，结果回去煮酸辣汤的时候每样辣椒我都放了一点，吃完后不久就“上火”感冒了，真是难忘的“事故”啊！

每次去买菜时我会自备塑料袋，都是将用过的袋子清洗后重用。可能也是这个原因，每次购物时摊档的阿姨们都会将零头给我免除了，虽

after eating it. It is really an unforgettable "accident."

When purchasing vegetables, I use my own plastic bags, which I wash and reuse. Maybe for this reason, vendors always give me a small discount. Though a few cents each time is not that much, but the accumulation of changes is not a small number anymore. It moved me a lot. The money has little impact on me, but these aunties are making their money by selling vegetables day by day. Sometimes I insisted to pay them the money, they always refused to accept it. Sometimes I did not have enough money with me, they will say: "Never mind, you can pay it later."

Moreover, the most attractive places in the market are the colorful fruit stalls. Fruits are my favorites, ranging from the strawberries in spring, peaches in summer to grapes in autumn and oranges in winter. When eating the fruits of the season, I am longing for the ones from next season. I frequented to a fruit booth, whose products are both fresh and reasonable in prices. The auntie there is warm-hearted and would like to help me pick. When I buy strawberries, she will carefully check each one. She was really a trustworthy person.

The Chinese pronunciation for the year 2020 sounds like "Love You Love You." Meanwhile, such a lovely year was ruined by a sudden epidemic at the beginning. I am really proud of China for taking decisive measures to curb the epidemic effectively and quickly. Hope that the outbreak will end soon, I can return to Beijing to step on the land of China and experience the passion of Chinese people.

北京中医药大学的五老上书纪念雕像 / 吕纯晶提供

然每次的几毛钱对我来说不多，可是积少成多，累计几年下来也是一笔不小的数目。对此我挺感动的，也许这些钱对我而言影响不大，但阿姨们却是靠卖菜很不容易地一笔笔攒钱。有时硬要将钱给她们，她们却拒收给我塞了回来。有时我身上带的钱不够，阿姨们会说："随便拿想要的，钱的事儿以后再说吧。"

每次最吸引我的当数五彩缤纷的水果摊档。春天的草莓、夏天的桃子、秋天的葡萄、冬天的橙子，都让我吃着当季的水果，想着下一季的。我固定光顾的是一间水果既新鲜价格又合理的摊档，里面的阿姨很是热情，我每次买水果时阿姨都会帮忙挑选，尤其是买草莓时她会一颗一颗地精心挑选，让我非常信任。

2020 年，用中国话可理解为"爱你爱你"年，可这么美好的一年一开始就被疫情笼罩。看到中国采取果断的措施，有效、快捷地将疫情控制住，我心里真是为中国感到骄傲。希望疫情早日结束，我能再次回到北京探望，再次走在中国的土地上，感受那浓浓的人情味。

透过疫情看中国

Witnessing China's Arduous Fight Against COVID-19 Pandemic

[巴基斯坦] 伊森　西北大学

[Pakistan] Muhammad Ihsan, Northwest University

This year is the fourth year of my studying in Xi'an, China. Just before my graduation, the sudden outbreak of COVID-19 pandemic shocked the world. During the epidemic, I stayed in China and witnessed Chinese people's gallant fighting against the virus. It has become a special memory of me. In February and March, which was at the very height of the epidemic, I browsed online news and videos to learn about what was happening outside.

The person who impressed me most is a doctor named Zhong Nanshan. In his 80s, Zhong often appeared in the news at the beginning of the epidemic. I was told that he had retired, but he returned to work and arrived to hardest-hit Wuhan helping guiding the fight against COVID-19, a virus that he had never seen before. There was also a female doctor called Li Lanjuan. At the age of an old granny, she still takes vital tasks for the nation. Just like them, numerous medical workers rushed to Wuhan and Hubei Province bravely from their homes in other provinces to help save people's lives without thinking of remuneration and personal safety. In contrast, when the pandemic broke out in the United

这是我在中国西安留学的第四年，在即将毕业之际，震动全球的COVID-19疫情袭来了。疫情期间，由于留在中国，我看到了中国居民抗疫的过程，这成了我的一段特殊记忆。在最严重的时期——2月和3月，我通过网上新闻和视频了解外面发生的事情。

我印象最深的是一位名叫钟南山的医生，他已经80多岁了。在疫情刚开始的那段时间，他经常出现在新闻里。我了解到，他原本已经退休了，但因出现了疫情，他又重返工作岗位，来到了疫情严重的武汉，参与指导抗击COVID-19这个以前没有见过的敌人。还有一位李兰娟女医生，她的年龄看起来已是一位老奶奶了，但仍然承担了国家的重要任务。和他们一样还有许许多多的医护工作者，他们抛家舍业，不计报酬，无论生死，从中国各地来到湖北省和武汉市，拯救他们的同胞。所以当我看到美国暴发疫情的时候，纽约和其他地区缺乏医护人员，美国的政府不得不花很多钱聘请各地有经验的人来补充医院的医生和护士，我觉得我们的中国兄弟姐妹有非常强的奉献精神和道德责任感。

我还看到有一位做眼镜生意的中国男人，在疫情来袭后，他来到武

States, there was a shortage of medical staff in New York and other areas. The US government had to invest massively to hire experienced personnel from all over the country to assist doctors and nurses. I feel that the Chinese people have a strong sense of dedication and moral responsibility.

After the outbreak of COVID-19, a glasses merchant arrived at a hospital in Wuhan to repair goggles for medical workers. Because there was a lack of goggles in hospitals, he managed to find some stock products and swimming goggles and distributed them to medical workers for free.

In China, governments and doctors respect life. No one was given up treatment because of old age or insufficient medical resources. No one was left to die in despair. In some wealthy European countries, many patients failed to receive treatment but waited for their death at home. When I discussed this issue with my Chinese friends, they said that China has a socialist harmonious culture, in which nobody will be abandoned from the socialist family. This

西北大学 / 伊森提供

伊森

汉的一家医院，为医护工作者修理眼镜。那时，医院里缺少防护镜，这位生意人就想办法找到一些储存的产品和游泳镜，免费送给医生和护士们。

在中国，政府和医生都尊重生命，没有人因年老或医疗资源不够被放弃治疗，没有人被抛弃在绝望中等死。而在一些富有的欧洲国家，竟然有很多患者得不到诊治，只能在家等死。当我和我的中国朋友讨论这个问题的时候，中国朋友说，中国有着社会和谐的文化，中国的社会主义是一个大家庭，不会有任何一个人受到这个家庭的抛弃。这与我所了解的建立在优胜劣汰自然选择思想上的西方社会很不一样。

同时，我看到了许多的科学技术成果被应用到了抗疫的过程中。比如，当武汉的居民在家中隔离时，社区派出了有热成像设备的无人机隔着窗户为他们测量体温。在其他很多城市，无人机飞行在街道和广场上空提醒人们在外面戴好口罩。在医院里，医生们利用网络会议为病人远程会诊，在护士忙不过来时，送餐机器人会将食物送到不同楼层的病房里。

is very different from the Western society that is established on the basis of "survival of the fittest."

At the same time, I noticed that many technological achievements have been applied to the fight against the epidemic. For instance, when residents in Wuhan were quarantined at home, the community used drones with thermal imaging equipment on board to measure their temperatures through the window. In other cities, drones flew above streets and squares to remind people to wear facial masks. In the hospital, doctors use online meetings to conduct remote consultations for patients. When nurses are too busy to look after all the patients, the robots delivered food to the wards on different floors.

Professor Wang, my Chinese mentor, often told us, "Attitude decides success or failure." In my view, China has adopted a positive attitude towards epidemic control and prevention. While in some Western nations, which are economically developed with more advanced medical equipment, the losses and death tolls caused by the virus have far exceeded those of China. This is because their hesitation missed the best time to control the epidemic. When the lives of the people were under threat, they kept to argue for their "freedom" and were reluctant to suspend recreational activities.

After four years of study in China, I realized that China is a truly friendly country. Both my friends and I who are studying in China hope that China can play a greater role and make greater contributions to mankind after the end of the pandemic.

伊森

我的中国导师王教授经常对我们说："态度决定成败。"我认为中国对于控制疫情的态度非常积极，而不是像一些西方国家虽然很富有，有很好的医疗设备，但是病毒造成的死亡和损失远远超过了中国，这是因为他们的犹豫不决错过了控制病毒最好的时间，在生命受到威胁的时候，仍然在为他们说的"自由"而争吵，不愿意放弃娱乐。

四年的留学生活让我发现，中国是一个真正友好的国家。我和一起留学中国的朋友都希望在疫情结束后，中国能发挥更大的作用，为人类做更大的贡献。

邂逅中国，邂逅精彩
Encounter Splendid China

[津巴布韦] 将森甫 浙江科技学院
[Zimbabwe] Zhomwa Joseph Nyasha, Zhejiang University of Science and Technology

I came to China in the summer of 2019. During the past months, I have experienced a lot of things. From the day I stepped onto this soil, my experience is good enough to inspire those who have never been to the nation. I strongly believe that after reading this article, many people will learn a lot from the Chinese culture and its business logic.

I have planned to study in China long time ago, but failed after three years of endeavor. However, there is no such a word as "give up" in the dictionary of a brave man. God bless those who help themselves. Finally, my application was accepted. I'm very interested in studying abroad, especially in a country that attracts me a lot even before I went there. It was a fresh and cool day when I arrived at Hangzhou International Airport. I was immediately attracted by the grand but exquisite buildings of the airport, the bustling but orderly flow of people and the clear and melodious voices that I could not understand. I thought I was dreaming until a customs officer helped me count my luggage that I realized that I have arrived at the correct place. In my motherland, we seldom use buses as public transportation. Meanwhile, on the day I arrived in China, I realized the comfort of sitting on the bus among local

2019 年的夏天，我来到中国。在这短暂的时光里，我经历了很多，从我来到这片土地的那天起，我的经历足以鼓舞那些未曾到过中国的人。我强烈地相信，在读完这篇文章后，很多人将会从中国文化及其商业思维的中肯性和可信赖度中有所启发。

我很早就开始计划来中国，但前后尝试了三年多仍以失败告终。然而勇敢人士的原则是永不言弃，哪怕直到最后一秒钟，所幸皇天不负有心人，最终我通过了申请。我对去异域留学很感兴趣，尤其是一个在我没去之前就觉得很有魅力的国度。在一个清风徐拂，分外舒爽的日子，我到达了杭州国际机场，霎时间我被这机场广阔却不失精巧的结构，被熙熙攘攘却井然有序的人流，被那些听不懂但却清脆动人的各种声音所深深吸引。我甚至觉得自己是在做梦，直到一名海关工作人员帮我清点行李时，我才清醒地意识到自己到了该来的地方。在我的祖国，我们很少会使用大巴来当作公共交通工具，然而就在我到达的那一天，我体会到了坐在公交车上，坐在一个当地人旁边的舒适感。我难以忘记在我去学校的路上听到的第一句中文“你好”，亲切的招呼让我觉得我的到来是美好的，我体验到了被尊重的感觉，我清楚地知道了我来了一个所有肤色都会被尊重的国

passengers. I can't forget the first Chinese greeting word "hihao (hello)" I heard on my way to school. The kind greetings made me feel that my arrival was a beautiful start and I have experienced the dignity of being respected. I realized that I have come to a country where people of all skin colors would be respected. I received a welcome that everyone in the world would crave for. My first day in China is a "sexy and charming" memory for me.

China is a pluralistic country, which brings together people from all over the world. In China, people from different cultural backgrounds can choose cuisines that match their stomachs. In many countries, few people realize that China is a strong economy that is not only industrially prosperous, but also developed in agriculture. I also noticed that the country is also very strict in food safety and has adopted stringent safety standards. In China, I can enjoy every meal that is unique and delicious. People from other countries can also eat the delicacies from their own country. Undoubtedly, this is a land rich in fruits and vegetables that will shine through the global food culture.

I can't help but be attracted by the hard-working Chinese people, whose businesses are either small workshops or large-scale manufacturing enterprises, which contain their diligent sweat. I've read stories about Jack Ma, who led a group of people to establish Alibaba. It would be a great honor if one day I could see him face by face and hear him explain how e-commerce has brought success to him and Chinese people. Chinese people come up new ideas every day, and the way they conduct and create art goes far beyond my imagination. In business, I've learned a lot and I will use it to inspire young people in our country to emulate China's hard-working people.

The sudden outbreak of COVID-19 attacked the lovely and beautiful country without warning, but Chinese government has spared no effort to

家。我受到了这个世界上每个人都会渴望的欢迎。我不会忘记我第一天来到中国的经历，它对于我来说仍旧是一段性感而又迷人的记忆。

中国是一个多元化的国家，因为它几乎汇聚着从世界各国而来的人。在中国，有着不同文化背景的人们可以选择符合自己饮食习惯的食物。在许多国家，人们几乎没有意识到中国是一个强大的经济体，它不但在工业上繁荣，而且在农业领域也很发达。我还发现这个国家在食品安全方面也是很严格的，有着苛刻的安全标准。在这里我享受着独特而美味的每一餐，我可以吃到自己国家的主食，同时其他国家的人也可以在中国享受到来自他们故乡的食品，毫无疑问这是一片盛产蔬果且全球饮食文化大放异彩的土地。

我情不自禁地被勤劳的中国人民所吸引，他们做生意的方式无论是小规模作坊还是大型制造业，都蕴含着他们辛勤的史歌。我读过关于马云带领一群人创办阿里巴巴的故事，如果有一天我能亲眼见到他本人，能听到他解释电子商务是如何为他和中国人民带来成功的，这将会是一种无上的荣耀和珍贵的经历。我看到中国人每天都在脑海中构思着新的

浙江科技学院学生活动中心 / 将森甫提供

浙江科技学院西蜜湖 / 将森甫提供

ensure citizen's safety. The Chinese people have provided all the needed for the fighting against the epidemic free of charge, which deserves the respect from everyone. At present, China has become the first country suceed in curbing the spread of the virus thanks to the responsible national leaders, rescue personnel working at the front line, and every citizen who has showed tenacity, bravery and active response during the epidemic.

For the above reasons, I would like to visit more places in China to appreciate more landscape of lakes and hills and cultural relics in the future. China is the second hometown of me and many other international students. China is like a bowl of wine, fragrant and mellow, which one need to taste carefully. I also hope that I can have the honor to meet some of the top businessmen and scholars, meet my life's soulmate so as to secure my life direction in this peaceful, happy country. Thank you so much, China.

想法，他们建造和创造艺术的方式远远超出了我的想象力。在商业领域，我学到了很多，会将它发扬光大，以此激励我们国家的年轻人来学习效仿勤劳的中国人民。

虽然新冠肺炎疫情毫无预兆地袭击了这个可爱美丽的国家，但是中国政府竭尽全力确保着这片国土上每一个人的安全。中国人民为抗击疫情无偿提供了一切必要的救援，值得每个人尊重。目前中国已经成为第一个成功遏制病毒传播的国家，这取决于负责的国家领导人，每一位冲在一线的救护人员以及每一个在疫情期间表现出坚韧、勇敢、积极响应政府号召的公民。

鉴于这一切，我想在未来去游览中国更多的地方，去领略更多的湖光山色、人文名胜。中国是我和其他诸多留学生的第二故乡，值得我们珍惜，我们对中国的眷恋宛如一碗酒，又香又醇，需要细细品尝。我也希望通过我不断的积累能够有幸遇见一些顶级的商业和学术上的成功人士，遇到我人生的知音，在这和平幸福美满的国度找到我的人生方向。深深地感谢您，中国。

不同的家乡，同样的热爱
Different Hometown, Same Love

[柬埔寨] 陈春 浙江大学
[Cambodia] Chhun Chansovan, Zhejiang University

I believe that everyone will have moments of getting lost, being painful, confused, hungry or helpless. Compassionate people are always willing to give a hand to a stranger, because they know what it's like to be in trouble. Chinese people are characterized by the willingness to help strangers. I have had several such experiences in 2020.

A Motherly Madam

One day I went to a supermarket to buy a few daily necessities but ended up with too many goods in the shopping cart since there were many of my favorite brands. After paying the bill, I realized that I was all by myself and these goods were more than I could carry, and I had to hold some items to my chest with the left hand, and carry the rest with the right hand, and I must look very funny. At this moment, someone patted my shoulder, and a madam smiled at me and said that she could help me. Her kind appearance reminded me of my mother's smiling face, and I handed her the items in my right hand. She carried it and walked with me towards the place where I put my electric bicycle. On the

我相信每个人都有迷路、疼痛、迷茫、饥饿或需要别人帮助的经历。当然，有同情心的陌生人都会伸出援手来帮助我们，因为他们知道遇到麻烦是什么样的滋味。中国人乐于助人的特点尤其明显，仅在2020年里我就曾遇到过许多感人的故事。

热心的阿姨像妈妈一样

记得有一天，我本来打算去超市买一点日用品。因为那里有很多我喜欢的品牌产品，所以我买了很多。付账后，才意识到我是一个人来的，可能拿不下这么多东西，于是我只好用左手把一些东西抱在胸前，剩下的一些拿在右手上，看起来很搞笑。正在这时我感觉有人拍了我的肩膀，这是一位阿姨，微笑着告诉我，她可以帮我。看着她亲切的样子，不知为什么我的脑子里忽然闪过妈妈的笑脸，我很自然把手里的东西给了她。她接过来一路提着，还慢声细语地叮咛，一次别买太多，注意保质期什么的，直到我停电动车的地方，还送了我一个帆布包装这些东西。道别的时候，我才回过神来，我的妈妈在柬埔寨呢！此时，我的心里涌出的不是淡淡的失落，而是身在异乡的暖暖的母爱，感谢您！像妈妈一样的

way she told me gently not to buy too much at a time and to pay attention to the expiration date, then gave me a canvas bag for these goods. It's not until we bid goodbye that I realized that my mother was still in Cambodia! At that moment, I felt motherly love in a foreign country rather than a sense of loss. Thank you, a motherly madam!

A Memory of Kindness

One day, it suddenly rained heavily when I was window shopping on Wulin Road near the West Lake, and I got soaked immediately since I didn't have an umbrella with me or have time to find a shelter. A passerby noticed and waved towards me and let me to take shelter from the rain at his porch. He offered me his chair and a cup of hot tea and said, "Have some tea! Be careful of the cold." Chinese people are just so kind! Without a word, I memorized their kindness in my heart. I love this country, and these moments stored in my heart are the seeds of love!

"Motorbike Man" of China

A few months ago, I went to Rui'an and worked as a Sino-Cambodian interpreter. After the work, it got dark, and the high-speed train I would take to Hangzhou was about to leave within only one hour left. I had waited for a taxi but couldn't find one for a long time. Then an old man on a motorbike nearby happened to notice my anxiety and nervousness with a pale face. He asked me what is the matter. Learning my situation, he immediately said to me, "Get on and I will take you to the railway station." I was extremely happy. What moved me most was that he rode the motorbike as flying to catch up with the train. Finally, we made it. I was so grateful of his help and insisted to pay him, but he

陌生阿姨。

一念善举记心间

有一天，我在西湖武林路逛街，突然天降大雨，当时我没带雨伞。来不及避雨，我就被这片刻间倾盆的大雨浇成了落汤鸡。一个路人发现我的窘境，便向我招手让我到他的门廊下躲雨。他不仅把椅子让给我坐，还给我倒一杯热茶，说："快喝了吧！别受凉了。"这让我看到中国人有多善良啊！我默默地记在心里，我热爱这片异乡的土地，这些收藏在我心里的点滴记忆都是爱的种子啊！

大爷，您是中国的"摩托侠"

几个月前，我去了瑞安市当中柬口译员。办完事，天也快要黑了，只剩一个小时我返回杭州的高铁也要开了。哪成想我等了半天出租车，连个影子都没有。这时在我旁边有一位坐在摩托车上的老人碰巧看到了这一幕。他发现我忐忑不安，束手无策，又着急又紧张，脸色也变得苍白。他热心

浙江大学 / 陈春提供

陈春

just smiled, shook his head and waved away.

There are so more touching tales in China that are shocking, changing, inspiring and reshaping me. Even though I couldn't repay all of them, I swear that I will help others if I have a chance, because I know what gratitude means. I also want to encourage you to join me – whenever a stranger helps you, you then help two persons in return. In the end one kind action will inspire countless kind actions. In my days of studying in China, I have a special feeling, "Although I am a foreigner, I've never been an outsider." Because a sentence is always in my mind, "Different hometown, same love."

地问我怎么回事，我告诉他我的具体情况。他马上说："上车来，我送你去火车站。"这时候我开心极了。最令我感动的是他因为怕我赶不上高铁，把摩托车开得飞一样快。最后，我终于到了火车站，谢天谢地赶得上高铁。我向他万分道谢，并再三表示给他钱来表达我的感激，他只是微微一笑，摇摇头就招手离开了。

浙江大学 / 陈春提供

在中国这片热土上发生了太多感人的故事，震撼着我，改变着我，启发着我，重塑着我。即使我无法回报他们，但我发誓以后一旦有机会，我就去帮助其他人，因为我懂了什么是知恩图报。我也想邀请大家跟我一起试着这样做：每当有陌生人帮助你时，你就主动帮助两个人作为回报。一次善举将会激发无数次善举。在中国留学的这段日子，我有一种特殊的感觉："虽然我是外国人，但我不是外人。"因为我的心里总是涌动着这句话：不同的家乡，同样的热爱。

停课不停学，隔离不隔爱

Suspend Schools but not Study, Isolate People but not Love

[俄罗斯] 夏旋 东北师范大学

[Russia] Ipatenkova Yulia, Northeast Normal University

On the train back home for the Spring Festival in January, I learned of the outbreak of the epidemic and my heart was overshadowed by unease. With the spread of the epidemic, I saw that the Chinese people put down the warm and sweet bowls and chopsticks of the New Year's Eve, bade farewell to their families and rushed to the front. When the world was enjoying comfort, countless "heroes in harm's way" chose to leave their families and went all out to contribute to the health and well-being of the people. The process of "fighting-epidemic" was arduous and required the participation of all people. All Chinese people quarantined themselves at home during the Spring Festival, which bought valuable time for the world epidemic prevention work.

On the third day of the Chinese Lunar New year, I flew back to my hometown. On the way to the airport, I saw more and more strict inspection and more and more epidemic prevention work. When the self-managing awareness became the norm, China was bound to overcome the epidemic soon. This epidemic has made me see clearly and thoroughly some matters,

回想 1 月回家过年，火车上得知疫情的出现，平添了很多不安。随着疫情的蔓延，我看到中国人在浓厚的年味下，放下除夕的碗筷，告别家人，奔赴前线。当世界正在享受安逸时，中国已经有了无数的“逆行者”选择离开自己的家人，全力以赴为人民健康和幸福奉献。抗疫的过程是艰苦的，是需要全民参与的，春节期间中国全民在家自主隔离，为世界防疫工作争取了宝贵的时间。

大年初三我坐飞机回家乡，去机场的路上我看到了越来越严格的检查与越来越多的防疫工作。当自主意识成为常态化，中国必然会很快战胜疫情。这次疫情也让我看清、看透了一些事，让我感受到常说的理想信念，体会到疫情考验下的制度优越性。

停课不停学，不仅是学习方式，更是学习态度。回到家的时候才逐渐明白，情况并非如我想象的那么简单，学校时刻都在关注我们的健康，及时向我们通报疫情发展及安排。春季学期不能按时开学，作为一名博士研究生，不能回到学校学习，没有同学和导师，知识怎么学？科研怎么做？这成为我最主要思考的问题。疫情下，在中国多年的学习环境让

understand the oft-told ideals and beliefs, and realize the superiority of the system under the test of the epidemic.

Suspending schools but not suspending study is not merely a way of learning, but also an attitude of learning. When I got home, I gradually realized that the situation was not as simple as I had thought. The college was always concerned about our health and kept us informed of the development of the epidemic and the arrangements in a timely manner. Spring semester would not start on time. As a doctoral student, not being able to go back to school, and without classmates and the supervisor, how should I study? How to do scientific research? These had become the most important questions for me. After years of study in China, I didn't know how to start in Russia. When I was hesitating, China's Ministry of Education immediately responded, advocating "suspending schools but not study" and guiding students to study independently at home through online platforms and live videos. Scientific research platforms and databases were opened to the public for free. Special time, special care. During the period of perfecting my doctoral thesis, I deeply felt the positive impact of Chinese efficiency on emergencies. Smooth transition from "offline" to "online" teaching took effect in a short period of time. The state also supported the development of free communication and collaborative software, such as "Ding Talk", to ensure the stability of online platforms. Since then, the weekly offline academic discussions of our study team have also been "upgraded". Online research and discussion were positive, effective and adaptable. The key to systematic change lied after all in the people, the learning attitude of the students and the way of teaching of the supervisor. Interactive development and common adaptation broke down the barriers of time and space. I was able

东北师范大学 / 夏旋提供

我回到俄罗斯以后不知从何下手。犹豫之际，中国教育部马上就有了回应，主张“停课不停学”，通过网络平台、视频直播引导学生在家自主学习。开放科研平台、数据库，特殊时期，特殊关怀。在完善博士论文期间，我深刻感受到中国效率在处理突发事件上的积极影响，短时间内能顺利做到从“线下”到“线上”教学的转变。国家还支持开发免费沟通和协同软件如“钉钉”，确保网络平台的稳定工作。自此，我们学习团队每周的线下研讨也“升级了”。线上研讨积极有效，适应性强。系统设备的转变关键还是在人，在学生的学习态度，在导师的授课思维。做到交互发展，共同适应，打破了时间空间的壁垒，我以这种方式与导师和学弟学妹“见面”。互相学习是一件非常幸福的事，在疫情的考验下，形式虽然变了，但是“质”和“量”绝对没有变。

隔离不隔爱，不仅是处理方法，更是大国担当。随着疫情全球化的蔓延，俄罗斯也开始采取相应的防控措施。生活变得不一样，但却又一

to "meet" my supervisor and the younger brothers and sisters in this way. It was a very happy thing to learn from each other. Under the test of the epidemic, although form has changed, "quality" and "quantity" have never changed at all.

Isolating the people but not isolating love is not only a solution, but also the responsibility of a big country. With the spread of the epidemic in the whole world, Russia also began to take corresponding prevention and control measures. Life became different, but seemed the same as well, as if I were holding on together with my relatives and friends in China. We were at home, and you were also at home, constantly extending warm greetings and care to each other, which made me feel the genuine affection and tenderness in distant Russia. Distance made us closer. I was also once a "cloud supervisor" who followed the construction of Mobile Hospitals on the internet. I saw and felt the greatness of China and the Chinese people in the control of the epidemic. China mobilized the people of the whole country to act in unison in a very short period of time to curb the development of the epidemic, assuming the responsibility to the people in their own country as well as other countries, which embodied the sense of responsibility of a great power.

In the common test, we saw the decline of lives and the brilliance of human nature as well. It is already six months, and I miss my relatives and friends in China very much. Spring will come eventually. The epidemic has changed our way of life. Perhaps we are now thousands of miles apart, but we are ties and friends closely connected with China. What remains unchanged is friendship and determination. In the face of the epidemic, we are firm in confidence and will overcome the difficulties together!

东北师范大学 / 夏旋提供

样，仿佛我在同中国的亲朋共同坚持。我们也在家，你们也在家，不断的是温暖的问候与暖心的关怀。这让我在遥远的俄罗斯感受到真情和温柔，距离反而让我们变得更近。我也曾是一名在网络上关注方舱医院建设的“云监工”。控制疫情时我看到也感受到中国和中国人民的伟大，在非常短的时间内能让全国人民统一行动，控制疫情的发展，对自己的国家，也对其他国家的人民担起了责任，体现了大国的担当精神。

经历过共同的考验，我们看到生命的凋零，也看到人性的光辉。六个月了，我很想念我在中国的亲人，想念我在中国的生活。春天终将会到来，疫情改变了我们的生活方式，或许现在远隔万里，但我们是纽带，是与中国紧密相连的朋友。不变的是情谊与决心，面对疫情，我们坚定信心，共克难关！

我的爱豆叫阿中
My Idol Is Called Brother Zhong

［越南］ 阮氏秋恒　贵州大学
[Vietnam] Nguyễn Thị Thu Hằng, Guizhou University

There is an idol called Brother Zhong and he has more than 1.4 billion fans.

In my heart—

He is both soft and tough, modern and traditional;

He has great views on his lands with grand mountains and beautiful historical relics. You can enjoy on his lands both the blossom of oriental cherries in spring and the yellow ginkgo leaves in autumn.

He can also recite traditional poems and play musical instrument for you to feel his inborn romance.

He is an amazing cook. Even if you have a picky appetite, you will still enjoy his various delicious food.

He is powerful, excellent in many aspects such as science, economics and education.

When I got the opportunity to come close to him, my happiness was beyond words.

Then who is Brother Zhong?

Brother Zhong is the nickname for China by the young people for their

有一个爱豆名字叫阿中哥，拥有了 14 亿多粉丝。

在我的心里——

他是个温柔中带着刚强，传统中带着现代的人；

他拥有大好河山，可以带你去享受名胜古迹的美丽，看春天的樱花盛开，赏秋天的银杏满地；

他还可以吟古诗，弹琴给你听，让你感受那份骨子里的浪漫；

他的厨艺惊人，让我相信就算你是个非常挑食的人，也会被他的美食吸引；

他的实力强大，不管是科学、经济、教育……哪个方面都很优秀；

能有机会来到他的身边，我说不尽我有多幸福。

那阿中哥到底是谁呢？

阿中哥其实是中国年轻人对祖国的昵称。在中国，不要怀疑这个称呼是否缺少礼貌，因为中国人民对祖国都特别亲切，没有什么距离。这样的称呼，让我感受到，在中国，人与人之间的关系很好，他们对生活充满爱。这份爱时时刻刻都在彼此之间传递着。告别故国，踏上异国留学的我，幸亏被这样的热情与相爱所拥抱，才不觉得孤单，才能让我安

motherland. In China, don't doubt if this nickname is impolite for a nation. Chinese people have a sense of warmth to their motherland, close and intimate. This nickname makes me feel the love and warmth between people in China. They love each other and convey their love all the time. Far away from my home country, I am embraced by their enthusiasm and love. This makes me feel not lonely anymore and be engaged in my study. This warmth and love are especially moving when I am in difficulty.

I recalled the day when I met across a security guard on my way to the back door of my university picking up my deliveries during the pandemic.

Hi, do you speak Chinese?

Yes, I do.

That's nice. I have been thinking that foreign students in the Western campus cannot speak Chinese.

That's how we started our conversation. We talked while walked.

He told me to take care of myself and study well. He mentioned that

贵州大学阅湖 / 阮氏秋恒摄

贵州大学图书馆 / 阮氏秋恒摄

心地学习。而且，在困难的时候，这份爱更令人感动。

还记得疫情期间的寒假去学校后门取包裹，路遇一个保安叔叔：

——同学，你会说汉语吗？

——我会的。

——那就好，我以为住在西校区的留学生不会讲中文呢。

……

就这样，我跟那位保安叔叔因为正好同路，就一起走了一段。

他贴心地告诉我要照顾好自己，努力把中文学好，以后可以回国当翻译，如果可以在大使馆工作那更好。因为这样对促进两国关系发展有大的帮助。当我们提到新型冠状病毒，我感叹中国政府对抗击疫情的举措做得非常好！如果是在别的国家发生，不敢想象后果是什么样。我在贵大被老师和宿管阿姨们照顾得很好。当他听我说了这些以后，非常有自豪感！

每个相遇都是最好的安排。我遇见的中国人，都是如此善良。

我也不知道学校的老师们为了我们失眠了多少个夜晚，每天都有人

maybe after graduation I could be an interpreter, or even better to work in the embassy, which would be greatly helpful to promote the friendship between China and Vietnam. When we talked about the Covid-19 pandemic, I told him how impressive and admiring I was for what the Chinese government had done. If this happened in other countries, I could not imagine what would happen next. Our teachers and apartment assistants had done an amazing job to protect us from the pandemic. He was very proud hearing my experience.

Every encounter is a God's arrangement. Every Chinese I met is kind and warm.

I did not know how many sleepless nights our teachers had been gone through to keep us safe. Every day someone was on duty and there were always someone performing sterilization and spreading knowledge about virus prevention, even in Spring Festival - the most important festival in China!

"Your teachers are always available. Any problem, don't hesitate to come to us for help. "

"Hope all of you are healthy. You can come to the Psychology Center to relax."

"I will not go back to my hometown for the Spring Festival since I will be on duty in the university. You must be missing your family. Just stick to your dream a bit longer, study hard and you can find a nice job after graduation."

"I will always be ready to help and you can find me all the time in the first floor of the apartment. If you need any help, come to us any time and I am always ready."

Delivery men are also great. Without their service, we will be having more troubles in daily life.

Our health and safety is put in the first priority in their minds. No matter how tired they were and how troublesome the tasks, they had been trying their

值班，每天都有人做好消毒与普及预防知识的工作，即便在春节——这个中国最重要的节日。

“有老师在，同学们有任何问题都请及时告诉老师。”

“你们都健康就好，同学们也可以去心理咨询中心放松一下。”

“叔叔今年不回家，留校值班。你们应该很想家了吧，坚持一下，好好学习，以后回国可以找到满意的工作。”

“阿姨一直在宿舍一楼，大家需要帮忙可以随时找阿姨。”

在我心中，快递小哥也是伟大的，这段时间如果没有他们，我们的生活将会遇到很多麻烦。

……

可以说，在他们的心中，我们的安全、平安是第一位的，他们不管有多累，有多烦恼，也会为我们而付出到底，这让我知道了什么是中国人的责任感！

不知不觉 2020 年已经过半了，虽然依旧在学校，哪里都不能去，

樱花下的贵州大学 / 阮氏秋恒摄

utmost to keep us safe and healthy. This made me get to know how responsible Chinese were!

The year 2020 has passed more than a half. Though still stuck in the university, I go through every corner of the university and record all of its beauty using my phone camera. Sometimes I walk casually under moonlight and sometimes sit on the grasslands besides lakes enjoying summer breeze. No one can see what has happened in 2020 from my life. However, I know deep from my heart, "there is no peace and happy life without the sacrifice of heroes who carry burdens for us." It is no doubt that behind my carefree life is the strongest shoulder I am relying on - China.

Mum, I want to tell you, Brother Zhong does and will protect your daughter well and don't worry.

Today there is bright sunshine outside and the magnolia flowers are in full blossom. I will go outside and take pictures now.

但我却可以跑遍学校的每个角落，用手机把美好的瞬间拍下来，偶尔在月光下悠闲地散步，偶尔会坐在湖边的草地上享受夏天的风。从我身上，也许没有人可以看出2020年发生了什么。但我知道，“哪有什么岁月静好，只不过有人替你负重前行”，我能像现在这样的无忧无虑，毫无疑问，背后是强大的依靠——中国。

妈妈，我想对您说，阿中哥会照顾好您的女儿，您放心吧！

今天的阳光特别好，学校的木兰都开花了，我要去拍照啦！

2020，在抗疫中前行

2020 Records Progress and Victory in Battle Against Pandemic

［哈萨克斯坦］ 文武 上海大学

[Kazakhstan] Bayanbayev Ilyas, Shanghai University

I believe, for many people, the memory of the outbreak of COVID-19 during the 2020 Chinese New Year festival will last a lifetime. We are all in this together. It is everyone's campaign to control and prevent the pandemic. No one is an "outsider," nothing is "none of your business." The pandemic has brought traumas to many families and affected the world economy. As an ordinary foreign student who has witnessed the pandemic in China, I would like share with you all with what I saw, heard and felt.

In January, Chinese and international media spontaneously covered the infectious disease that broke out in Wuhan. At that time, people did not know if the new virus was SARS or not. They were uncertain about its "human-to-human transmission", for the virus seemed like something we saw in a movie or in a computer game. Foreign netizens joked about it, they failed to understand the impact it would bring us all.

At the same time, the coronavirus pandemic started to spread all across China. Control measures escalated accordingly. Living in China as a foreign

相信2020年的春节，新冠肺炎疫情的突然袭来让很多人终生难忘。在疫情防控的当下，没有谁是“局外人”，也没有事是“分外事”。这一特殊的事件给很多家庭带来了创伤，也给世界经济造成了一定的影响。作为目睹疫情的一位普通外国留学生，我希望通过这篇文章分享自己的所见、所闻、所感。

2020年1月，中国和国外的媒体都不约而同地报道了武汉发现的传染病，那时的人们还不知道这个新的病毒到底是不是SARS，到底会不会“人传人”，因为病毒似乎是我们在电影或者电脑游戏里常见的东西。国外网民还曾就这件事开玩笑，不理解它可能带来的深远影响。

与此同时，新冠肺炎疫情开始在中国各地迅速蔓延。在中国留学的我也在第一时间感受到了疫情对国内生活的影响。幸好在老师和同学的帮助下，我提前备好了口罩和酒精，才安下心来。

在医学专家确认新型冠状病毒可以通过人与人之间传染之后，中国政府和世卫组织开始采取相应的措施——“封城”来控制疫情的发展。

“2020的庚子春节，疫情打乱了所有人的生活节奏。街道上看不见

student, I could feel the impacts the pandemic was putting on life. Thanks to the help of our teachers and classmates, I stocked some masks and alcohol for disinfection, and then I felt less anxious.

Medical experts later confirmed the human-to-human transmission of the coronavirus. In response, the Chinese government and World Health Organization took some relevant measures including "city lockdown" to control the spread of the pandemic.

"During the 2020 Chinese New Year break, the pandemic disrupted the pace of life for everyone. Streets were almost empty with very few pedestrians and vehicles. People wore facial masks and kept social distance, their eyes on alert. In Shanghai, the pandemic took heavy toll on the third industry. Since people dared not venture out for partying and gathering, many shops and restaurants were closed, out of business." – This is the voiceover I wrote for a short video I made on the pandemic and its affect on people's life.

There were some unstable elements in the society and rumors were spreading across the Internet. These noises, although hard to believe, were disturbing people's mind. I believed at that moment the government could monitor all channels of information so as to help people tell the true from the false. My university did play a big role in this respect. Wasting no time, the head teacher set up a WeChat group to include all foreign students in the class. Latest developments of the pandemic were shared in the group to bring us up to date on the COVID-19 pandemic and strengthen our confidence in defeating the pandemic.

As the pandemic spread across China and beyond, more and more countries started to evacuate their nationals in China. My country Kazakhstan's embassy in Beijing also advised its nationals to take a charter plane to return home. After

上海大学钱伟长图书馆 / 文武提供

熙熙攘攘的人群和车水马龙的繁忙，行色匆匆的人们都面戴口罩、眼神中增加了戒备和疏离。在上海，致命的疫情给第三产业带来了沉重打击，因为大家都不敢出门、不再聚会，很多店铺、餐厅纷纷闭门谢客，停止营业。”——这是我为疫情制作的短视频所写的“台词”，描写了当时的生活状态。

当时社会情况确实出现了一些不稳定的因素，网上流传着一些谣言，虽让人难以置信，但还是很影响人的心态。我相信在这个时候，政府可以监管所有的信息渠道帮助人们辨明事实真相。学校也在这方面发挥了很大作用。比如，班主任迅速建立了外国留学生的微信沟通群，在群里及时发布最新疫情状况，帮助大家了解这个新的病毒，增加大家战胜疫情的信心。

随着国内外疫情局势的发展，越来越多的国家开始撤侨。我的祖国哈萨克斯坦大使馆也建议同胞乘坐包机返回祖国。我在和父母商量后，觉得没必要动身回国，只要严格按照中国政府建议的防护要求，勤洗手、多通风、少出门、少聚会、戴口罩，我相信中国人民一定会取得抗疫的

discussions with my parents, I believed there was no need for me to do so. As long as we strictly followed the Chinese government' advice to take prevention measures (wash hands frequently, keep the room ventilated, go out less, attend fewer gatherings and wear masks), I believe, Chinese people could finally succeed in defeating the pandemic and life would soon return to normal as before.

As expected, within just two months, the Chinese government took swift decisions, commanded unified fight, deployed national resources and mobilized the whole society to launch a super-scale public health safeguarding campaign. Thanks to the swift deployment and general mobilization of the people, the pandemic was effectively controlled in China, with daily confirmed cases on a decline. In a foreign country, it usually takes years to build a hospital, however in just 10 days China built a 1,000-bed hospital in Wuhan. The Chinese government has made greatest nationwide efforts to fight against the pandemic, not only to save lives of Chinese people, but also to contain the spread of the pandemic so as to save lives in the rest of the world. As the world closely watched on, heart-touching stories of Chinese people making unselfish sacrifices to help control and prevent the pandemic became widely known. The credibility of the Chinese government in prevention and control of the pandemic was remarkably enhanced accordingly.

The success in control and prevention of the pandemic lies not only in the governance capability of the Chinese government, but also in the solidarity and sense of responsibility in the hearts of Chinese people. We all have heard stories of medical teams and professionals braving their way to Wuhan, they were truly heroes in harm's way. Actually there were many people around us who silently made contributions and unselfishly helped others, among them were my teachers and classmates and

最后胜利，生活很快就会恢复到从前的状态。

果然，短短两个多月的时间里，中国政府迅速决策、统一指挥部署、全社会动员，展开了一场超大规模的公共卫生维护行动。凭借着快速部署与全民动员，中国的疫情得到了很好的控制，确诊人数每天都在下降。在国外，建成一座医院要用几年时间，而武汉仅用 10 天就建造了一座拥有 1000 张病床的医院。中国政府举全国之力去抗击这场疫情，不仅仅是为了中国人民的安全，也是为了阻止疫情蔓延，保护世界上其他国家的安全。那些为防控疫情而无私奉献的故事一瞬间就在全世界变得家喻户晓，也提高了中国政府在防控疫情方面的公信力。

防控疫情的成功不但在于政府的治理能力，更在于中国人心中的团结信念和责任感。大家都听说过前赴后继去武汉的医疗队和抗疫勇士的故事，其实我们自己身边也有很多默默付出、舍己为公的人，包括我的

上海大学教学楼 / 文武提供

other Chinese students who volunteered to buy daily necessities online for foreign students locked on campus and had the purchases delivered at their doorsteps. At the beginning of the pandemic, there was a shortage of facial masks in China. Alumni abroad were mobilized to buy masks and send them to China to be donated to their universities and their younger alumni on campus.

For students who lived outside the campus like me, they were unable to work as volunteers on campus, nevertheless they proactively cooperated with the prevention and control work of the pandemic. We handed in our "daily report" every single day online, which recorded individual health conditions and latest itinerary. We showed a special permit to leave and enter the residential compound where we lived, had our temperatures scanned in public areas, washed our hands with disinfectant and wore masks. These had become the new norms of our daily life. In February I shot a video to capture how an average Shanghai resident complied with the government rules during the pandemic. When my family and overseas friends watched this video, they were shocked because at that time they had not yet experienced what life would like during the pandemic. Later on, more and more countries learned from China's successful anti-pandemic experience. China became a role model.

Several weeks ago, I attended an online seminar with the theme of "The Advantage of the Chinese System in Governing a Major Pandemic". The seminar believed China's phased victory in the battle against the coronavirus pandemic depended on its unique state system capable of launching swift and large scale nationwide actions, including the central leadership of the ruling party and the power of mobilizing and deploying nationwide resources to address great challenges and achieve victories. I think only through this kind of "big test" can

文武

老师和同学们。还有的中国同学主动当志愿者，帮助不方便出校门的外国同学网购生活必需品并快递给他们。疫情初期，当中国国内口罩奇缺的时候，身在国外的同学还自发组织起来，积极购买口罩，寄回国内捐助学校和同学。

更多像我一样住在校外的同学，虽然没办法在校园内做志愿者，也用自己的实际行动配合防疫工作。大家每天在线提交“每日报告”，在线记录自己的健康状态以及最近的行程。每天凭出入证进出小区、在公共场所量体温、用抗菌洗手液洗手、戴口罩等，这些都成为我们生活的常规。2020 年 2 月，我拍了一个视频，通过短视频反映了疫情期间的上海，每一位普通市民是如何遵守这些规定的。我的家人和外国朋友看到视频的时候都感到很惊讶，因为当时他们还没有真切感受到抗疫时期的生活。后来，中国人的抗疫经验成为许多国家纷纷效仿

we see the real advantage of the state system of China, a country with its own unique national conditions and anti-pandemic practices.

The pandemic did not affect our studies. The university was proactively restoring the teaching orders with online courses being launched step by step. It took some time for the teachers and students to adjust themselves to online courses. The truth was the online courses successfully replaced the face-to-face teaching. They worked.

I gradually got used to online courses, and I felt online study demonstrated a favorable comparison with teaching in the classroom, and in some ways, it provided us a new way of thinking. And the teachers well understood the challenges the students encountered, so they adjusted the timing of the online courses and deadlines for handing in their homework to help students in different time zones. If some students still had problems with the Internet or others, the teachers would opt for other way of teaching. Our teachers could even fix up the experiment classes. Since we could not use the professional equipment in the lab, the teachers instructed us to use some simulation apps which perfectly demonstrated the steps and result of the experiment. I believed these new exploration effects paved the way for broader perspective of online education.

Above are what I heard and seen as a foreign student in China. My sincere thanks to our Chinese teachers and classmates for their selfless help, with which I smoothly survived the test of this aggressive pandemic. Through this pandemic, I firmly believed when faced with a common enemy, the world people must work together in solidarity so as to defeat the virus. As a foreign student living and working in China, I truly acknowledge the truthfulness of "Breathe the Same Air and Share the Same Fate", and I am even more soberly

上海大学溯园 / 文武提供

的榜样。

几周前，我参加了一个在线讲座，报告的主题是“重大疫情治理下的中国制度优势”，报告认为中国人民抗疫的阶段性胜利在于其速度快、规模大，以及独一无二的制度优势，包括执政党的集中统一领导、集中力量办大事的举国体制等。我觉得，只有通过这种“大考验”才能够透过中国的特殊国情和抗疫实践看到制度带来的真正优势。

疫情也没能影响到我们的学习。学校也在积极恢复教学秩序，循序渐进地开展在线教学工作。虽然让老师和同学们适应了一段时间，但不可否认在线教学成功代替了面对面授课。

我也慢慢地习惯了在线上课，甚至觉得比起在课堂上面对面授课，在线学习毫不逊色，一样完备充实，甚至在某些方面还能提供学习的新思路。老师们也能体谅同学们碰到的困难，调整上课和作业截止时间来帮助有时差的人，如果有同学依然存在网络或其他问题，老师还

aware of the fact that only when we seriously understand and cooperate with the government's requirements for prevention and control of the pandemic can we finally prevent the invasion of the virus and make progress and move forward in the battle against the pandemic.

会通过别的方式进行授课。即使是实验课，老师依然想办法帮我们解决无法使用学校各种专业设备的问题，指导我们使用仿真软件进行实验，完美地达到了实验目的。相信这些探索能给在线教育打开更广阔的发展空间。

以上就是我作为一位外国留学生在疫情期间的真实见闻感受。衷心感谢老师和中国同学提供的无私帮助，让我顺利通过这场来势汹汹的疫情的考验。通过这场疫情，我也深切地感受到，面对共同灾难之时，世界人民需要团结合作才能战胜病魔。作为在中国生活学习的外国留学生，我们更深刻地体会到什么才是“同呼吸、共命运”，更清醒地认识到只有认真了解、配合政府疫情防控要求，才能防止病毒的侵害，并在抗疫中前行！

相思湖畔浅浅忆
Lakeside Memory

［越南］ 黎氏浅　广西民族大学
[Vietnam] Lê Thị Thiển, Guangxi University for Nationalities

It has always been my dream to "learn Chinese well and walk across China". Cherishing this dream, I picked up Chinese as my major when I attended college. Last September when I learned I could study for one year at Guangxi University for Nationalities as an exchange student, I was so thrilled. Happiness descended on me all of a sudden and I was so excited to start my journey in China. I trust it would be a beautiful encounter.

When I just arrived, I was excited and thrilled. However, in a new environment I naturally had some fears. The campus is so large. In the morning it was hard for me to follow the right path to go to the classroom. My largest headache was I could not make head or tail of what the canteen menus said. I was dazzled by these Chinese dish names. At that time, I had no courage to communicate with Chinese because I feared they could not understand my poor Chinese pronunciation. And I also feared that some bad guys might take advantage of me if I spoke poor Chinese. In a word, at that time I felt anxiety. But when I got the courage up to communicate with Chinese, all my worries evaporated. Chinese people are very enthusiastic. Whenever I was not sure of

“学好汉语，走遍中国”一直是我的梦想。怀着这样的梦想，大学时我毫不犹豫选择了中文专业。2019 年 9 月，得知可以作为交换生到广西民族大学留学一年，我真是兴奋不已。没想到幸福来临得这么突然，我终于也可以和中国来一次美丽的“邂逅”了。

我刚到中国的时候既兴奋又激动，但是在一个陌生的环境生活总还是会有一些恐惧感。校园很大，早上去上课时不知道要走哪条路，最让我头疼的一件事就是食堂菜单上的菜名很多我都看不懂，看着看着就眼花缭乱了。那时我还没有勇气跟中国人交流，怕自己的汉语发音不好他们会听不懂，也担心会因为汉语说不好而遇到坏人，所以在那一段时间里，我有些焦虑。但是当我鼓起勇气开始跟中国人交流的时候，我才发现自己真是杞人忧天。中国人都很热情，每次去吃饭不知道那些菜的特点时，他们都会很耐心给我们介绍；如果不小心迷路了，随便问一个行人，他都会很热情地告诉你怎么走，完全不用害怕和焦虑。就这样我每天都有收获，生活过得充实又有趣。

广西民族大学是一个非常美丽的学校，我每天都能发现它不同的美。学校的建筑，既有中国传统的雅致风格，也有壮乡的民族特色，还令人意

what to order at the canteen, they would patiently introduce the food to me. When I got lost in the street, whoever I asked for help would enthusiastically tell me the right direction. No fear or anxiety at all. Each day I had new gains. And I lived a fulfilling and interesting life.

Guangxi University for Nationalities has a very beautiful campus. Each day I can find its different beauty. And university buildings display an interesting mix of elegant Chinese style, ethnic *Zhuang* style and even exotic Southeast Asian style, which was a surprise for me. The campus actually shelters under a canopy of tall trees. Lined with these tall and big trees is the beautiful Xiangsi Lake. Our dormitory buildings and classrooms are all located by the side of the lake. Every morning, I looked out of the window from my dormitory building. I could see the lake is veiled in dreamy foggy air like as if in a fairyland. All of a sudden, I cheered up. It was so hard not to fall in love with such an environment for study.

Those who learn the Chinese language naturally have an interest in Chinese culture. I am no exception. So during the winter vacation, although I missed my family, I decided to stay in China to experience the Chinese New Year. However, something unexpected happened. When I was looking forward to the upcoming Spring Festival, the coronavirus broke out. Everyone was required to stay indoors and was not allowed to venture out unless they had something really urgent. I was rather panicked and as calls from my parents, relatives and friends flooded in, I became even more panicked. What's more, the university and dorm administrators always required me to fill out lots of forms every day. I did not know what to do and I had worries and felt depressed. Luckily, I have a very nice head teacher of my class. Although she could not

外地带着东南亚的异域风情。校园里绿树成荫，环境优美，在那些既粗壮又高大的树木掩映中，可以看到美丽的相思湖。我们的宿舍和教室都在相思湖旁。每天清晨，从楼上窗口望出去，湖面烟雾笼罩，如梦似幻，人的心情一下子就变好了，我能不喜欢在这样的环境中学习生活吗？

学习汉语的人总对中国文化很感兴趣，我也不例外。所以，放寒假时，尽管非常想家，我还是下定决心要留在中国过年，感受一下中国春节不一样的氛围。但是，人算不如天算，当我充满了期待等到春节到来的时候，一场突如其来的新冠肺炎疫情降临了。每个人都要待在家里，没有什么重要的事儿都不能出门时，我当时很慌张。加上听到这个消息时的爸妈、亲戚朋友老打电话问我，更让我恐慌。不仅如此，学校、宿舍管理员总要求我们填很多表格报告每日的情况。那时的我，不知道要怎么办，心里既烦恼又郁闷。可幸运的是我有一位温柔、体贴的班主任老师，虽然在这个特殊时期她不能来看我们，但常常给我们发短信，鼓

广西民族大学 / 黎氏浅摄

visit us during this special period, she often sent us messages to encourage us and introduced some Chinese movies for us to learn Chinese. As time went by, I calmed down. Our dorm administrator aunties also gave me timely care and comfort. Just like every Chinese, I made my due little contributions to the society– staying in the dorm room. My dorm room quarantine lasted around one month. I felt no bored at all. I had lots of time reading and worked out some smart ways to study Chinese. I also often watched the news and learnt that many Chinese doctors and volunteers made great contributions to the battle against the pandemic. Some even lost their lives. I was so touched, they were great heroes. And I believe thanks to these people China would surely recover from the pandemic. By the end of April, China gradually controlled the spread of the pandemic. So I returned to my home country.

It has been just two months since I left China. I feel as if a long time had passed, and I cannot help missing China. If someone asks me: "If you have a chance to study in China, will you still go there?" I am sure with no hesitationI will reply "Yes, I will". As time went by, my encounter with China, unforgettable and unusual, had already become a lasting memory.

励我们，给我们介绍适合学习汉语的中文电影，让我的心慢慢平静下来。还有宿管阿姨，她们的关爱和安慰也让我安心，因此我就和每一个普通的中国人一样，每天待在宿舍里就是为社会做出了小小的贡献。就这样连续宅了一个月，但我一点儿都不无聊。我不仅有时间读书，而且还自己琢磨出了一些学习汉语的方法。我也经常看新闻，中国的很多医生、志愿者在为这场疫情付出甚至牺牲，让我很感动，他们真是了不起的英雄，有这样的人在我相信中国一定会好起来。到 4 月底，在中国的疫情慢慢控制住了的时候，我也回国了。

2020 年春天的相思湖 / 黎氏浅摄

到今天，离开中国只是两个月的时间，但是我总觉得已经过了好久了一样，有空的时候常会想念。如果有人问我：“假如有机会的话，你还愿意去中国留学吗？”我肯定会毫不犹豫地回答：“我愿意。”原来在不知不觉中，与中国那段难忘又不寻常的邂逅早已成了我心中难忘的印记。

我的 2020
My 2020

[阿富汗] 伊克巴尔 中国科学技术大学
[Afghanistan] Mohammad Eqbal Rizaie, University of Science and Technology of China

My name is Yi Ke Ba Er and I am 25 years old. I come from Afghanistan and have studied in China for more than four years

I had longed for studying abroad since high school. Once my teacher asked me where I wanted to study. I replied without any hesitation, "China." Later when I knew that I got an opportunity of a government-sponsored program to study in China, I was overjoyed.

I used to be an army man, studying at PLA Army Academy of Artillery and Air Defense. Because I loved China and Chinese culture so much, I then returned to study for my MPA at the University of Science and Technology of China (USTC) after a short period of staying in Afghanistan.

I had learned a lot in my studying in China, including but not limited to textbook knowledge, humanity, history and food, and I had also had many interesting and beautiful experiences. What my family and I were most proud of was that I won the Belt and Road Initiative Award of USTC. Though it was quite a challenge to study abroad, it was also a marvelous opportunity for me to realize my dreams.

我叫伊克巴尔，今年25岁，来自阿富汗，在中国生活学习已四年有余。

高中时期，我就很想去国外学习。记得有一次，老师问我想去哪个国家留学？我毫不犹豫地回答说："中国！"后来知道能有机会公派到中国留学，我真的开心极了！

我曾是一名军人，本科就读于陆军炮兵防空兵学院。因为热爱中国、热爱中国文化，短暂的回国后，我又来到中国科学技术大学，就读MPA。

回想过去将近五年的求学经历，我收获颇多，不单单是大学校园的课本知识，人文、历史、美食，还有很多美好有趣的经历。当然，最让我和全家人开心的还是我获得了中国科学技术大学"一带一路"的奖学金。离开了家乡到异国读书很不容易，但是这对我来说是求之不得的、实现梦想的好机会。

然而，本想着热热闹闹过个中国新年的我，在2020年1月经历了一场突如其来的新冠肺炎疫情。按照学校安排，除了必要的采买，我们必须尽量留在宿舍。疫情让我们校区、宿舍也变得像机场、车站一样：

I was expecting a bustling Chinese New Year at the beginning of 2020 when the COVID-19 pandemic broke out in January. According to the instructions of the university, we should stay at our dormitories unless we had to purchase necessary daily supplies. The pandemic forced the university to perform health checks like airports and railway stations: A 3-step health check was required, that is, room card, temperature and health code. Though very strict, the working staff were also warm. There were smells of disinfectants everywhere and deliveries were required to pick up in dedicated areas. I knew all these strict measures were carried out to protect our safety and health and to fight against the pandemic so as to win the fight as soon as possible. Therefore, we did not complain about these measures. However, we felt much grateful for what the Chinese government had done for us.

I saw all Chinese people, as well as all foreigners in China, were united to dedicate their utmost to fight the pandemic. Doctors and nurses were beautiful heroes who put themselves in harm's way; press industries brought real-time news day and night; our teachers launched "air classrooms" immediately after the pandemic spread; delivery men were busy running about to deliver supplies for the needed. All these people were ordinary but great and lovable Chinese. I was greatly touched by what they did and wondered what I could do in return.

深圳 / 伊克巴尔摄

长城 / 伊克巴尔摄

进入需要三步检查——房卡、体温、健康码。虽然很严格但工作人员也很热情，到处都有消毒水的味道，快递、外卖都要到指定的地方去拿。我知道，这是为了我们的安全，更是为了与病毒做斗争，早日赢得国家和人民的胜利。所以，我们心存感恩。

不仅是我们，我看到所有的中国人，团结在一起，都在尽自己的全力与这场疫情进行着艰苦卓绝的斗争：医护人员们是最美的“逆行者”，媒体人夜以继日地为人们带来实时消息，老师们给我们在第一时间开始了“空中课堂”，快递员们奔波在传送物资的道路上……是这些人，这些平凡又伟大的可爱的中国人，深深感动着我，让我也想为他们做些什么……

记得疫情伊始，我刚领了学校给我们发的口罩，正好需要去超市买些生活用品。在超市很多人看见我手上抓着的一沓口罩，急切地问我：“朋友，请问你的口罩是在哪里买到的？”中国给了我这么好的求学机会，中国的朋友曾经给过我那么多无私帮助，尽管我自己也买不到口罩，

On the first day when we knew the pandemic, I went to a supermarket to buy some daily supplies with mouth masks I just got from my university. Seeing the masks in my hands, some people asked me earnestly, "Hi, could you tell me where you bought those mouth masks?" China granted me such a good study opportunity and my Chinese friends had given me so much selfless help, how could I return their favor? Though I could not find more mouth masks either, I could save some if I reduced the times of going out. Thinking of this, I handed out most of masks to the elderly around me. They said thanks to me, excitedly. At that moment, from their glittering and thankful eyes, I came to understand a sentence by Confucius my Chinese teacher had taught me, "Cherish our lives to wait for opportunities for contribution to the society." Now I, as an Afghan, could contribute my even minor efforts to help some Chinese during the pandemic, and this greatly comforted and satisfied me. I wish I could do more to help China and Chinese people since I, an Afghanistan, no longer regarded myself as a foreigner after spending more than 5 years here in China.

Now the pandemic has long been tamed. However, the Chinese people and their government were still working hard to keep everyone in its nation safe and healthy. Living in a nation like this, I was greatly moved and amazed. I even started to envy the Chinese people for their having such a great government. I truly hope Afghanistan could have such a great government with such high administration capability to keep its people safe, healthy and united with abundant life. This experience further strengthened my determination to study in China. I will certainly tell my family, friends and Afghanistani people how great a nation China is. China is beautiful, with warm and determined strength, and with caring and nourishing culture running through the history like a stream.

但是如果我尽量少出门，完全可以省下一些口罩……想到这，我将手中大部分的口罩分给了周围的一些老年人，他们激动地向我连声道谢。也正是那一刻，从老人家们闪烁的目光中，我才顿悟了中文课老师给我们讲的："爱其死以有待也，养其身以有为也。"能尽自己的微薄之力，在疫情肆虐时，不忘初心，帮助哪怕很少的几个中国人。这，给了我这个阿富汗人莫大的安慰和满足。我是外国人，但在中国已生活了五年的我，早已不再认为自己是外人。

现在，中国的疫情已经得到控制。然而，政府和所有中国人仍在为了所有人的安全、健康，团结着、努力着，丝毫没有倦怠、丝毫没有松懈。正是身在这样的国度，才让我的内心既震撼又敬佩，既感动又羡慕……真的希望，希望我们国家的政府也能有这样的执政能力，人民也能过上这样安定、团结、富足的生活。这更加坚定了我努力求学的决心，我会告诉我的家人、朋友、国家，这是一个怎样的美丽国度，这里涌动着怎样温暖而坚强的力量，这里传承和发扬着怎样如涓涓细流滋养人心的文化……

中国科学技术大学东区 / 伊克巴尔提供

"封闭"生活中的感动
Heart Touching Moments in Quarantine

［俄罗斯］ 夏小夕 中央财经大学
[Russia] Pavlenok Irina, Central University of Finance and Economics

For four years I always dreamed of seeing the real China. Having read about China and seen its pictures in textbooks, I already envisioned a China in my mind. I wanted to come to this amazing land and enjoy real Chinese food. In September 2019 my dream came true. Rapt in admiration for Chinese culture, I arrived in the Chinese capital of Beijing, where history meets modernity. Standing on the soil once ruled by emperors in various dynasties, the majestic land created by *Pangu* according to the Chinese Creation Story, I saw the sun shine brilliantly on the way ahead of me. A brave new world awaited me.

On the way from the airport to the university, the beauty of Beijing was gradually unveiled before my eyes. I remember the pop song *Beijing, Beijing* was played in the taxi. So whenever I hear of this song, I will naturally recall my first day in China. My friend treated me with Chinese food for lunch on my arrival day. The first course was *malatang*, a spicy Sichuanese food. Till today the flavor still lingers at my taste bud.

The year 2020 is a special year for the whole world, during which the pandemic has changed people's way of life. Facial masks and disinfectants have

期待了四年，一直梦想着与心目中的中国见面，梦想着亲眼看到课本上图片所描述的独一无二的中国，梦想着亲口品尝一下真正的中国菜。2019 年 9 月，梦想成真，满怀着对中国文化的向往，我来到了中国的首都——北京，一个充满历史和现代气息的地方。站在各朝各代的皇帝曾经生活过的大地上，看着中国神话中盘古开创的天地，灿烂的阳光照耀我的新世界的道路。

从机场到学校的路上，北京渐渐展开了她的美丽景色，美轮美奂地呈现在了我的面前，我激动万分。记得在出租车上听到的第一首歌就是《北京，北京》，现在每次听这首歌，我都会想起刚来中国的那天。中午朋友带我去品尝中国菜，第一道菜就是麻辣烫，现在那道菜的味道还在我的舌尖上。

2020 年，对整个世界来说都是特殊的一年。疫情改变了人们的生活方式，口罩、消毒液成了生活的常用品，封闭隔离成了生活的常态。

事实上，“封闭”不是一个可怕的词。校园封闭期间，我一直留在了学校，特别感谢我们的老师，为我们组建起了第二个家，我们在学校不仅感到安全，而且非常舒适。朋友常问我：“你整天待在房间，不出去

become daily necessities. Lockdown and quarantine have become a new norm of life.

In fact, quarantine is not a terrifying word. My campus was shut down to control the spread of the pandemic. I remained on the campus throughout the lockdown period. Thanks to our teachers who helped construct a second home for us. We felt safe and comfortable staying on campus. My friends often asked me: "You stay indoors all day long, having nowhere to go, no one to talk to. Are you bored?" I always beamed: "If you are a smart person, you have your own hobby. Even if you are alone by yourself indoors, you will not feel bored or lonesome." In fact, quarantine life can be interesting too. From morning to midday, we attend online courses, have interactions at a study platform the university has built for us. We study online, contact the teachers, raise questions just like in normal times. For foreign students, this way of study is very convenient. If I fail to catch some parts in the course, I can playback the course and take detailed notes. This helps the test. What amazed me was the variety of distance learning platforms in China, as well as excellent teachers who are committed, well poised and resourceful capable of providing good solutions to meet students' needs.

I happened to have my birthday during the pandemic. Two days before the day, I thought with no family members, no friends with me – even most classmates had returned to their home countries – there would be no birthday cake for me this year. However when my birthday came, my teachers sent me a birthday cake, and classmates who stayed on the campus also sent me another one. What a great surprise! They were with me and we had a great day together. We sat on the meadow in our university stadium. Everyone was wearing a facial

玩儿，不跟人聊天，不寂寞吗？”我总是笑着回答：“如果你是个聪明人，有自己的爱好，即使一个人待在房间，也不会无聊和苦闷。”另外，谁说封闭生活没趣儿？从早上到中午，我们在网上学习，学校提供了平台，我们可以通过平台学习知识、联系老师、提出问题，就像在正常生活中一样。对留学生来说，这种学习方法非常方便。如果不了解课程中的某些内容，那么可以回看课程并做出详细的笔记，这对考试有很大的好处。使我感到惊奇的是中国不仅有各种各样的远程学习平台，而且还有很多优秀的专业老师，他们尽职尽责，沉着应对，在非常时期想出好的办法，保证学生的学习需求。

疫情期间，正好赶上我的生日，生日前两天我一直在想：今年身旁没有家人，没有朋友，同学们大多数也回国了，连生日蛋糕也不会有了。可是让我惊讶又感动的是，生日当天，不仅老师给我送来了蛋糕，在校的同学也送来了蛋糕，陪我度过了特别开心的一天。那天我们坐在学校体育场的青草地上，虽然戴着口罩，但大家眼中都闪烁着快乐的目光。

中央财经大学 / 夏小夕提供

mask, but I found their eyes all glowed with joy. That moment I felt at home as if I was not away from home. That moment you look up in the blue sky, with a smile on your face, you feel so grateful to all who make you smile in the diffcult time.

During the quarantine, we only had our walking distance limited. All the study channels remained open. When spring arrived, the magnolia blossomed brilliantly in the yard. Gratitude and devotion are the hallmarks of the time, each and every day. Faced with the public health crisis, mankind are united together regardless of nationality or race. Our common enemy is the virus and fears only. I have no fear because I am fully confident. I am not panicked because I have full hope. I know one day I will walk out of the campus to embrace the beautiful season, to explore the beautiful city. I know one day I will return to my home country and will share with my family and friends my experience here. I will tell them how we were united and made our contributions to the anti-pandemic campaign. By then I will recall the azure sky and the blooming flowers.

Victory will come. As a foreign student, I will continue my study here, plunging myself into the learning. I will not fail the time, nor fail these who had made great efforts and contributions and even lost their lives to control the pandemic. I may not know all their names. But when I am able to walk out of the campus, I will say thank you to them all, to the time that is full of hope, to the world that is full of love. Thank you for this precious experience! I shall remember by heart throughout my whole life!

那时我感到了家的味道，就好像没有离开祖国。那时候你仰望蓝天，面带微笑，在你的心里会感谢所有在此艰难时期让你保持微笑的人。

其实，被“封闭”的只是我们的行走范围，学习知识的渠道依然畅通。窗外的玉兰花如约绽放，感恩和奉献依旧流淌在时光的每一帧里。危难之下，人类不再分国界和肤色，我们的敌人只有病魔和恐惧。我不恐惧，因为我充满自信；我不惊慌，因为我充满希望。我知道有一天我会再走出校门去拥抱这美好的季节，去探寻这美丽的城市；我知道有一天我回到我的祖国，和家人朋友谈起这一段经历，我会将这段齐心抗疫的日子娓娓讲述，那时候我还会记得天正蓝，花正开。

胜利终将到来，作为留学青年的我会继续投身到学业中，不负这大好韶华，不负一切曾经为我付出过时间、精力甚至生命的人。也许我不会知道他们所有人的名字，但当我能够再次走出校门的时候，我想对他们，对这个充满希望的时代，对这个充满爱的世界说一声：谢谢！谢谢这段宝贵的经历。我，终生难忘！

中央财经大学 / 夏小夕提供

阿中的蒲公英
——给中国的一封信
Dandelion of Azhong
—A Letter to China

［哥伦比亚］ 岑冠浩 北京理工大学
[Colombia] Cen Cen Andres Guan Hao, Beijing Institute of Technology

Dear Sister Azhong[a]:

How are you doing?

Do you still remember when I first floated onto this land 13 years ago? That was the first time I really knew you, not through my parents' mouths, documentaries, books nor other people's comments; Instead, I completely integrated myself into you. In the following years, I got acquainted with our culture, knew what hometown means, and learned that blood of heroes flew in our veins. It's you who let me know whom I really was, made me realize that I also belonged to Chinese nation, and reminded me that we should be proud of our 5,000-year of history. Most of myths and fairy stories of our culture, such as King Yu Taming the Flood, Houyi Shooting the Excessive Suns and the Foolish

① Azhong is a personification of China in Chinese pronunciation, so Sister Azhong means Sister China.

亲爱的阿中姐姐：

你好呀！

还记得13年前我第一次飘到这片土地的时候么？那是我第一次真正地认识你，不是从父母的口中描述，不是从纪录片，不是从书籍，不是从别人议论中的七拼八凑，而是完完全全地把自己融入其中，那些年我学习到了我们自己的文化，那些年让我认识到了什么叫作故乡，那些年我知道了我们的血统是英雄的血液，是你让我知道我是谁，是你让我意识到了我也是中华民族的一员，是你让我觉得我们应该为我们自己的五千年历史而感到骄傲，并让我看到我们这五千年的文化中大部分的神话故事都是让我们勇敢地跟大自然对抗，如大禹治水、后羿射日、愚公移山等，而不是叫我们愚昧地把自己的生命交到神灵手中，正所谓我命由我不由天。

我很幸运父母把我送到这片土地上，让我有机会好好地认识你。一开始我不理解为什么非得来，为什么不在我的出生地学中华文化，但随

Old Man Who Removed the Mountain, called on us to confront bravely the natural difficulties rather than to surrender to them, in other words, we're the owner of our own destiny.

I was so fortunate that my parents had sent me back to this land so that I had a chance to know you well. At first, I didn't understand why I had to come back instead of learning Chinese culture in my birthplace. As I gradually grew up, I came to understand the reason and my parents' efforts as well. Azhong, you were a clay sculpture at the first sight, wrapped with clay, vague and mysterious. As I slowly approached you and uncovered the mud around you, I was shocked! You were such a beauty, in an implicit, euphemistic and pure manner rather than in a shining way...

As a dandelion, I have made so many flower friends the first time I set foot on my homeland. Whenever I said that I was a dandelion, they would be surprised. Instead of isolating me, they all asked why I had the same habits as theirs, without even the slightest differences. I always told them that's because we shared the same root. They would then inquire whether the soil outside was pleasant and fertile, and I told them the soil was truly fertile, but it's too difficult for us to absorb the nutrients. In many lands, to gain the same nutrients we had to work much harder than other plants. We wouldn't wander around had we not been dandelions. But even if we were far away from home, our hearts were always with Azhong. We worry so much about you this time when you were hit so badly by pests. You always stand behind us when we're away from home. We will try our best to help you recover as soon as possible when you are sick, even if our efforts might

着我慢慢地长大，我懂了，也理解我父母的苦心，阿中，最初的你就像一个泥塑艺术品，被泥包裹着，我看不清你的模样，很神秘。等我慢慢地靠近你，揭下裹在身上的泥土时，我惊呆了！你是一个漂亮的姑娘，不是艳惊四座的那种美，而是含蓄的、委婉的一种美，耐看，清纯……

虽然我是蒲公英，但我第一次踏上阿中这片故土，我就交了很多花朵朋友，每当说到我是蒲公英，他们都会觉得很惊讶，神奇的是没受到排挤，而是问我为什么我的习惯跟他们一样，甚至感觉不到丝毫差别，我就跟他们说我们的根是一样的啊，他们还会问我外面的土地是不是很好，很肥沃，我就跟他们说外面的土地以前确实很肥沃，但对于我们来说太难吸收养分了，在很多土地上我们为了获得养分要比别的植物付出更大的努力，要不是我们蒲公英不得不背井离乡，我们也不会跑到外面去。但即使是在外面我们还是心系着阿中你的，这次姐姐受到这么严重的虫害，我们还挺担心你的，我们在外面你就是我们的后盾，如果你生病了，我们会想方设法，即使是微小的一点点力量也要帮你快快康复。

北京理工大学 / 岑冠浩提供

be insignificant. Likewise, I would long for your assistance if I were sick or in trouble. After all, blood is thicker than water.

Dear Azhong, at the last connecting flight every time I come back to visit you, the Butterfly Lovers is always played as background music on the plane. Whenever hearing that music in typical traditional Chinese style, I feel like "Great! Almost there!" I am so excited that I could only fall asleep until the last two to three hours of this 11-hour-trip. Now Azhong, I am back again! And I may stay longer this time than my first time. And I find that you have changed a lot this time – you are even prettier, stronger and more confident.

Could you please take good care of me during this period? I have come back to appreciate your beauty again...

Sincerely,

Yours dandelion

西安夜景 / 岑冠浩摄

我生病了或者遇到麻烦，我也希望得到你的帮助，这恐怕就是骨肉相连，血浓于水吧。

阿中呀，每次来看望你的时候在最后一次转机快到的那一刻，飞机上总会把梁祝当作背景音乐，每当我听到那有浓厚的中国古风的曲子，我就觉得快到了，真好！在时长 11 小时的旅程中兴奋到只剩下两三个小时才舍得睡过去。现在阿中，我又来啦！这次待的时间可能会比第一次来的时候还要久，这次回来发现你又变了不少，漂亮了，坚强了，并且越来越自信了。

这段时间就拜托你多多照顾喽！我又来欣赏你的美了 ......

此致

敬礼！

你的蒲公英

我愿搭起中日桥梁

My Labor of Love: Building Bridge between China and Japan

［日本］ 松叶佳子　中央民族大学

[Japan] Matsuba Yoshiko, Minzu University of China

The year 2018 marked the 40th anniversary of the signing of the China-Japan Treaty of Peace and Friendship. It was that year that I decided to come to China for further study and to experience the greatness of this powerful country in the East. I was also curious to know how Japan was perceived in the eyes of the Chinese people.

Throughout history and till today, the China-Japan relations are complicated. Both countries have boycotted each other. And the media coverage and online discussions are rather vehement. My original understanding of China came from Japan's news coverage, much of which was negative. However, when I finally arrived in China and communicated with Chinese people with sincerity, I found they are straightforward, honest and gentle. They are by no means that nasty as portrayed by Japanese media. My personal experience in China has made me realize that the friendly and candid exchanges between Chinese and Japanese students help promote China-Japan friendship. So, in 2019, I joined a volunteer team named Pia-Smile whose

2018 年是《中日和平友好条约》缔结 40 周年，而这一年，我也决定来中国留学，来感受这个东方大国的气派，也想深刻了解一下中国人眼中的日本到底是一个什么样的国家。

中国和日本的关系，无论是从历史还是当今来看，都处于一种错综复杂的关系中，双方都曾展开过大规模的抵制活动，而媒体报道和互联网上的议论更是异常激烈。我对中国最开始的了解来源于日本的新闻报道，而报道内容很多也是负面的，但是当你真正走进中国，真正用心与中国人交流时，你会发现接触到的中国人既友好，又爽快，既真诚，又温和，并没有像日本媒体所说的那样糟糕。而在中国留学时的所见所闻，也让我意识到中日学生之间的友好交流、坦诚交流，对中日友好关系的促进至关重要，于是 2019 年我参加了一个叫“Pia-Smile”的志愿团队，志愿通过该活动，搭建中日之间的桥梁。

“Pia-Smile”的活动主要是在华的日本留学生去访问中国农村的希望小学，并和当地的小学生进行中日文化交流。2019 年的第 25 次访问活动是我第一次作为组织成员参加的访问活动，因为“Pia-Smile”是由

mission was to build a bridge between China and Japan.

Pia-Smile's main activities center on organizing Japanese students in China to visit Hope Schools in China's less-developed rural areas and to hold China-Japan cultural exchanges with local pupils. In 2019, I joined Pia-Smile's 25th tour. It was also my first time to join the tour as a member of the Pia-Smile team. Since Pia-Smile was founded by Japanese students, language and funds remain as two big challenges when we set out to organize activities. We worked hard to raise funds and design interesting sessions capable of touching the hearts of both Japanese students and local Chinese pupils. The whole process usually takes three to four months in advance. Each week, we had a meeting of four to five hours to discuss the details of the activities. Between the meetings, we approached some Japanese companies for financial support. Raising funds is not easy. Nevertheless, we feel so grateful to those Japanese companies who gave us support. They share one thing in common with us, that is deep affections for China and willingness to make contributions to China-Japan friendship.

Frankly speaking, it is so hard to plan each event. However, when I see everyone has a smile and cry happy tears, all my hard work pays off and I feel so proud of being part of the winning team behind the great event. For Chinese pupils in the primary school built under the Project Hope, it is their first time to know Japanese people. In the beginning, they were unfamiliar with us. As the event went on, the friendship grew between Japanese students and Chinese pupils. We chatted with each other, took part in some small games and enjoyed ourselves. It was a cozy atmosphere. At the end of the event, we found it so hard to say goodbye to each other. Some Chinese pupils started to cry. In tears,

在中国的日本留学生组成的，所以语言和资金成为我们准备活动时面临的最重要的两个问题。我们每天都会抽出一些时间去解决这些问题。如何筹措资金，如何能更有效地让参加的日本留学生和当地的学生有一个心连心的交流活动，往往需要我们提前三到四个月去准备，并于每周召开四到五个小时的会议去讨论活动的内容。没有讨论会的时候，我们会找一些日本公司，请求他们给予我们资金上的支持，虽然拉赞助的过程并不是很顺利，但是我们很感谢支持我们的日本企业，他们同我们一样对中国有着浓厚的感情，愿意为中日友好做出力所能及的事情。

说实话，每一次活动的筹划都是艰辛的，但是，当在活动中看到大家的笑容和眼泪时，我觉得我的努力并没有白费，同时也觉得这个活动意义非凡。对于在希望小学学习的学生来说，他们是第一次接触日本人，刚开始的时候对我们很陌生，但是随着活动的进行，日本留学生和小学

中央民族大学春景 / 松叶佳子提供

they told us: "I don't want you to leave us. Can we meet again?" Whenever I heard such words, I had tears running down my cheeks. Although we are from different countries, there is a deep tie of emotion that connects us regardless of nationalities, cultural backgrounds and psychological barriers. I guess this is what President Xi Jinping of China had called for building "a community with a shared future for mankind," a community that is based on materials as well as in the hearts of people all over the world.

China launched Project Hope to build primary schools in the less developed rural areas to educate the students and inspire them to pursue their dreams. Visits of these Hope Primary Schools have opened eyes of Japanese students to the reality of China's rural education. We came to understand the ideal of the Chinese education is to make sure that "No single student shall be left behind." Through these activities, we realized that people to people exchanges play an important role in enhancing the China-Japan relations. So, we are determined to carry on these activities of amity. We will keep building and strengthening a China-Japan bridge of friendship. This is our labor of love.

中央民族大学冬景 / 松叶佳子提供

生之间的感情逐渐升温，大家一起聊天，一起参加各种小游戏，沉浸在温馨的环境中。访问活动结束时，双方亦表达出不舍之情，很多中国小学生开始哭，哭着跟我们说：“我不想和你们分开，我们还能见面吗？”每当听到类似的话语时，我的眼泪也会情不自禁地流出来，我觉得虽然我们来自不同的国家，但是彼此之间却有着深厚的感情，这种感情已经超越国度、超越文化、超越心理的束缚，它让我们在此刻联系在一起，不会分离。我相信这就是中国国家主席习近平所说的“人类命运共同体”吧，这种“命运共同体”已经不仅仅存在于物质层面，同时也深深地烙印在世界人民的精神世界中。

希望小学是为了发展中国农村教育而兴建起来的小学，通过对希望小学的访问，我们日本的留学生也深刻了解了中国的农村教育，这就是中国所倡导的“教育一个也不能落下”的观念的体现。而通过与他们的交流，我们也深刻了解到民间交流对促进两国关系的重要性，我们决定将此类活动继续办下去，志愿在搭建中日两国友谊桥梁的道路上坚定不移地走下去。

中国！只想说爱你

China, I Just Want to Say I Love You!

[加纳] 陈坤 上海海洋大学
[Ghana] Akyampong Ernest Wilson, Shanghai Ocean University

Dear China, I'd like to say thank you sincerely. It was two years ago in that early autumn that we first met, and you, like a burning light, illuminated my future. And today, at this quiet night, sweet and bitter memories poured into my heart. Although I want to say love you, it is always difficult to open my mouth, however, on thinking of what happened in the past two years, I have to say: China, I love you!

In confusing life, you are the lamp of hope for me. When I graduated from senior high school, just like most young people, I imagined a promising future. But to my astonishment, the reality woke me from my dream. I didn't like the medical major I chose in college, so I decided to drop out and then I worked in the harbor for over a year. For lacking of skills, I can only do porters, count the goods, work more than 10 hours a day, which is very tough for me. And the next day I had to repeat what I had done yesterday. There is no hope for me to return university again. But just at this time, you came from the Far East, smiling to illuminate a way to the future for me. After passing the examinations, I finally got a Chinese government scholarship and I excitedly told my mother the good

亲爱的中国，我由衷地感谢你。两年前，我们相识的那个初秋，那时的你，像是一盏明灯，点亮了我的未来。今天，在这个宁静的夜晚，酸甜苦辣的回忆又涌上了我的心头。虽然想说爱你，总是口难开，但想起这两年发生的事，我只想对你说：中国，我爱你！

在迷茫的生活中，你是给我希望的明灯。当时我高中毕业，像大多数年轻人一样，想象着美好的未来。但让我没想到的是，现实把我从美梦中叫醒。大学选择的医学专业我并不喜欢。我决定退学了，然后在港口工作了一年多。因为没有技能，只能做搬运工，清点货物，每天工作十多个小时，非常辛苦，第二天又重复昨天的工作。上大学对我来说没有了任何希望。但就在这个时候，你来了，你在遥远的东方，微笑着为我照亮了一条通往未来的路。通过考试，我终于获得了中国政府奖学金，我激动地告诉妈妈，我至今还记得她听到这个消息后惊喜的表情。

刚到中国，你是我“有问必答”的汉语老师。因为签证问题，我上学迟到了将近一个月，同学们的功课早就远远领先于我。巨大的压力下，我不得不加倍努力才能赶上他们。俗话说“有志者，事竟成”。这时候你来了，你是我的汉语老师，白天课间帮我补习，晚上在繁忙的工作中

news, and I still remembered the surprised expression on her face.

After just arrived in China, you are my Chinese teacher who answers all my questions. Because of the visa problem, I was nearly a month late for school, and my classmates were far ahead of me. Under great pressure, I had to redouble my efforts to catch up with them. As the saying goes, "Where there is a will, there is a way." At this time, you, my Chinese teacher came, during the day you tutored me, and at night, you still helped me correct homework in your busy schedule, and you are seriously and responsibly explained every question I asked. I didn't want to disappoint you or leave this class. Finally, through hard work, I gradually caught up with the other students. Thank you very much, my teacher!

When I got ill for the first time in China, you were the angel in white in the hospital. In Beijing, I spent the first winter of my life and saw snow for the first time. But since I was not used to the sudden change of temperatures, I was ill soon. It was the first visit for me to a Chinese hospital, I cannot understand what the doctor said. I became particularly anxious, so I called my Chinese friend for assistance and he was happy to help me out, which made me very happy. The doctor and me used translation software and body languages, as well as the help of Chinese friend, finally understood each other's meaning. This "performance" let the people next to laugh, I was also very happy. Finally, although I have understood, you told my friend, over and over again, how to let me take the medicine. At that moment, you are like an angel, gentle and kind. Great thanks to everyone on the site.

On the outbreak of the COVID-19 pandemic, you are our considerate "escort." When the corona virus was prevalent all over the world, you informed me in time, and I rushed back to school. I would never forget the quarantine

仍然在帮我批改练习题，我问的每一个问题，你都认真负责地讲解。我不想让你失望，也不想离开这个班。终于，通过努力，我渐渐赶上了同学们的进度。真的非常感谢您！我的老师。

第一次生病，你是医院里“手舞足蹈”的白衣天使。在北京，我度过了人生中的第一个冬天，也是第一次看到下雪。但由于我还不习惯这温度的突然变化，没多久我就生病了。第一次到中国的医院就诊，我听不懂医生在说什么，我特别着急，于是我打电话给我的中国朋友，没想到他很乐意来帮我，我高兴极了。我和医生用翻译软件和简单的动作，并在中国朋友的帮助下，终于明白了彼此的意思，这场“表演”让旁边的人哈哈大笑，我也很开心。最后，尽管我已经明白了，但你还是不放心，一遍又一遍地告诉我的朋友该如何让我用药，那一刻，你好像一位天使，温柔善良。感谢在场的每一个人。

疫情袭来时，你是我们体贴周到的“保护神”。疫情在全世界流行的时候，你及时地通知了我，我立刻赶回了学校。我永远也忘不了在宿

上海海洋大学 / 陈坤摄

days in the dormitory, volunteers sent us meals on time every day, teachers sent us bread and milk, schools delivered face masks, counselors did their duty to check our body temperatures every day. In order to win the struggle against death, everyone is working so hard. I was deeply moved, and although I knew I couldn't do much, I wanted to do something. Following the rules of the school, I report body temperatures every day, maintain environmental hygiene, seperate dry and wet garbage, which I will try hard to do my best. As I read before, "China is always well protected by their bravest people." So many people protect China in silence. Although I am not Chinese, at the moment, I stand with all Chinese people. Wuhan, come on! China, come on!

I have encountered a lot of difficulties during the past two years, but you always appear in the first time. I didn't regret it, even I am glad for what I have decided. The way I chase you is high and long, but there are always passers-by who will giving a helping hand in time; your knowledge is as deep as the sea, let me continue to harvest growth here. I will say hello to you on next meet, you are still so mysterious to others, and I will have become your bridge with the rest of the world. China, I love you!

陈坤在绍兴兰亭

小雨中的上海海洋大学 / 陈坤摄

舍隔离的那段时间，志愿者每天准时为大家送来饭菜，老师给我们送来面包和牛奶，学校送来了口罩，辅导员尽职尽责地每天检查我们的体温，宿管阿姨也每天来宿舍消毒……为了赢得这场与死神的斗争，大家都在努力付出着。我被深深地感动了，尽管我知道自己做不了多少，但也想做点什么。遵守学校的规定，每天报告体温，保持环境卫生、分类干湿垃圾，这些我都会做到，并且尽力做好。就像我之前读到的一句话“中国总是被他们最勇敢的人保护得很好”，很多人默默地保护着中国。虽然我并不是中国人，但此刻，我和所有的中国人站在一起。武汉，加油！中国，加油！

这两年，我遇到了很多困难，但是你总能在第一时间出现。我没有后悔，甚至庆幸当初的决定。追你的路山高路远，但总有路人会雪中送炭；你的知识深似海洋，让我在这里不断地收获成长。下次见面我向你问好，在别人看来你还是那么神秘，而我已经变成了你与世界的桥梁。中国，我爱您！

我看中国
China in My Eyes

［马来西亚］ 陈诗吟　北京理工大学
[Malaysia] Tan See Ying, Beijing Institute of Technology

One question has puzzled me for quite a long time: Why do I choose to study in China? Now I got the answer: I want to face those unknown challenges – challenge of loneliness without family by my side; challenge of desolateness when I was ill in a foreign land; challenge of tiredness when I study hard. I want to test whether I have the courage to overcome all these challenges. One could never improve herself and become mature without living on herself.

Now I'm more than confident in speaking or writing Chinese. It's my privilege to have learned to speak Putonghua fluently and write down what I want to express to China. China, you have gorgeous scenery, splendid history, numerous great souls and heroes who have affected the world from generation to generation.

A total of 1.4 billion people live in China, as perseverant as the Yangtze River and the Yellow River that ceaselessly flow across this land. Born in Malaysia, I am actually a Chinese descendant too. In a war, my great-grandmother had to take my grandfather and her siblings to flee from Guangdong Province to Malaysia, where they settled down since.

一直以来我都有一个困惑：是什么让我决定去中国留学呢？现在我有了答案——是希望自己去面对那些未知的挑战。挑战在中国留学，没有家人在身旁的寂寞时刻；挑战孤身在异乡生病时手足无措的孤独时刻；挑战学业繁重时心力交瘁的疲惫时刻。我要考验自己在这些挑战来临之时，是否有经得住考验的勇气。人生的路只有自己去走，才会在漫长时光中提升自己，让自己变得更成熟。

每当我说起中文、写下汉字时，我都会无比自信。我很庆幸自己学会了说一口流利的普通话，有能力写下我想对中国说的话。中国，您有美丽的风景，有悠久的历史，从古到今有多少伟人诞生在这里，有多少豪杰生长在这里，是您孕育了一代代影响了世界的华夏人。

这片土地上生活着 14 亿生生不息的中国人，他们有着坚忍不拔的精神，犹如盘虬卧龙，滚滚长江黄河才会川流不息。生在马来西亚的我其实也是炎黄子孙，在某一次战争中，曾祖母为了保住一家的性命迫不得已带着爷爷和兄弟姐妹们从广东逃到了马来西亚。后来，就在马来西亚安顿了下来。

2019 年，我来到北京。北京这座城市是很多年轻人梦开始的地方，

北京理工大学 / 陈诗吟提供

In 2019, I came to Beijing, a city where most young people's dreams set sail. I strolled on Beijing's streets and alleys and by its skyscrapers and was amazed by the charm of this metropolitan. I can't help thinking – how many years of ups and downs it has weathered! From here I have seen kaleidoscope of society and varieties of life. Beijing is always an exciting city with magnificent buildings and solemn history, and it will never let you down if you want to learn the excitement of the world.

Due to the COVID-19 epidemic, I came to Shanghai by chance in 2020. There are three stainless steel sculptures on The Bund: "Light of Pujiang River", "Sail" and "Wind." Located at the green corridor of the Bund, they glitter in the sunlight. The car lights and neon of skyscrapers form a continuous picture scroll, so beautiful and vibrant. I waited until dusk and saw the lights turned on one by one. The Oriental Pearl Tower is pretty and colorful like a fairy, while Jinmao Tower and Shanghai World Financial Center stand there proudly like two giants. I was completely indulged in this dreamlike night view and would say this was the best light show!

There is a beautiful park near my residence, Gucun Park, which has a touching story of "10 Years of Love." The cherry blossoms at the park are like clouds in the sky and the fragrance of flowers are everywhere. Taking a closer look, you could see they blossom in clusters and fragrance smell even better. The falling cherry blossoms are like small dancing butterflies. In the park,

那一年我漫步在北京的大街小巷，穿梭于高楼大厦之间，领略了北京这座城市的魅力。不禁感慨，多少年的风风雨雨才有了如今繁荣的北京啊！在这里，我看到了人间百态，看到了变化多端。北京是个时刻都能令人心潮澎湃的地方，宏伟的建筑，庄严的历史，世界有多精彩，来北京便知。

2020 年，因为疫情的原因，机缘巧合之下我来到了上海。外滩城市雕塑群由“浦江之光”“帆”“风”三座不锈钢雕塑组成，位于外滩绿色长廊中，在阳光下熠熠生辉。车灯伴着高楼大厦的灯光，像一幅绵绵不断的画卷，那么的美丽动人。我从天亮等到了天色渐渐暗淡，灯光一个一个亮了起来。东方明珠塔绚丽多彩，犹如仙女下凡。巍然屹立，傲对碧空的金茂大厦和环球金融中心就像两个巨人。这一幕让我陶醉在这片如梦如画的夜色中，最佳灯光秀非这莫属！

在我的住处附近有一个美丽的公园，那就是顾村公园。它有着一

北京理工大学 / 陈诗吟提供

picnic families, kite-flying children, young photographers and girls in Chinese traditional costumes, are all enchanted in nature and are unwilling to leave.

Chinese food culture has stretched for thousands of years, and the colorful feasts and abundant cuisines have earned China the reputation of "Kingdom of Cookery." White and tender steamed buns, mushy roasted sweet potatoes, stinky tofu with a strong aroma, red candied haws... it's said that in this world only love and delicious food should not be missed. Having missed a lot of love, I could no longer afford to miss any delicious food.

I enjoy the days of studying abroad in China, which is both a journey of learning and that of tracking my roots. My future is still a long way to go and I hope I could remain calm no matter what difficulties I might encounter. The purpose of my study here is to learn to be independent, gain experience and improve my thought. If I have sufficient money, I would like to travel to every corner of China, challenge myself and record all the merry experience.

上海街景 / 陈诗吟提供

上海外滩 / 陈诗吟提供

个“十年之恋”的感人故事。公园里的樱花烂漫似天霞，花香四溢天涯。往近处一看，它们一簇一簇地绽放，一簇一簇的花儿散发出的清香更是令人着迷。落下的樱花像小花蝴蝶，扭动着美丽的翅膀翩翩起舞。公园里野餐的一家人，放风筝的小朋友，照相的青年，穿着汉服的女孩，一个个陶醉在大自然的怀抱中，流连忘返。

中国饮食文化绵延几千年，五光十色的筵宴和五花八门的风味流派，使得中国获得“烹饪王国”的美誉。白白嫩嫩的小笼汤包，糊糊的烤红薯，浓郁烈性香味的臭豆腐，红彤彤的冰糖葫芦……人世间，唯有爱与美食不可辜负，爱已经辜负得太多了，美食就不能再辜负了。

我喜欢在中国留学的这段日子，这不仅是求学之旅，更是寻根之旅。未来很远，岁月很长，愿自己不管遇到任何人生路上的小插曲都得以从容淡定，沉得住气。我留学的目的就是学会独立，收获经验，提高自己的觉悟。如果资金充裕，我愿走遍中国的每一个角落，“折腾”一下自己，把美好的一切都记录下来。

我的中国情缘
My Attachment to China

[马里] 马杜 中国石油大学(华东)
[Mali] Kouma Mamoudou, China University of Petroleum (East China)

Time flies. I have successfully completed my undergraduate studies as a foreign student in China.

My Chinese name is Ma Du, and I have just graduated from China University of Petroleum (East China). Just like Ancient China's two great poets Li Bai and Du Fu (also known as Li Du in short in Chinese), Ma Du of UPC loves art and culture. You see I am a rugged man who studied engineering. Yet I have a delicate heart inside and I am an arty guy. Well my motherland is the Republic of Mali, a beautiful country in Africa, China's good brother country in the continent. It has been 60 years since China and Mali established diplomatic ties.

My attachment to China came from my dad. He is a businessman travelling between China and Mali. In 2004, I got a movie DVD "The Heaven Sword and Dragon Saber." It ignited my dream of coming to China. To prepare myself for my future adventures in the Middle Kingdom, I learned Chinese *kungfu* for three years at a Chinese Martial Arts House.

Finally, in September 2016, I came to the beautiful country of China, my second homeland. I became a student of China University of Petroleum (East

时光飞逝，不知不觉，我在中国的本科留学生活，画上了圆满的句号。

我叫马杜，刚刚毕业于中国石油大学（华东）。中国古代有李杜，今天石大有马杜。我是一名在粗犷外表下隐藏着一颗细腻的心，满载工科知识的脑袋中还有一点文艺气息的非洲小伙儿。我的国家，她也姓马，是马里共和国，一个美丽的非洲国家，是中国的好兄弟，和中国建交 60 年了。

中国石油大学（华东）图书馆夜景 / 马杜提供

China) and thus joined its open, tolerant and excellence-pursuing big family. I worked hard. When I was still a freshman, I passed Chinese proficiency test HSK Level IV. My major courses scores were also among the highest in the class. I felt good. However, when I compared myself with Chinese students, I was taken aback. Oh my goodness, how come they are so outstanding? I am no match for Chinese students. But, am I better than other foreign students? The answer is surprisingly NO. Look at Kajia of Russia, winner of 2020 UPC President Award, Shaweishi of Yemen, Runner-up of Chinese Bridge – Chinese Proficiency Test for Foreign Students, doctoral student Asefu of Pakistan, China's Nationwide Foreign Student of Excellence. I love playing basketball. However, when my university's foreign student basketball team won the national championship of 2018 China Foreign Students Basketball 3VS3 Competition, I was not even a substitute... I lag far behind them. You can imagine the pressure on me. So, I constantly reminded myself to work harder and harder so as to catch up with these models. My hard work pays off. In 2020, I myself became one of 582 China's Nationwide Foreign Students of Excellence. And I have realized that pursuing excellence is a lifelong endeavor. Upon graduation from university, my journey has just started.

马杜

University education has changed my way of thinking. Since my country

我的中国情缘始于我的爸爸。他是一名往来中马之间的商人，2004年的那盘DVD电影——《倚天屠龙记》，点燃了我来中国的梦想。于是，我去中国武馆学了三年的中国功夫，准备来中国笑傲江湖。

终于，在2016年9月，我来到了人生的第二个故乡——美丽的中国，加入了中国石油大学（华东）这个开放、包容、追求卓越的大家庭。我学习挺努力的，大一的时候就通过了汉语水平四级考试，专业课成绩也是班里的前几名，感觉自己还可以嘛。结果，和中国学生一比，我的天哪，他们怎么那么优秀？！我就想，比不过你们，总比我身边的外国学生强吧？没想到也比不过他们：俄罗斯的卡佳，2020年中国石油大学校长奖获得者；也门的沙卫诗，全国汉语桥大赛亚军；巴基斯坦的博士生阿瑟夫，全国优秀来华留学生；我这么喜欢打篮球，当学校留学生篮球队夺得2018年“留动中国”篮球3vs3全国总冠军的时候，我竟然连个替补都不是……和他们比，我都有这么大的差距，我的压力瞬间就大了呀。于是，我时刻提醒自己：学学学、追追追。功夫不负有心人，2020年我也获评了全国优秀来华留学生，成为全国582名获奖者中的一员。

中国石油大学（华东）校园南门俯瞰 / 马杜提供

中国石油大学（华东）体育馆俯瞰 / 马杜提供

is less developed, China's steady path toward xiaokang, a moderately well-off society has left me with deep impressions. As President Xi Jinping pointed out, "Poverty alleviation starts with boosting people's morale. Poverty alleviation must go hand in hand with education support." Happiness is something that is hard-earned through work and perseverance. Roll up your sleeves and work hard! Seize the day, seize the moment.

University education has changed my way of life. I came from a tropical country, where the highest temperature can be 50℃ and the lowest above 14℃. When I came to China, alas! There is truly winter and big snow in this world. I never drank boiled water back in my home country, now I often carry a thermos bottle. China boasts an advanced Internet network. During the COVID-19 pandemic, online office, online course and online test mushroomed. Students even attended online graduation ceremony. China takes lead in internet technology. A mobile phone in hand opens the door to a classroom, a library and a university.

University education has changed my fate. It guides the direction of

中国石油大学（华东）/ 马杜提供

到现在毕业，我发现，追求卓越，我才刚上路呢。

大学教育改变了我的思维方式。我的国家不发达，中国的小康之路给我留下了深刻的印象。习大大说得很对，“扶贫先扶志，扶贫必扶智”，幸福是奋斗出来的，撸起袖子加油干，只争朝夕，不负韶华。

大学教育改变了我的生活方式。我来自一个热带国家，最高气温可达 50℃，最低气温也不低于 14℃。来到中国后，啊……世界上真的有冬天和大雪呀！从没喝过热水的我，现在经常背着保温杯。发达的网络，尤其是疫情期间，网络办公、网课、网考，还有现在的网上毕业典礼，强大的网络技术再次展现了中国的硬核力量。一部手机，就是一门课、一座图书馆、一所大学。

大学教育改变了我的命运，指引了我人生的方向。我是一粒来自非洲的种子，在中国大地上破土而出，茁壮成长。如果有机会，我会继续在中国读研、读博。在中国优秀的大学里读书是一种荣幸，留学生的入学申请竞争真的很激烈，不优秀根本进不来；不用心，根本留不下；不努力，绝不会成功。

路漫漫其修远兮，吾将上下而求索。收拾行囊再出发，秉持中国精

my life. I am an African seed springing up from the Chinese soil, growing and thriving. If I have the opportunity, I will pursue a mater degree and a doctor degree in China. Studying at a top Chinese university is an honor. For foreign students, applying for admission to a top Chinese university is truly an acute competition. Only top students are admitted. No diligence, no graduation. No pains, no gains.

The way ahead is long and tedious, I shall search high and low. My graduation marks a new beginning in my life. Cherishing a Chinese dream, I now start a new journey. I believe one day I will return to my beautiful motherland and bring home all knowledge and skills I learn here. I will feel proud as a foreign student in China. In the capacity of an international alumnus, I will tell a good story of China to the world.

My forever blessings for China, my second homeland. May her be prettier, stronger and wealthier.

中国石油大学（华东）/ 马杜提供

神，怀揣中国梦想，伴着中国力量，开启人生新征程。我相信，有朝一日我将满载而归，去建设我美丽的国家。我为是一名来华留学生而自豪，做一名杰出的国际校友，讲好中国故事。

永远祝福我的第二故乡——中国，越来越美丽，越来越富强。

我的第二故乡
My Second Hometown

[柬埔寨] 艾金花 中央民族大学
[Cambodia] Ek Sovannbopha, Minzu University of China

I began to study Chinese seven years ago, and gradually a dream grew in my heart – studying in China one day. The year 2019 was an extremely lucky year for me because I was admitted to Minzu University of China. Since then I have embarked on the long-awaited road of studying in China.

When I first got to China, the familiar environment and native accent seemed to have left me far away, and all that was left was the word "unfamiliar." But what is wonderful is that loneliness has never been with me, and my life is full of freshness and vitality in Beijing.

Before I came to China, I learned about China through the internet, movies, TV dramas and other channels. Such new inventions as mobile phone code-scanning payment, sharing bicycles, high-speed railway, subway and so on had been repeatedly talked about by my teachers, and had been fantasized by me countless times. Once in China, I found that it was even better to see than to hear. They are more special and wonderful than I thought. Although I was always clumsy because of rustiness when I tried for the first time, the novelty brought me great happiness. I even had the feeling of falling into a fantasy, as if

七年前我与汉语结缘，渐渐地，我心中便有了一个留学中国之梦。2019年，对我而言是极其幸运的一年，因为我被中央民族大学录取了，自此，我踏上了期盼已久的中国留学之路。

初次来到中国，熟悉的环境、熟悉的乡音仿佛都已离我而去，剩下的只有陌生二字。但奇妙的是孤独感从未与我做伴，我的生活充满着新鲜与活力。

来到中国之前，我通过网络、影视作品等渠道来了解中国。手机扫码支付、共享单车、高铁、地铁等，这些新时代的新发明，我曾无数次听老师提起，也曾无数次幻想过它们的模样。来到中国之后，我发现果然百闻不如一见，它们比我想象得更特别、更奇妙。虽然第一次尝试的时候，我总会因为生疏而笨手笨脚，但新鲜感给我带来了莫大的快乐。我甚至有种掉入幻境的感觉，仿佛自己穿越到了更加发达的时代。我想，这些新发明不仅提高了人民的生活质量，方便了人民的日常生活，它们更意味着中国科技的崛起与进步，意味着中国人民的努力和智慧。

在留学中国的这段时光里，我最难以忘怀的，是10月1日新中国成立七十周年的阅兵仪式。记得国庆那天，我同学院的中国学生一起，

I had crossed into a more developed era. I think these new inventions have not only improved the life quality of the people, but also mean that China has risen and advanced in science and technology and that the Chinese are intelligent and hard-working people.

During the time when I study in China, what impresses me most is the October 1 military parade on the 70th anniversary of the founding of the people's Republic of China. I remember that on that National Day, I sat with the Chinese students in the lecture hall in front of the big screen and watched the live broadcast. It was the first time that I had seriously watched the whole National-Day military parade. The soldiers' neat pace, firm eyes, and walking posture with their heads held high all revealed China's strong national strength, which awed me into admiration. Although across the screen, I felt as if I were at the venue and was inextricably immersed in the mighty and majestic cry. I was deeply moved by the "mass parade" part. A total of 36 phalanxes, 70 groups of floats and 100,000 people marched across Tiananmen Square. The prosperity and stability of the country, the freedom, joy and happiness of the people and the brotherhood and harmonious coexistence of the 56 ethnic groups were vividly and thoroughly presented in this part. I couldn't help but give the thumbs-up.

Sometimes I wonder why I love China so much and what magic it has to make me enjoy my stay in a foreign country. Maybe because I love Chinese? Maybe because of China's broad and profound culture and high-quality life? I think these are among the reasons, but what really moves me is the simple but loving greetings from the teachers every day, the warm smiles from the uncles and aunts in the canteen, and the lovely students who always lend me a helping

坐在报告厅的大屏幕前观看现场直播，那是我第一次认认真真地看完中国国庆节的阅兵仪式。军人们整齐的步伐、坚定的眼神、昂首挺胸的走姿，无一不透露出中国强大的国力，令我震惊赞叹。尽管隔着屏幕，但我仿佛身临其境一般，沉浸在威武雄壮的呐喊声中难以自拔。阅兵仪式的“群众游行”环节深深打动了我。36个方阵、70组彩车与10万游行群众浩浩荡荡地走过天安门前，中国的繁荣富强、国泰民安，人民的自由、欢乐与幸福，56个民族亲如兄弟、和而不同的状态，在这个环节中得到了淋漓尽致的呈现。我情不自禁地为这个伟大的国家点赞。

有时候我在想，为什么我会如此喜爱中国？它到底有什么魔力，让我在异国他乡却仍然甘之如饴？或许，是因为我喜爱的中文？或许，是因为中国博大精深的文化和高质量的生活？我想这些也是原因之一，但真正打动我的，是老师们每天一句简单却充满爱的问候，是食堂的叔叔阿姨一次次向我露出的温暖的笑颜，是总在我需要的时候向我伸出援手

中央民族大学 / 艾金花提供

hand when I need it. It is these tiny details that constitute the ordinary but warm happiness in my life.

"Hometown is where your heart rests." Fortunately, I found a colorful China, and also met such a beautiful university. This is my second hometown. If this studying abroad is a precious journey in my life, then in the following time, I will, as always, embrace more unknown wonders.

中央民族大学 / 艾金花提供

的可爱的同学们。正是这一个又一个微不足道的小细节，构成了我生活中平凡而温暖的幸福。

“此心安处，便是吾乡。”很幸运，我发现了多姿多彩的中国，还遇见了如此美好的民大，这儿就是我的第二个故乡。如果说这次留学是我人生中的一次珍贵的旅途，那么在接下来的时光里，我将一如既往，拥抱更多未知的奇妙。

魅力中国，我眼中最美的风景
Charming China, the most Beautiful Scenery in My Eyes

[巴基斯坦] 常德 哈尔滨工程大学
[Pakistan] Chand Kishore, Harbin Engineering University

It is said that nostalgia is poets' privilege. With a civilization of 5,000 years, China is a country full of poetry and culture. Poetic love bathes every grass, tree, mountain and river. I am immersed in such idyllic setting and never remembered that I was a foreigner. In my eyes, this charm of China is the most beautiful scenery.

In 2018, I departed Pakistan for ice-city Harbin in Northeast China's Heilongjiang Province. Seeing is believing. My sensitive heart has turned into a time-carving pen to express my impression of China.

Maybe it is because I stay ten thousand miles away from home, or maybe it was a long journey, I felt hesitant about the upcoming study in a new country. After the plane just landed, two students from the Harbin Engineering University had been waiting at the airport. Their enthusiasm moved me a lot, reminding me the saying "It is always a pleasure to welcome friends coming from afar" During the following days, everyone I met has given me a helping hand, which enables me to settle down from unknown to known, from strange

有人说，诗人的天职是返乡。于我而言，拥有五千年文明的中国是个充满诗情画意，富有文化底蕴的国度。一草一木，明艳动人；一山一水，脉脉含情。我沉醉在这样的诗情画意中，从未记起自己是个异乡人。在我眼中，这魅力中国，就是那道最亮丽的风景。

2018 年，我从巴基斯坦的迪普洛出发来到了中国的冰城哈尔滨，极尽视听，游目骋怀，将一颗敏锐的心化作雕刻时光的笔，来抒写我的中国印象。

或许是因为离家万里，又或许是因为航时稍久，我开始对这次异国求学的选择心生犹疑。但飞机刚刚落地，两位哈尔滨工程大学的同学早已等候在机场，他们的热情使我感动于“有朋自远方来，不亦乐乎”的礼遇。连日来，从未知到已知，从陌生到熟悉，从慌张到从容，所接触的每一个人都给予我莫大的帮助。与他们有关的所有记忆，即便岁月匆匆，也无法抹去。可爱的中国同窗，就像杜甫笔下“润物细无声”的春夜细雨般，帮助我适应这里的一切。《学记》中说：“独学而无友，则孤陋而寡闻。”2019 年 5 月，我与哈尔滨—齐齐哈尔工业考察团一起到哈

to familiar, from panic to calm. All the memories about them will never fade with the passage of time. Lovely Chinese schoolmates are like the spring drizzle depicted by Tang Dynasty poet Du Fu "to moisten things silently," help me adapt to everything here. "Study alone with no friends makes him cut off from the world," read the On Learning.

In May 2019, I joined a delegation to visit the Harbin Electric Co Ltd and Qiqihar Heavy CNC Equipment Co Ltd. In August of the same year, I went to China Women's University and Beijing International Chinese College for an exchange visit, which gave me the opportunity to interact with my friends in other universities. It also opened a window to better understand each other, through which I felt more of the Chinese academic atmosphere and also found another self. It turned out that I was as small as a grain of dust in the wind, but I could gain something in a certain field. Maybe one day, I can also be somebody I admired. I feel comfortable and happy to be able to study in China.

常德在重庆武隆天坑地缝

A Chinese saying goes He who has never been to the Great Wall is not a true man. With the aim of looking for relics, I went to the Chinese capital – Beijing. I was deeply lured by the prosperity of Beijing without losing its charm of traditional

尔滨电气公司和齐齐哈尔重型数控设备公司参观学习。同年 8 月又赴中华女子学院和北京国际汉语学院进行交流访问，这让我与其他高校的朋友们有了倾心交流的机会。我的世界里打开了一扇增进彼此了解的窗，透过这扇窗，我更加感受到中国学术氛围的浓厚，同时也发现了另一个自己。原来就像风中一粒尘埃般渺小的我，也可以在某个领域里有所收获。或许某一天，我也可以成为那个被仰望的自己。能够留学于中国，我感觉快然自足。

人们常说，不到长城非好汉。于是怀着寻访古迹的心情，我去了北京。北京繁华而不失古韵的气度使我流连忘返。驻足在长城深处，我为古人的智慧和成就而赞叹不已。这气派古朴的建筑虽与自然之力无关，却已然和自然凝结在一起，它代表了人类的卓越匠心。千年以前，那第一个站在长城上瞭望远方的诗人是谁？他那明月下的影子，映入了谁的梦境，又装饰着怎样的梦？而当时的我，应该会成为他人眼中的一缕目光，传递着无限的崇敬。

常德在黑龙江哈尔滨索菲亚教堂

民以食为天，《舌尖上的中国》着实好看，其中的各种美味更为诱人。来到中国，怎能不满足口腹之欲！想来，街头小吃称不上玉盘珍馐，但这色香味毫不逊色的大众美食已成为我休闲时光中的陪伴。煎饼果子中那炸得

culture. Standing on top of the Great Wall, I was marveled by the wisdom and achievements of the ancient people. Although the grand architecture has nothing to do with the power of nature, it has condensed with nature as it represents the excellence of mankind. A thousand years ago, who was the first poet to stand on the Great Wall? Whose dreams are reflected in his shadow under the moonlight, and what kind of dreams are decorated his life? If I appeared at that time, I should express my admiration in the eyes of others.

Food is the first necessity of the people. The popular TV documentary A Bite of China has provided various delicacies in China. Living in China, it is not difficult to satisfy the desire for good food. Come on, street food is not expensive at all but both its color and flavor are so delicious and has become my favorite choice. Just as crisp fritter is the essence of pancake, sesame paste is indispensable seasoning of spicy hotpot, which is loved most by young girls. The flavor of stinky tofu is unforgettable. You will have to wait in long line before eating a modem popsicle in hot summer; while in chilly winter, the red, sweet sugar-coated haws represent happiness and reunion. No matter which country you are from, the food in China is sure to live up to your expectation.

Charming China, nobody can depict your beauty with words. You are the story that I can't finish in my heart, the song that repeats in my life. You are the most beautiful scenery in my eyes. I am only a passerby, who wishes to record your appearance with lens. Your beauty will not lose any luster even if it has been weathered.

哈尔滨工程大学 / 常德提供

刚刚好的薄脆是点睛之笔，是灵魂；女孩们钟情的麻辣烫中最不可或缺的就是那香醇的芝麻酱；臭豆腐那意想不到的口感更令人觉得奇妙；夏日里能消解人们心中酷暑的是那有时需要为之排队的马迭尔冰棍；冬日里能甜到心里的永远是那根红通通、象征着幸福团圆的冰糖葫芦儿……无论是哪方来客，来到中国，美食定然不可辜负。

魅力中国啊，纵有千言万语也无法将您描绘。您是我心中说不完的故事，是我生命中单曲循环的歌。您是我眼中最美的风景，我不愿只是一个过客，我要用最好的镜头记录下您的样子，就算泛黄，您的美依然不减半分。

铁杆兄弟
Blood Brother

［柬埔寨］ 龚少杰　中国地质大学（武汉）
[Cambodia] Kong Phearon, China University of Geosciences (Wuhan)

When I was young, my grandfather and my father ever told me stories between China and Cambodia. Though too young to understand the diplomacy between countries and the changing of world situation, I still remembered they called China Blood Brother. My grandfather told me Blood Brother meant the two countries were having very good relationship, helping and supporting each other even if in hardship. No matter how hard the situation was, the two countries were like blood brothers. Yes, it is true. The saying Blood Brother made me look forward to China with beautiful image in my head.

I am an 18-year-old boy from Cambodia. Though I am young, coming to China to study is an objective that I have stick to for longest years. The experience is more complicated than I have imagined. However, to write down how I feel in such a historic moment is to memorialize it.

Before I came to China, my knowledge about China came from my grandfather and my father as well as books both inside and outside classrooms. Both China and Cambodia have long history and the mutual relationship can be traced back to more than 2,000 years ago. During the coup in 1970 in Cambodia,

在我很小的时候，爷爷和爸爸就给我讲过柬埔寨与中国的故事。那时的我，还不懂国家间的外交，也不懂世界风云的变幻，但是我记得他们告诉过我一个称呼——铁杆兄弟。爷爷说，所谓铁杆兄弟，就是两个国家的关系相当好，患难与共，互相帮助和扶持，无论遇到什么事儿，它们都像风雨同舟的兄弟似的。没错，中国和柬埔寨就是铁杆兄弟，这个称呼也让我对中国有了更多美好的想象。

我是一个来自柬埔寨的男孩儿，今年 18 岁。别看我年纪小，来中国留学可是我坚持最久的一个目标。今年的留学之路比我想象得要崎岖得多，不过在这个时刻记录下我的心情，更是具有纪念意义。

来中国留学前，我对中国的认知来自爷爷、爸爸的故事，来自课内外的书本里。中国和柬埔寨都是拥有着悠久历史的国家，两国双边关系的建立可以追溯到两千多年前。1970 年柬埔寨政变时，西哈努克亲王流亡北京，受到了中国的大力支持和帮助。而今，中柬合作也是随处可见。在中国政府的帮助下，我们有了第一条全线四车道的国道，有了第一家水泥厂、火电站、最大规模的水电站……有很多中国人民来到柬埔寨旅游、投资、做生意，还为我们解决了不少就业问题。这样一个真心实意

Norodom Sihanouk went into exile in Beijing, and was supported and helped by Chinese government. Now cooperation between the two countries can be seen everywhere. With the help of Chinese government, we have built the first four-lane national highway, the first cement factory and thermal power station, and the largest hydro-power station. Many Chinese come to Cambodia for traveling, investment and business, which creates a log of job opportunities. Such a genuine and sincere Blood Brother, who will not love him?

Last September, I finally came to China. My first stop was Wuhan where I would spend one year in studying preparatory courses before I went to the university. Before I came to China, I learned Chinese by myself. Though still poor in Chinese, I quickly adjusted myself into the strange yet also familiar environment. China was just like what I had imagined, warm, co-operative and friendly. It made me feel like home. Wuhan was a bit different from what I had imagined. It has distinct four seasons, high buildings, advanced public transport network, as well as beautiful views such as mountains and lakes. Its beauty was far beyond words to describe and you can never see enough of it.

I went back to Cambodia during the winter vacation when Wuhan was seized by the COVID-19 pandemic. The pandemic was spread to many other countries and regions in the world. Though far away from Wuhan, I was still deeply concerned by my beloved Wuhan and China. I was eager to know how I could help those people in hardship in Wuhan and China. I was bewildered and eager to help people.

In February 2020, the Prime Minister of Cambodia Hun Sen visited China. He carried with him all good wishes from the Cambodia people, including mine. Cambodia was not a developed country. However, as a blood brother,

的“铁杆兄弟”，谁会不喜欢呢？

去年 9 月，我终于来到了中国，第一站是武汉，我将在这里度过一年的预科学习时光。来中国以前，我自学了汉语，虽然水平不高，但是让我快速融入了这个陌生又熟悉的大环境。中国跟我想象得差不多，人民热情、团结友爱，四处充满了家的熟悉感。武汉跟我想象中有点儿不一样，四季分明、高楼林立、交通发达，山川湖泊美景遍布，怎么也看不完。

今年放寒假，我刚刚回国，武汉便遭遇了新冠肺炎疫情。世界上有不少国家和地区也受到了病毒的侵害。虽然身处异地，我的心却紧紧地牵挂着我的武汉、我的中国。我不知道要用什么方式才能帮助到身处困境的人们，那时的我手足无措、心里干着急。

2020 年 2 月，柬埔寨首相洪森赴中国访问。他是带着我们全体柬埔寨人民的心意去的，当然也有我这颗微不足道的真心。柬埔寨不是一个发达的国家，但作为铁杆兄弟，面对困难，我们绝对是第一个冲上前去献出关怀的国家。首相洪森告诉我们：“贫穷时相亲相爱，困难时识真心朋友。”在这个特殊时刻，真正的兄弟会一起战胜困

黄鹤楼 / 龚少杰提供

we were the first to give a helping hand when China was in difficulties. Hun Sen told us, "True friends love each other when they are poor and help each other when in difficulties." In this special period, blood brothers fought against the pandemic and went through hardship together. When the pandemic broke out in Cambodia, China sent their medical teams to us immediately and donated large quantity of medical supplies. Such deep love and friendship moved millions of Cambodia people. They used slogans such as "Forever Sino-Cambodia Friendship" and "Heart Together, China and Cambodia" to express their gratitude. My relatives and friends all thought of my decision of studying in China a definitely correct decision.

In China, I learned a new phrase, "a community of shared future for mankind." We live on the same planet, breathe the same air, look up to the same sky and our destiny is closely related. No one is a separate island, entire of itself, in this complicated and changing world. It is precious to have a genuine friend who can go through hardships together. I wish the Blood Brother friendship between China and Cambodia can keep on and keep refreshing itself no matter how time flies and how the world situation changes.

Though I still cannot go back to my university, I believe we will overcome all the difficulties with the joint efforts of Chinese and people of other countries. My second hometown, Wuhan, will break through the darkness before dawn and finally light up the special dark period.

China, please wait for me to come home.

武汉东湖 / 龚少杰提供

难。即使在这么困难的时刻，当柬埔寨出现疫情后，中国马上派出医疗团队来帮助我们，还捐赠了大量的医疗物资。这样的深情厚谊感动了万千柬埔寨民众，大家纷纷表示“中柬友谊，万古长青”“中柬同心，守望相助”。我周围的亲戚朋友，都觉得我选择去中国留学是万分正确的决定。

在中国，我学会了一个新词——“人类命运共同体”。我们生活在同一个地球上，呼吸着同样的空气，仰望着同样的天空，每个人的命运都是息息相关的。于这个纷繁复杂的世界之中，我们都不是孤立存在的。能有一个患难与共的真心朋友，是多么珍贵的事情啊。我希望这份“铁杆兄弟”情谊能一直持续下去，无论风云变幻、时间更迭，感情只会历久弥新。

尽管现在还回不去学校，可我相信，在中国人民和世界人民的共同努力下，我们终将战胜一切困难！而我的第二家乡——武汉，也一定会冲破黎明前的黑暗，把这幽暗的岁月点亮。

中国，等我回家。

爱上温情的中国
Fall in Love with Tender China

［俄罗斯］ 瑞吉娜　安徽师范大学
[Russia] Shaekhova Regina, Anhui Normal University

I am a girl from Russia studying in Wuhu, a beautiful river city in Anhui Province.

There were very few people learning Chinese in Moscow back in 2012. For some reason, I grew a sudden interest in China, so I went to the Confucius Institute to sign up and embarked on the road of learning Chinese courses. In 2013, I studied as an exchange student at Ocean University of China in Qingdao, Shandong Province for a month, which was my first time going abroad. When I arrived in China, I instantly fell in love with this ancient and modern country! Although the study time was limited, it left me an unforgettable memory in my heart. Later, I returned home, graduated from university and started to work. But I simply couldn't forget China and was secretly determined to return to China when I had the opportunity.

In 2019, I was admitted by Anhui Normal University! When the news came, I danced with joy. On the first day at school in China, I was very nervous in class. But the teachers' kind smile, gentle tone and warm manner melted my unease in an instant like opportune spring wind and rain.

我是一位来自俄罗斯的姑娘，在美丽的江城——芜湖留学。

2012 年在莫斯科，当时学汉语的人很少，不知什么缘故，我突然对中国非常感兴趣，于是去孔子学院报名，从此走上了汉语课程学习之路。2013 年，我作为交换生在青岛的中国海洋大学学习了一个月，这是我第一次出国。初到中国，我就爱上了这个古老而又现代的国家！学习时间虽短暂，但在我心中留下了难忘的记忆……后来我回国大学毕业开始工作，但我心里却始终割舍不断，暗下决心有机会一定要重返中国。

2019 年，我被安徽师范大学录取了！消息传来，我高兴得手舞足蹈，飞回中国到校后第一天去上课，我非常紧张，但老师讲课时温柔的微笑、温和的语气、优雅的仪态有如春风化雨，瞬间将我的不安化解得无影无踪。

这种“温情化”教育模式不仅带给我们温暖，更带来高效！毫不夸张地说：我遇到的最专业的老师是中国老师！他们很讲究教育方式方法，特别是善于一下子就发现各个留学生的学习短板，因材施教，循循善诱，帮助你一步步把“绊脚石”挪掉。我在俄罗斯学汉语的时候，怎么也学

This "affectionate" education mode brings us not only warmth but high efficiency! It is no exaggeration to say that the most professional teachers I have met are Chinese teachers! They stress educational means and methods and are especially good at quickly discovering the learning shortcomings of each foreign student. They personalize their pedagogy, teach with patience, and help you remove the "stumbling block" step by step. When I was learning Chinese in Russia, I wasn't able to make sentences. But when I took a quiz only a few months after I was in Anhui Normal University, the sentences I made were all correct. The teachers had taught me the skills of making sentences in such a short time, and more importantly, let me know the how besides the what. I deeply realized that learning Chinese in Russia for five years was not even as good as studying in China for one year.

China's affection is reflected not only in education, but also in all other aspects. When it comes to friendliness and hospitality, China is indisputably one of the most enthusiastic countries! Confucius said, "It is a pleasure to have friends coming from afar." For thousands of years, Confucian civilization has deeply permeated the spirit and soul of this oriental power. Its idea of "benevolent people loving others" is also reflected in its foreign policy, which is embodied in the famous concept of "kindness, sincerity, benefit, and tolerance" and "be kind to the neighbors and be companion with the neighbors". This "kind and friendly" atmosphere is reflected everywhere in daily life. The people around would give us bright smiles every day and wholehearted help would be offered when it is needed. Once when I was in Nanjing, it suddenly rained. I was waiting for a taxi by the road side. At that time, a Nanjing madam came over, held her umbrella for me and even offered to give her umbrella to me. I

不会造句，但进入安徽师范大学学习不过数月，当我拿到小测验后的试卷——我造的句子居然全对！如此短的时间老师就教会了我造句技巧，关键还让我知其然更知其所以然！我深深体会到：与其在俄罗斯学汉语五年，不如在中国学习一年！

中国的温情不仅体现在教育上，还体现在其他方方面面——若论到友善好客，中国无可争议是最热情的国家之一！孔子说过："有朋自远方来，不亦乐乎？"数千年来，儒家的思想深深浸透了这个东方大国的精神灵魂，其"仁者爱人"思想也体现在外交政策上，即著名的"亲、诚、惠、容"理念和"与邻为善，以邻为伴"。在日常生活中，也无处不体现这种"亲睦"的氛围，周边的人每天都给我们灿烂的微笑，需要帮助的时候都竭诚相助。有一次我去南京，突然下雨了，我在路边打车，一位南京大妈路过主动为我撑伞遮雨，并说把伞送给我，我当时好感动，眼里噙满热泪，我坚决没要伞，但衷心感谢这位"南京大萝卜"（当

安徽师范大学敬文图书馆 / 瑞吉娜提供

was so moved and tears filled my eyes. I firmly resisted her offer. But I sincerely thanked this "Nanjing big radish" (a local nickname for a good person). When seeing me off, my Russian relatives and friends said, "You will be very lonely when you are alone abroad." But I don't feel it at all. On the contrary, I think it is really good to study in China, like enjoying spring breeze.

Chinese cuisine is famous in the world, and hotpot is one of my favorites. I often go to a Hai Di Lao hotpot restaurant. Every time I went there, I felt like I was at a relative's home. As soon as the waiter saw me, he would come to greet me happily. Sometimes I ran into activity occasions when gifts were being given to children, they would also give me one, which made me feel at home!

I was deeply impressed by China's customs and conventions as well as the simplicity, sincerity and kindness of the Chinese people. I know through learning that there is a kind of "home" ethical culture in China. From individual

安徽师范大学 / 瑞吉娜提供

地对好人的别称)。出国时俄罗斯亲友们曾说“你一个人在国外会很冷清的”，但现在我丝毫感觉不到，相反觉得在中国留学真的很好，如沐春风！

中国的美食是世界出名的，火锅是我的最爱之一，我常去一家海底捞火锅店，每次去都像到自己亲戚家一样亲切，服务员一见到我就高兴地跑来招呼，有时候举办活动给小孩子们发礼物，他们也会特别送我一份，使我有一种回家的感觉！

中国的风土人情，中国人的淳朴、真挚、善良，无不给我留下深刻的印象。我通过学习知道：中国有一种“家”的伦理文化，由小家及大家，由家人及他人，由个体及社会，每个人都乐于增进华夏整体的“大善”，在这样的文化熏陶中，自然会孕育出一个充满亲情、和睦、关爱、礼仪的国度！这是一个日渐走向强大的国家，但更是一个不断走向和平、文明、进步的国家。我深深地爱上了中国，我的心留在了中国。这学期由

瑞吉娜在宁波

homes to public homes, from family members to other people, from individuals to society, everyone is happy to contribute to the "great goodness" of China as a whole. Nurtured by such a culture, a country full of affection, harmony, love and etiquette will naturally be impregnated! This is a country that is becoming more and more powerful, but it is more a country that is constantly moving towards peace, civilization and progress. I am deeply in love with China, and my heart stays in China. Due to the COVID-19 epidemic, I cannot study in China this semester. I miss China, miss our university, miss our teachers. I deeply pray that if there were afterlife, I would like to be a happy Chinese girl!

安徽师范大学敬文园 / 瑞吉娜提供

于新冠肺炎疫情无法在中国读书，但我很想中国、想我们的学校、想我们的老师，我深深祈愿，如果人生有来世，我希望能做一个幸福的中国女孩！

留学生活掠影
A Glimpse of My Study Life in China

［越南］ 阮氏庆璃 广西民族大学
[Vietnam] Nguyễn Thị Khánh Ly, Guangxi University for Nationalities

On September 5, 2019, I stepped on the Chinese soil for the first time and thus began my journey in China. That moment I clearly realized that I would spend some time living and study in a foreign country. And I felt so excited.

The Secret of Happy Learning

I remember at my first Chinese literature class, the professor lectured on Confucius and selected readings from *The Analects*. He patiently explained all the details in a graceful manner. "Confucius said: Isn't it a pleasure to study and practice what you have learned?" – These were the first two lines the text started. I was totally perplexed. For me, whenever the teacher asked us to review what we have learned, I felt great pressure. How come could it be a pleasure? While feeling bewildered, I heard the teacher asked us if we were ever happy when reviewing our studies. Since the teacher asked this question, I felt that I must tell him the truth. So I did. And I was eager to know why Confucius so. Then the teacher told us a story of how Confucius learned to play the Chinese *qin* zither. Finally it all clicked. There are different levels of study. Some

2019年9月5日，我踏上了中国的土地，从那一刻起，我就清醒地认识到，以后的一段日子我将在一个陌生的环境中生活和学习，我感到莫名的兴奋。

一、学习何以快乐？

还记得第一次上中国文学课，老师给我们讲孔子和《论语》选读。老师讲解得很仔细，很耐心，很有范。子曰："学而时习之，不亦说乎？一上来这两句话就把我搞蒙了，学习然后按时练习、复习，不也很愉快吗？每当老师说要复习的时候，我就感觉压力很大，哪有什么愉快的感觉？正当我还在犯嘀咕的时候，老师说："你们复习功课的时候愉快吗？"既然老师问了，我当然不客气地说出了我的真实想法。但孔子为什么那样说呢？老师给我们讲了一个孔子学琴的故事，终于让我们明白，原来学习的境界有高低之分，孔子达到了学习的最高境界，所以他能享受学习。

短短两句话，让我对孔子有了一些了解。果然圣人就是圣人。我幻想着有一天自己也能像孔子那样，快乐地学习，学有所成。老师精彩的

are lower and some are higher. Confucius reached the highest level of study, so he enjoyed studying.

These two short lines gave me some initial knowledge about Confucius. He is truly the greatest of the ancient Chinese sages. I imagined that one day I can take delight in study, learn well and achieve something, just like Confucius. Guided by knowledgeable teachers at class, I gradually developed an interest in Chinese literature.

广西民族大学相思湖 / 阮氏庆璃提供

Word of Courtesy and Encouragement

As days passed, I made some Chinese friends. When I chatted with them, I can often hear their comments on my Chinese, something like "Your Chinese is so *niu*, you talk like a local." And they looked sincere and their tones were rather honest, so I believed they told me the truth and I felt so good. However when I heard so much of it, I was sort of confused. The Chinese *niu* literally means cattle. Why they did not say "your Chinese is excellent" or "your Chinese is so fluent"? I wondered.

I searched in Baidu and got two explanations: one is sincere praise as

授课让我一步步地喜欢上了中国文学。

二、你太牛了！

我交了几位中国朋友，跟他们聊天的时候，总是听到“你的中文太牛了，你说话像本地人一样”之类的话。他们认真的表情和诚恳的语气让我信以为真，心里美滋滋的。后来听多了我就有点儿想不通了，他们为什么不说“你中文太好了”或者“你中文说得很流利”呢？

我上百度搜索了一下，有两种解释：第一种解释是你做得非常好，没有人能比得过你；第二是他在嘲讽你。所以要看着情况来判断是贬义还是褒义。我想，中国人也会玩这一招吗？他们是不是在嘲笑我的汉语水平差？从那以后每次听到“你太牛了”我就闷闷不乐。后来我发现几乎每个中国人都这么对我说。而且不仅是对我，对其他外国人也这么说，

在广西民族大学（左二为阮氏庆璃）

you have done something great and you outperformed all others while the other is a satire. It depends on the real situation to decide whether it is sincere praise or a satire. I wondered if the Chinese played a trick with me. Were they actually laughing at my poor Chinese? They said so, not only to me, but to other foreigners. Later on, I realized that this was a word of courtesy. As long as you are a foreigner and you open your mouth and utter Chinese, no matter good or poor, you will receive praises from Chinese people. Well, that's awesome. I'm just loving it. I can make believe that I am doing well. I can feel great the whole day.

Nuoc Mam and Mobile Payment

Once we visited a night market and entered a noodle restaurant. At first glance, the boss found we were Vietnamese students and asked "Would you like some Nuoc Mam in the noodle soup?" His words made us feel so warm in a foreign country away from home. They seemed to know the Vietnamese fish sauce. Although the Nuoc Mam taste was not authentic, we felt grateful for his warm-heartedness.

We used cash to buy clothes. The landlady smiled and asked us if we were foreign students. She said Chinese people now seldom use cash, they pay with their cell phones. Later I got a bank card, and now when I want to buy something, I use my cell phone to scan the code and make the payment. So easy□Chinese people also like sending each other WeChat *hongbao* (red envelopes containing money) as festival blessings. One night I received quite a few *hongbao* and I was super happy that night. I hoped that every day was a festival in China. China's Internet is so advanced. It has affected all aspects

我慢慢了解了这是他们的礼貌用语，原来无论你说得好还是不好，只要你是老外，一开口说中文他们就会不停地夸你。这一点我还是挺喜欢的，因为这会让我沉浸在自欺欺人式的满足感中，一整天心情都舒畅无比。

三、鱼露与手机支付

有一次去逛夜市的时候，我们进了一家拉面馆，老板一眼就看出我们是越南留学生，直接问："你们要加鱼露吗？"似是不经意的一句话真的让在异国的我们倍感温馨。原来他们知道鱼露是我们越南的特产，虽然鱼露味道不纯，但是他对我们的这份热情已经让我感激不尽了。

买衣服的时候我们用现金支付，老板娘就笑着问道："你们是留学生吧？"她说中国人现在很少用现金了，直接用手机支付就可以啦。后来我办了一张银行卡，买东西时用手机扫一扫就可以完成支付，真的太方便了！过节时中国人也喜欢用微信发红包祝福，我曾经一个晚上就收到中国朋友的几个微信红包，那个晚上我超级开心，恨不得在中国天天过

广西民族大学 / 阮氏庆璃提供

of life in the country. A cell phone at hand can solve many problems. The convenience of life in China is truly adorable.

My days in China have changed my perception of Chinese people. I will always remember this interesting experience, probably the most beautiful memory during my school years. I sincerely hope one day I will return to China in the near future. I love China!

节。中国互联网非常发达，它影响着中国生活的各个方面，一部手机几乎可以解决所有问题。中国人生活方式的便捷令我羡慕不已。

我在中国学习的日子改变了我对中国人民的看法，我永远都会记得这段有趣的经历，它也许是我学生时代最美的回忆。我真的希望能够在不久的将来再回到中国。我爱中国！

邂逅中国，邂逅爱
Encounter China, Encounter Love

[日本] 铃木雅子 东北财经大学
[Japan] Suzuki Masako, Dongbei University of Finance and Economy

At the beginning of each year, Dalian is covered by silver snow, and it is also the time for me to return to Japan for holidays. In order not to miss out on the beautiful scene this year, I decided to stay in school. After the final exam, I said goodbye with reluctance to my classmates who will go back to their homelands and expect to meet them again on the campus in the new semester.

At that time, we all thought friends would gather in school again when spring returns. Some may come back late but they can still catch the cherry blossoms on the campus at the latest. However, what we never thought of was that the sudden outbreak of the novel coronavirus not only leaves me alone to enjoy the cherry blossom from flourishing to declining, but even now, my lovely classmates have not returned to the campus. On this rainy spring day, the heavy clouds, just like my low mood, are always hanging there. The lush avenue turns to be very silent. No cars passed by. Even if on the small path, you can only see few people. There are more wild kittens on the campus than students. I miss the time so much when my friends and I shared learning, chatting and roughhoused randomly under the trees. Breathing the fresh and pleasant air

每年年初，正是大连银装素裹、白雪皑皑的季节，也是我假期回日本的日子。为了不再与美景错过，今年我选择了留校。期末考试后，我和回国的同学们依依不舍地道别，期待新学期的到来，再次重逢在财大校园。

那时的我们都以为到了春天朋友们就都会回到学校，也许有人回来得晚，但最晚也来得及一起赏校园盛开的樱花。但是，令我们万万没有想到的是：突如其来的新冠肺炎疫情，不仅让我独自欣赏了校园的樱花由繁盛到衰落的全部过程，甚至到现在，我可爱的同学们也没能回到财大的校园。在这个阴雨连绵的春季里，阴沉沉的天气正如我低落的心情一样无法散去，郁郁葱葱的林荫道变得静悄悄，大道上没有车，就连小路上也很少见人，校园里的小野猫比学生还多。我很怀念曾经和朋友们在林荫树下讨论学习、畅快聊天、肆意大闹的时光。在雨水、树木与阳光一起散发出清爽而怡人的空气中，我们一起快乐地享受着在中国留学的日子。

虽然留校的生活很孤单，但是随着疫情的一天天好转，我的心情也渐渐好了起来，特别是我每次去学校西门拿快递的时候。这是为什么

mixed with the smell of rain, sunshine and trees, we enjoyed our days together in China.

Though the life of staying in school is lonely, I feel better and better with the improvement of the epidemic situation day by day. My mood is especially good when I go to the west gate of the school to pick up a delivery, as the kind doorman uncles remembered my name. When I was waiting for a package at the west gate one day, the delivery didn't come for a long time. I was wondering if I should wait for 10 minutes before going back to dormitory. A handsome and responsible doorman came over and called out : " Hi little girl (Xiaoyatou)?"

I asked with surprise:" Why do you know my name?"

The doorman felt puzzled and replied:" I have no idea what your name is."

I responded in doubt: "You just said my name, that is Yazi"

东北财经大学 / 铃木雅子提供

The doorman and his colleagues laughed. The explained what the doorman said is "Xiaoyatou" in dialect. Plus, he spoke very fast, I mistaken it as Yazi.

As we chatted, my package arrived. The doorman who called me "Xiaoyatou" noticed I had a lot of staff and kindly helped me carry them all the way back to my dormitory.

呢？是因为西门和蔼的门卫叔叔们记住我的名字了。记得有一天，我去西门等外卖，等了好久都没有来，正在我纠结要不要花10分钟再走回宿舍的时候，门岗帅气负责的门卫小哥哥走过来，与我闲聊起来，他喊我："小丫头！"

我惊讶地问他："您为什么知道我的名字？"

小哥哥纳闷地说："我不知道你叫什么呀！"

我半信半疑地回答："可是您不是刚才说了我的名字吗，我就叫雅子呀。"

小哥哥和别的门卫叔叔都哈哈大笑，他们跟我解释：刚才说的"小丫头"是方言，而且他说得比较快，所以我错把"小丫头"听成了自己名字"雅子"。

聊着聊着，我的外卖到了，叫我小丫头的门卫小哥哥看见我的东西很多，又好心地帮我把东西一直拿回了宿舍。

从那以后，每当我经过西门，保安和门卫的哥哥叔叔们都亲切地和我打招呼，问我："雅子你去哪儿？""又买了冰激凌吗？""拿快递吗？"现在，他们都知道我的名字，让我感觉又有了好多新朋友们。以前我以为在东财校园里能交到的朋友只有东财的留学生和中国学生。但是现在我知道了：原来我有幸遇到的所有中国人都可以成为我的朋友！

门卫小哥哥和叔叔们每次都会帮我拿东西，也常常问我需不需要帮助。有一次，我与他聊天，问他："你们为什么对我这么亲切？"门卫小哥哥告诉我，这是中国人的美德。中国人都很热情，喜欢帮助别人。就这样，我在校园里，邂逅了中国的美德、中国最美丽的风景。这种美德也时刻感染、影响着我。有一天，我又一次去西门拿快递，遇到了一位有很多件快递而正在发愁的老师，好不巧门卫叔叔们正忙着入校检疫，于是我跟老师说："我帮您吧！"于是我一直陪着那位老师拿着快递走回

Since then, every time when I pass the west gate, the guards and doormen often greet me amiably: "Where are you going? Yazi." "You bought icecream again?" "Pick up your package?" Now, they all know my name and It makes me feel I have more new friends. In the past I have thought I could only make friends with international and Chinese students in my university. In fact, all the Chinese people I met may become my friends.

The guards and doormen, whom I called uncles and brothers, always assist me in carrying my things and often asked if I need any help. One time I asked one guard why they all are so kind to me. He told me it is the virtue of Chinese. All the Chinese people are warm-hearted and willing to help others. Thus, I encounter the virtue of the Chinese people, that is the most beautiful scenery of China. The virtue around me is influencing me all the time. One day I went to pick up a delivery in the west gate and came across a teacher who was worried as there were too many deliveries for her. The guards were busy with quarantine inspection for school entry. I offered help to the teacher and carried her packages. On the way to her office, I learned some packages belong to other teachers. I was moved again by warmheartedness of Chinese people.

The epidemic has no mercy but people harbor love. In the days of the epidemic, I would like to thank my new Chinse friends, who taught me Chinese virtue and gave me selfless help and love. I look forward to the day when the epidemic is over and friends come back to the campus from all around the world. I will share the virtue and love I encountered in China with them. I wish more and more people could enjoy and appreciate the beauty of China.

东北财经大学之远楼 / 铃木雅子提供

了她的办公室。在路上得知，这么多快递，也不是这位老师自己一个人的，有很多是她帮助其他老师拿的，我又一次深深地被中国人的热心肠所感动。

疫情无情人有情，在疫情肆虐的日子里，我感谢这些新的中国朋友，感谢他们教会我的中国美德，对我的帮助和无私的爱。我好期待疫情过后，朋友们从世界各地回到东财校园，我要把我邂逅的中国美德与爱，与他们分享，和更多人共赏美丽中国！

我在中国的成长故事
Growing up in China

[印度尼西亚] 郑伊晴 广西华侨学校
[Indonesia] Angelly Julie, Guangxi Overseas Chinese School

I am Zheng Yiqing, 19 years old and I come from Indonesia. Yijing is the Chinese name given by my Chinese teacher on the first day I arrived at Guangxi Overseas Chinese School. I like this name a lot and my family also call me Yiqing when I have conversations with them.

I came to Guangxi Overseas Chinese School for study in September 2019. My Chinese was so poor at that time that I could barely understand anything when I went out shopping or taking a bus. I relied on others to interpret for me. My teachers were so patient and they spoke very slowly and clearly so that we could understand them. They repeatedly correct our pronunciations and encouraged us to express our thoughts freely in Chinese through various means. After two months, I could understand Chinese language easily and went out shopping, strolling and sightseeing easily. My life and study in China became happy and easy. I would like to use this opportunity to thank all my teachers! Thanks to all for your great efforts!

After almost one year in China, I felt the big gap between China and Indonesia and came to love China deeply.

我叫郑伊晴，今年 19 岁，来自印度尼西亚。“伊晴”是我到广西华侨学校开学第一天我的汉语老师给我取的名字，我非常喜欢，平时和家人通话时他们也会这么叫我。

我是 2019 年 9 月到广西华侨学校学习的。记得刚到中国时，我的汉语水平很差，外出坐车、购物时什么都听不懂，都需要别人帮忙翻译。我的老师们都非常有耐心，教学时讲得很慢、很清晰，一遍遍纠正我们的发音，同时通过各种方式鼓励我们用汉语表达思想。两个月之后，我能够很轻松地听懂中国话，可以随便出去玩，去坐车、去市场购物、去公园散步等。我的学习生活变得轻松愉快起来。在此，非常感谢我的老师们，你们辛苦了！

在中国学习生活近一年的时间，我感受到了印尼与中国的巨大差距，并深深地爱上了中国。

中国的电子支付，让我感觉非常方便。吃、住、玩，以及平时外出购物，无论是大超市，还是小商店，都可以使用微信或者支付宝支付，平时出门只要带一个手机就够了。印尼在这方面比中国已经落后了很多，平时出门都要带钱包和现金，非常不方便。当我和家人说起来时，他们

China's e-payment is very convenient. You can use e-payment anywhere at any time, including but not limited to shopping or travelling, no matter you need to pay in supermarkets or small shops. You can use WeChat pay or Alipay no matter it is for food, hotels, travelling, or shopping and all these can be done through a cell phone. Indonesia lags far behind China in this aspect. And we have to carry purses and cashes with us when going out and that's very inconvenient. When I talked about this with my family, they do not believe my words until they see my pictures and videos. They are all amazed incredibly.

I enjoy online shopping too in China. Online shopping and fast delivery in China are very advanced. Though my school is very strict in management especially in frequent going out, online shopping made our life rich. We can buy anything we need through online shopping. China's delivery service is quick and convenient. When we are in class or out of school, the delivery men can put our stuff in delivery boxes and we can pick them up when we are free. We do not need to waste our time in waiting for our parcels. However, in Indonesia, delivery men often deliver parcels door by door and sometimes they even have to re-deliver again and again if the recipient is not at home. This is not very efficient.

Nanning has a very advanced transportation network especially, subway system. In Nanning, you can go to every corner of the city by subway. However, Indonesia's first subway went operation just in the last year. Buses in Nanning are punctual and have an extensive network. You can even know the number of buses and their arrival time in the electronic displays of bus stops. There are sharing bicycles everywhere in the city. We can easily go to subways or bus stops using sharing bicycles, which also helps exercise ourselves. In addition, I

还不相信，但是在收到我拍的照片和视频之后，他们都感到非常惊奇和不可思议。

我很享受中国的网上购物方式。中国的网购和快递很发达，虽然我的学校管理很严格，外出不是很方便，但是网上购物让我们的生活变得丰富起来。各种好吃的、好玩的都可以在网上买到。而且中国的快递服务很便捷，当我们在上课或者不在学校时，快递员可以把快递放到快递箱里，等到有空的时候再去取就行了，不需要把时间浪费在等待接收上。而在印尼，快递员得一家一家地把快递送上门。有的人常常不在家，快递员需要跑几趟才能完 1 个包裹的送达，这样做效率很低。

南宁的交通很发达，特别是地铁。在南宁可以坐地铁到达这座城市的每个角落，而印尼的地铁去年才刚刚开通。南宁的公共汽车又多又准时，在站台的电子屏幕上还能看见汽车到站的数量和时间。共享单车随处可见，使用共享单车不仅可以锻炼身体，还可以很快地到公交站和地铁站。另外，我还很喜欢中国的秩序，各种车辆都自觉地遵守交通规则，

广西华侨学校 / 郑伊晴提供

also like public manners in China. All cars and buses follow public transportation rules and there are seldom traffic jams. However in Indonesia, there are traffic jams in many cities especially in rush hours.

I had an unforgettable Spring Festival in China. The pandemic COVID-19 broke out right after the Spring Festival and spread quickly. This terrified me and my family worried about me very much. They expected me to go back to Indonesia as soon as possible. However, the care and concerns the school took for us relieved our fear and worries. I tracked the everyday status of the virus through my mobile phones. Though the numbers of infection cases were increasing every day, the anti-virus capability of Chinese government was increased even more quickly. China built hospitals to fight against the COVID-19 within several days and almost all doctors and nurses gathered in Wuhan. Village and road block measures took effect very soon and all infected patients were treated well. China controlled and ended the pandemic within three months. Through this fight against the COVID-19, I saw the union, devotion and sacrifice spirits of Chinese people and was greatly touched by their national integrity and confidence.

I was greatly moved by the experience in China in fighting against the COVID-19 and I was even more confident in my study in China. No matter what difficulties will be confronting me in the future, I will face up to them bravely and help the needed one without any hesitation. Wish all other countries to win the fight against the pandemic with the help of China and wish our normal life and study can soon resume.

广西华侨学校 / 郑伊晴提供

很少有堵车的情况发生。在印尼，很多城市都常常堵车，上下班时间更是拥挤不堪。

在中国，我度过了一个难忘的春节。春节过后，中国突然遭遇了新冠肺炎疫情，而且疫情发展得很快。这让我感到很害怕，家人也非常担心，希望我能够尽快回国。在这段时间里，学校对留学生无微不至的关心和照顾让我们慢慢地把心放回了肚子里，也让远方的家人渐渐放下心来。我每天都通过手机关注疫情的发展，虽然感染人数每日都在增加，但是中国的抗疫能力很强，几天时间就建成医院，整个中国的医生护士赶往武汉，封城、封村、封路快速有效，所有病人都得到了救治，只用三个月时间就基本控制了疫情。通过中国武汉的抗疫行动，我看到了中国人的团结、奉献和牺牲精神，看到了中国的民族凝聚力和民族自信心。

通过在中国亲身经历的抗疫过程，我受到了深深的感动，对生活也更加的自信。在今后的人生道路上，无论面对任何困难，我都会勇敢面对，同时当别人需要帮助的时候，我也一定会毫不犹豫地伸出援助之手。希望在中国的帮助下，各国的疫情能尽快结束，尽快恢复正常的学习和生活。

哦，我亲爱的中国
Oh, My Beloved China

［加纳］ 武扬 南京邮电大学
[Ghana] Ezekiel Young Uwumborbi, Nanjing University of Posts and Telecommunications

Oh, my beloved China, your winter was put to a stop last year, and happy celebrations suspended. Your streets were deserted like a desolate wilderness, lying motionlessly. You displayed your beauty in spring, but no one was there to appreciate it. The hugs we had shared vanished, and an invisible bridge was built between closest friends and loved ones. But never did you lose your patience because your love never wavered. You watched us flee from your arms with wretched eyes, but you knew it was just for the time being. And you waited and hoped that we would return with you to the glorious days of love, hugs and smiles, like a wife waiting for her husband to return.

Your land was laden with tears mourning for the loss of their beloved ones. Your love endowed us with the strength to defeat a monster like the beast of Nian. This enemy is different, which, like a colorless smoke, came to despoil our happiness. But your care nourished our heart and soul and made us unite and fight. We will win, as always.

This is what we learned about China from the COVID-19 epidemic. Now let me describe my beloved China to you.

哦，我亲爱的中国，去年您的冬天停止了，欢乐的庆祝停止了。您的街道荒凉如旷野，躺着一动不动。您在春天展现了您的美丽，却没有人去欣赏。我们分享的拥抱消失了，最亲密的朋友和所爱的人之间建立了无形的桥梁。但您从未失去耐心，您的爱从未动摇。您带着悲伤的眼神看着我们从您的怀抱中逃走，但您知道这只是暂时，您等待并希望我们会再次和您一起回到充满爱、拥抱和微笑的光辉岁月，就像一个妻子在等待她的丈夫归来。

您的土地承载着为我们失去的亲人哀悼的泪水。您的爱给了我们力量去打败像年兽一样的怪物，这个敌人是不同的，就像一团无色的烟雾，来抢夺我们的快乐。但您的关怀滋养着我们的灵魂，让我们团结起来战斗。我们一定会赢，一如既往。

这是我们从新冠肺炎疫情中了解到的中国，现在让我向你介绍我心爱的中国。

让我们回到 18 个月前，当我第一次来到中国。

在成长过程中，每个孩子都出于各种各样的原因梦想和渴望去其他国家旅行。不用说，我也不例外地怀着这个童年的梦想。然而，问题是：

Let us go back to 18 months ago, when I first came to China.

When growing up, every child would dream and desire to travel to other countries for a variety of reasons. Needless to say, I was no exception to this childhood fantasy. However, the question is "When should I leave and for which country?" Friends often talked about the U.S. , the Caribbean and Europe. Only a few mentioned Asia as their destinations, and Singapore and Malaysia had always topped their dream places. No one seemed to be interested in China.

However, after earning a bachelor's degree in political science and economics, I changed my views on world politics, especially on how the influence of such Asian powers as Japan and China has gradually shifted. Over the past 20 years, China has gradually and steadily established its status as a world political superpower. I am both impressed and awed by the quick changes China has accomplished. I knew, out of question, I wanted to go to China. To learn and experience for myself how this transition has come about, what would be more effective than receiving education in China? If I could study in China, I would have a better understanding of Chinese culture, professional ethics and the Chinese way of thinking, which seemed to be the cornerstone of transformation and hard work. Besides, my love for Chinese movies like "Journey to the West" and movie stars like Jackie Chan further reinforced my desire to study in China.

南京邮电大学 / 武扬提供

I finally entered Nanjing

我应该在什么时候出发？去哪个国家？朋友们经常谈到美洲、加勒比和欧洲。只有少数人说过亚洲是他们的目的地，而新加坡、马来西亚一直是他们的梦想之地。似乎没有人对中国感兴趣。

南京邮电大学 / 武扬提供

然而，在获得政治学和经济学的学士学位后，我对世界政治，特别是对日本和中国这样的亚洲大国的影响力是如何逐渐转变的有了不同的看法。在过去的20年里，中国逐渐稳步确立了自己作为世界政治大国的地位。中国如此迅速地改变了自己的命运，这既让我印象深刻，又感到敬畏。毫无疑问，我知道中国是我想去的国家。我需要自己学习和体验这种转变是如何发生的。还有什么方法比接受教育更有效呢！如果我能在中国学习，我会更好地了解中国文化、职业道德和中国人的思维方式，这些似乎是转型和努力工作的基石。我对《西游记》这样的中国电影以及成龙这样的影星的喜爱，进一步增强了我想在中国深造的愿望。

随着时间的推移，我终于进入南京邮电大学攻读工商管理硕士学位，我的最后一块拼图完成了。从我的国家经由上海国际机场进入中国，我对中国的一些偏见很快就消失了。首先，我认为中国人太矮小的想法被否定了，因为我在机场遇到的大多数人都和我一样高或者更高。其次，

University of Posts and Telecommunications to study for a master's degree in business administration, with which my last piece of jigsaw puzzle was completed. When I entered China from my country through Shanghai International Airport, some of my prejudices against China disappeared immediately. First of all, my idea that the Chinese were too short was refuted because most of the people I met at the airport were either as tall as I am or even taller. Secondly, I had thought that Chinese was very difficult, but when the taxi driver taught me a few Chinese words, it became so easy. I was welcomed by thousands of loving smiles on the street and in subway, which soon made me realize how friendly and magical the Chinese people were. The urge to help others seemed to be deeply ingrained in the Chinese genes. Almost everyone you met was willing to help you solve any problem. I was particularly impressed by the fact that a young man spent more than half an hour buying train tickets for us and stayed with us until making sure we didn't miss the train. I immediately felt as if I had never left my country, as if I had just been to another part of my country.

Be yourself and you can adapt with almost all ease. The hustle and bustle of the day embraces you, and the warmth of the night is like a mother hugging her newborn and caressing you with love.

I am pleased to add that after months of pain, the glory of the past is gradually returning. Handshake is no longer forbidden. Smiles are finally back. Parents and lovers can hug their children and partners without worrying that their way of expressing love might put them in danger.

主持中外学生文化交流活动（中为武扬）

我认为中文很难，但当我的出租车司机教我几个中文单词时，它变得如此清晰。在街上和地铁上，我受到成千上万充满爱的微笑的欢迎，我很快意识到中国人是多么友好和神奇。帮助他人的冲动似乎在中国人的基因中根深蒂固。几乎每个你遇到的人都愿意帮助你解决任何问题。让我印象特别深刻的是一个年轻人花了半个多小时和我们一起买火车票，在我们离开之前和我们待在一起，以确保我们没有错过火车。我立刻觉得自己好像从未离开过自己的国家，就好像我刚刚去了自己国家的另一个地方。

做你自己，你几乎可以毫无障碍地适应。白天的喧嚣拥抱着你，夜晚的温暖像母亲拥抱着她的新生儿，用爱爱抚着你。

我很高兴地进一步补充：经过几个月的痛苦后，昔日的辉煌正在逐渐回归，握手不再被禁止，微笑终于又回来了。父母和爱人可以拥抱他们的孩子和伴侣，而不用担心他们表达爱意的方式是否会危及他们。

我与中国的美丽邂逅

——志愿服务的变革力量

My Beautiful Encounter with China

—Change Power of Volunteering Services

[新加坡] 张苏仪　清华大学

[Singapore] Zhang Suyi, Suzie, Tsinghua University

Every great cause requires heartfelt devotion to gain sincere returns. When you devote your valuable time, knowledge and focus to your truly beloved cause, beautiful things will always happen. Volunteering service is a great cause, beyond material interest and nationality difference. It binds us closely with a spiritual tie. It not only pushes our social society to progress, but also promotes our personal development. Meanwhile it also arouses our inborn aspirations to serve other people.

When I was pursuing my graduate study in Tsinghua University, I participated in a teaching program for schools for migrant workers' children, sponsored by the Youth League of the School of Economics and Management , School of Social Science and Department of Electronic Engineering. We went to the suburb by bus where I saw houses made by metals and crowded simple shanty town areas. The facilities there shocked me, which made me feel aching and sad.

每一项伟大的事业，都只有发自内心地投入，才会收获最真挚的回馈。特别是当你为自己真正热爱的事业投入宝贵的时间、知识以及专注时，美好的事情将随之发生。志愿服务就是一项伟大的事业，它超越了物质利益、种族隔阂，用一条精神纽带将我们紧密联系。它不仅推进着我们人类社会，还促进我们的个人成长，同时激发我们与生俱来为他人服务的渴望。

在清华大学读研期间，我参与了一个由经济管理学院研团总支、社科学院研团总支和电子系研团总支三院联合筹办的文华打工子弟学校支教活动。我们从学校坐公共汽车到郊区，来到了用波纹金属构造的房子和密集的简易棚户区，所见所闻的硬件设施令我震惊，也有些心疼和愧疚。

每逢周四下午，志愿者们一起前往打工子弟学校为学生授课。我们教授的课程包括数学、美术、文学鉴赏、音乐和手工艺课等。我和其他两位同学负责教授小学六年级的英语课。令我印象最深刻的不是孩子们

Every Thursday afternoon, the volunteers of the teaching program went to those schools to teach the children there, including math, drawing, literature, music and handcraft etc. Two of my classmates and I were responsible for teaching English for Grade 6. Despite all the difficulties and hardship, the children had gone through, and the passion they showed to their life and friends greatly impressed me. The children I taught opened their hearts and arms to me and I experienced their enthusiasm and vitality. Their smiles, curiosity and fire-like enthusiasm equipped me with more determination in my dreams and more enthusiasm for life. Every Thursday afternoon, we brought joy and knowledge to these children, opened their eyes to a greater and better world and helped them experience a more colorful life and more happiness.

To me the volunteer teaching experience was very valuable and meaningful. What we were doing was contributing to the efforts to achieve educational resources equality for children of migrant workers. We were showing our care to the next generation and improving their confidence in acquiring knowledge and in efficient learning. I also learn from the children their optimistic and active attitude toward life during my teaching. Their resilience, hard-working spirits and

张苏仪在清华大学

张苏仪在清华大学

对生活的悲观和失望，而是他们对生命与同伴的热情。由我负责支教的孩子们向我敞开了心扉，让我感受到他们的热情与活力。他们的微笑、好奇心以及似火的热情，让我在心疼他们的同时，更学会了对理想的坚定和对生活的热情。我们利用每周四下午的时间，为孩子们带去了很多的快乐和知识，让他们看到更丰富、更美丽的世界，体验到更多彩的生活和更多的快乐。

在我看来，这样的支教经历是非常有价值的，同时也是意义非凡的。我们正在为解决打工子弟学校的学生面临的教育资源不平等问题做出贡献，关怀下一代，提高他们获取知识的自信心和学习方法的效率。我在传授这些孩子学问和经验的同时，也从他们身上学到了乐观、积极的生活态度。孩子们的韧性、奋斗精神以及为自己和家人创造更美好生活的信念，激发了我对人类社会贡献自我价值的决心。我怀着对生活的热情和孩子们的美好愿望离开了校园，决定将我的精力和时间继续投入志愿

confidence in creating a better life for their families and themselves motivate me in bringing more values to human society. After the teaching program, with more enthusiasm toward life and beautiful wishes from the children, I decided to devote more to volunteering services.

My study in China had to come to a stop due to the pandemic. However, the volunteer service there is so unforgettable that it will stay with me in my whole life. Teaching the children of migrant workers made me understand their education conditions. Indeed, they did not have sufficient education resources and their environment was shabby. However, their enthusiasm toward knowledge was high. Wish I could have an opportunity in the future to visit them again. Meanwhile, I wish they could walk out of their shabby environment and had their own incredible life.

I believe that every volunteer can see their contributions in education through their experience of volunteer teaching. We have different experiences and our own way of contributing to the society. However, if we converge our wisdom, we can jointly promote the great education cause.

A youth that pursues no fame or money, but devotes the wisdom and vitality to children's education is the most valuable and meaningful one. A youth that teaches children how to study and how to love study is the most encouraging one. My experience of teaching the children in Wenhua Migrants' Children School enables me to look forward to my future with more confidence and to end my study in China with a perfect full stop.

张苏仪在清华大学

服务中。

因疫情缘故，在华留学的旅程可惜被迫暂停。然而，这次的志愿服务经历令我毕生难忘。走进了课堂使我深入了解了打工学校学生的教育现状。的确，他们的教育资源是匮乏的，环境是陈旧的，但他们对学习的热情是炽热的。希望自己将来有机会回去探望他们，更希望他们能努力走出那里，走出不平凡的人生。

我相信大家在志愿服务的经历中都可以体会到自己为人类教育事业所做出的贡献。虽然每人回馈社会的方式和经历不尽相同，但只要我们把智慧汇聚在一起，就能共同推进伟大的教育事业。

为孩子们奉献自己的青春和活力而不是追名逐利才是最有价值的青春；教授孩子们学会学习、爱上学习才是最令人振奋的青春。在文华打工子弟学校支教的经历让我对未来的生活更憧憬，对未来的人生更自信，也为我在华留学画上了一个完美的句号。

美丽的邂逅
——我与中国的故事

A Beautiful Encounter
—*My Story with China*

[巴基斯坦] 阿福 中国科学院大学
[Pakistan] Saud Uz Zafar, University of Chinese Academy of Sciences

In my childhood, whenever China was mentioned, the first thing that came to my mind was long noodles. The staple food in our country, Pakistan, is large flat bread and rice, but I like eating noodles. So much so that my mother used to say at that time, "I wish Allah would send you to China one day!"

In March 2016, I've really come to China! I was accepted by the University of Chinese Academy of Sciences and became a PhD student.

I started to feel homesick when I ate at a restaurant in Beijing. There were only chopsticks in that restaurant, which I didn't 'know how to use. That experience made me feel like it was so hard to be fed in China. Now, not only am I skilled at using chopsticks, I can't even live without them. Another mind-blowing thing was China's mobile payment. I used to keep the people in line behind me waiting for a long time because of cash change. Now, I'm completely proficient at scanning QR code and paying. Greek philosopher Heraclitus said, "Change is the only constant in life." We live in a time where we are faced with

小时候，只要提到中国，我脑子里想到的第一件事就是长长的面条。我们国家巴基斯坦的主食是大饼和米饭，但是我却特别喜欢吃面条，以至于那时候妈妈常常挂在嘴边一句话："真希望有一天真主把你送到中国去！"

2016 年 3 月，我真的来到了中国！我被中国科学院大学录取，现在正进行博士阶段的学习。

第一次想家是我第一次在饭店里吃饭的时候。那个饭店里只有筷子。那时候我还不会用筷子，所以那顿饭让我感觉，填饱肚子是如此困难。现在，我不仅能熟练地使用筷子，我甚至离不开筷子了。另外一件让我大开眼界的事是中国的移动支付。以前，我经常因为现金找零而让后面排队的人久等。现在，我已经完全可以熟练地扫码支付了。希腊哲学家赫拉克利特说过："变化是生命中唯一的常数。"我们生活的这个时代，每时每刻都在面对各种变化，与其逃避，不如接受它，世界会变得越来越简单。

我在读硕士期间开始学习汉语。那时候，感觉自己像三四岁的孩子，

changes at every moment, and rather than running away from it, we should accept it and will find the world is becoming simpler and simpler.

I started to learn Chinese during my master's education. At that time, I felt like a 3 or 4 year old child and the teachers were like parents, teaching us to babble. Tone was so hard for me! I often made mistakes. The worst and most unforgettable thing was the oral Chinese test. The task was to complete a conversation using the words given by the teacher. I walked into the classroom and somehow my brain went blank. After thinking about it for a while, I had to say, "Sorry, teachers, I forgot." At that moment, I felt so ashamed. Walking out of the classroom, I remembered that I was responsible for organizing the class ending dinner. All the teachers and students came, and I kept greeting them in Chinese. One teacher noticed and asked, "A Fu (my Chinese name), you couldn't speak a word of Chinese during the test, how come you speak it so well now?" I laughed awkwardly and said, "Teacher, I don't have to worry about intonation and pronunciation at this moment, I can say whatever I want, there's no pressure at all." Everyone laughed.

When I just arrived in China, people around me can recognize I was a foreigner right away. Even when I traveled to cities outside of Beijing, the local elders would mistake me for a Xinjiang native. Instead of being surprised, I'm glad to hear this. This means that I've become more and more Chinese after spending more time in China. China has become my second hometown. Understanding and respecting Chinese culture has made a person to act as a Chinese people. How good it is. I enjoyed the changes very much that China has brought to me over the past four years.

For the people's happiness, China is developing better and better. With an open and inclusive attitude, the Chinese government has provided a variety

而老师就像父母，教我们咿呀学语。对我来说，声调太难了！我常常出错。最糟糕也最难忘的事是汉语口语考试。题目是用老师给出的词完成一段对话。我走进教室后，不知怎么了，大脑一片空白。憋了一会儿，我只好说："对不起，老师们，我忘了。"那一刻，我感觉好丢脸啊。走出教室，我想起自己还要负责组织班里的结课聚餐。所有的老师和同学都来了，我不停地用汉语招呼着他们。一位老师注意到我的汉语，问："阿福（我的中文名字），考试的时候你一句汉语都说不出来，现在怎么说得这么溜啊？"我尴尬地笑笑，说："老师，我这会儿说汉语不用担心声调和发音，想说什么就说什么，完全没有压力啊。"听到这，大家都笑了。

刚来中国的时候，人们一看就知道我是老外，甚至，我到北京以外的城市去旅游，当地的老人还会误以为我是新疆人。听到这个，我一点都不觉得惊讶，我甚至还挺高兴的。这说明，随着我在中国待的时间越长，我已经越来越像中国人了。中国成了我的第二故乡，理解和尊重中国文化让我变成了自己人，这是件好事。我特别享受这四年来中国带给

雁栖湖畔的中国科学院大学 / 阿福提供

阿福（右二）参观两弹一星纪念馆

of jobs and opportunities to give full play to their talents, not only for Chinese people, but also for foreigners. China equally takes in people of different cultural backgrounds, colors and races in the world. In fact, all people in this world are like the five fingers in our hands. Although they are different in lengths, they can form a joint force. Only when all people unite and cooperate sincerely can we make the world a better place. The development of science and technology in China is making the life of Chinese people more convenient.

In 2020, the novel coronavirus was rampant. It was an extremely difficult year for every country. I have been in China all this time because of my studies. Like every Chinese, I followed the call and request of the government and actively fought the epidemic at home. I have witnessed the effective measures taken by the Chinese government, which puts the safety and health of its people in the first place. Compared with many developed countries and other developing countries in the world, China's epidemic prevention and control efforts are highly effective. Here, I sincerely pray that China, together with the rest of the world, will succeed in defeating the epidemic and ushering in a better tomorrow.

中国科学院大学 / 阿福提供

我的这些变化。

为了人民生活幸福，中国正发展得越来越好。中国政府以开放包容的姿态，不仅为中国人，还为外国人，提供了各种充分发挥他们才能的工作和机遇。中国平等地接纳着这个世界上不同文化背景、不同肤色和不同种族的人们。其实，这个世界上的所有人就像我们手上的五根手指头，虽然长短不一，但却可以形成合力。只有所有的人都团结起来，精诚合作，才能让这个世界变得更加美好。中国的科技发展正在让中国人的生活变得越来越便利。

2020 年，新冠病毒肆虐，对于每一个国家和民族来说，这一年都是异常艰难的一年。因学习需要，这期间我一直在中国。我和每一位中国人一样，遵从政府的号召和要求，积极居家抗疫。我目睹了中国政府把人民生命安全和身体健康放在第一位而采取的有效抗击措施。与世界上许多发达国家和其他发展中国家相比，中国的疫情防控工作卓有成效。在此，我真诚地祈祷中国和世界各国一道，成功战胜疫情，迎来美好明天！